From the Japanese

From the Japanese

A Journalist's Encounters

CATHERINE BERGMAN

M&S

Originally published as *L'Empire désorienté*, by Art Global/Flammarion
   Québec, 375 rue Laurier ouest, Montréal, Québec, H2V 2K3
Copyright © 2001 Art Global
       © 2001 Flammarion Québec

Translation copyright © 2002 by McClelland & Stewart Ltd.

National Library of Canada Cataloguing in Publication Data

Bergman, Catherine, date
    From the Japanese : a journalist's encounters /
Catherine Bergman.

Translation of: L'empire désorienté.
ISBN 0-7710-1207-1

1. Japan – Social conditions – 1945-.   2. Japan – Civilization – 1945-.
3. Social values – Japan. I. Title.

DS822.5.B4713 2002   952.04'9   C2002-902362-9

We acknowledge the financial support of the Government of Canada through
the Book Publishing Industry Development Program for our publishing
activities. We further acknowledge the support of the Canada Council for the
Arts and the Ontario Arts Council for our publishing program.

Typeset in Janson by M&S, Toronto
Printed and bound in Canada

McClelland & Stewart Ltd.
The Canadian Publishers
481 University Avenue
Toronto, Ontario
M5G 2E9
www.mcclelland.com

1 2 3 4 5   06 05 04 03 02

To Donald W.

Contents

Acknowledgements

With my warmest gratitude to:
Gamil Sadek

Yoichi Higuchi
Shuichi Kato
Ken and Makiko Kuwahara
Hiroshi Meguro
Tom Sekine
Yu Serizawa
and the Montreal Nippon Shokokai

"Around us, there is no longer any landscape."

– Yochiaki Uchida

Preamble

Under the heavily laden branches of cherry trees in bloom, I am proceeding slowly along the Philosopher's Path, as do the millions of visitors to Kyoto every year, vaguely intimidated, in search of Japan eternal.

The famous canal runs through the hills of the Old Capital. Over the still water, century-old cherry trees planted on either bank form a pale canopy that belongs to another world: it seems not quite solid, not quite vaporous either, liquid almost, impalpable, with ethereal and fleeting contours . . . and when a petal separates from a blossom and lingers weightlessly in space, it's as if gravity itself no longer applies under the cherry trees.

On the Philosopher's Path, in the spring, one tumbles into another universe, senses fail, and so do words.

I came to live in the Empire of the Rising Sun with my diplomat husband, whose task it is to represent his country to the Japanese. By association, I now belong to this strange tribe of international nomads that are diplomats. Honoured by some for their titles, vilified by many for their privileges, envied by all for the petits fours, they meet, they part, and meet again from country to country, according to the vagaries of their postings, carrying with them the same solitude of professional exiles.

My own trade is to tell stories. To observe and hope I saw right, to listen and hope I heard right, and then recount, the way a witness does, what I saw and heard. From my years as a daily news reporter, I learned to take into account the inevitable subjectivity of the observer, the relativity of cultures, the fragility of absolutes, and the shortcomings of the spoken word. Yet none of this is sufficient to adequately prepare the visitor, even the professional journalist, for what awaits one in Japan.

As under the magic cherry-blossom canopy, Japan offers the image of a world where everything is different, even the most elementary laws of physics, a world where time and space belong to other dimensions.

Quite literally, Japan is inexpressible. Our terms of reference become irrelevant, our grids of comprehension of the real world become useless, and more often than not, the words in our language prove inadequate to describe smells, tastes, and colours, as well as feelings, values, and norms.

It is with this caveat that I launched into the adventure of telling the story of what I saw and heard in this country, where, every day, I found myself doubting my own senses and my own understanding.

Introduction

The nail that sticks out will be hammered down.

This common saying is one of the first things one hears in Japan. Everyone makes a point of mentioning it, as if to suggest that, if you intend to survive in this society, you are going to have to keep your head down, accept the rules, avoid attention. In short, you are going to have to learn not to stick out.

To be convinced, just look around you: well-behaved schoolboys in quasi-military uniforms walking two by two on the sidewalk; waves of beige raincoats unfurling every morning from far-away suburbs into Shinjuku station; young rebels loitering in Shibuya's lanes, sporting the same black rags for a perfect little anti-conformist look. This swarm of people who seem to be wearing a uniform even when they are not are constant reminders of the nail that sticks out, and provide so many reasons to become convinced that the fate of this unfortunate nail symbolizes that of all the Japanese.

Indeed, what attracts the attention of the foreign visitor is, first and foremost, the care, the caution, with which everyone in this country applies himself to behave according to the rules, even in the most trivial activities.

It is no easy thing, for there are rules for all gestures of daily life, starting with the difficult bows whose angles are codified within five degrees according to the age, profession, and gender of the person to whom you are trying to say good morning. Add to that the complex protocol of giving: gifts are exchanged often and in large quantity, and it is essential to know what is the appropriate gift for each occasion, its value, how to present it, and when. The minute specifics of gift-giving have been the object of entire treatises on social anthropology. For the foreigner just off the boat, it is a mine-field, yet it is unavoidable.

Mistakes should also be avoided when it comes to symbols associated with colours, tastes, and seasons; one must remember at all times the thousand and one ways of not saying "I" and to avoid saying "no."

I should also mention the famous shoes ritual (remove them before entering a house, wear the slippers handed to you, change slippers to go to the bathroom), the rules of the dinner table (how to set your chopsticks, how to pour sake, etc.), and those of the bath (there is only one way to soap down, and posters describe it in detail in hotels and public baths). For the newly arrived visitor, learning the rules can become a full-time occupation.

And when the newcomer realizes that, when dealing with public officials (police officers, for instance), one must first apologize, then apologize again, and in the end apologize once more, absolutely, whatever the circumstances, he or she will become thoroughly convinced of the relevance of the nail that sticks out.

Of course, all of this is true. But it is also true that there exist in this country many nails that stick out with a defiance and a vigour that would shame most of our own free spirits. Could it be that the fear of the hammer leaves only the most determined to speak up?

In any case, I was surprised by the intensity of societal debates, the multiplicity and energy of activism, and the sheer courage of intellectual thought.

The issue of national identity is central to all this ferment. Whether the topic of the day is general elections or the correct way to cook rice, the future of nuclear-power plants or that of the Pill, a dam project or the elementary-school curriculum, the debate always ends with the same question: Who are we? It is altogether painful, exasperating, and inevitable.

Some of these anxieties have a familiar sound to them. Can our traditional values survive globalization? Is our cultural identity threatened by modernity? Is it possible to be modern without being Western? Occidental without being American? Are we all doomed to learn English in order to become citizens of the world? Do we have to choose?

But to the Japanese, the debate comprises yet another question, and it is a most thorny one: granted, we must protect our traditional values, but . . . which ones? Those that remained after the big postwar upset? Those that helped us survive during the dark years of the military regime? Those that allowed Japan to transform itself, in less than thirty years at the end of the nineteenth century, from an ancient feudal regime to a world power? Buddhist values imported from China by a handful of monks in the sixth century? Or, going back even further in time, the values of this people of sea and mountain who venerated the son of the Rising Sun?

At the end of the war, the Americans gave the Japanese what is closest to their heart: their constitution. Layered over a civilization far removed from Judeo-Christian values, this often results in odd juxtapositions. More than half a century later, the Japanese are still trying to put together the pieces of that puzzle, and no one knows for sure if it can be done. The exercise absorbs them completely. It is often confused and frenzied, it involves questions that are sometimes ill-thought-out and answers that are contradictory, but it always exhibits the same anguish, the same sense of urgency.

In this disorderly debate, many nails get hammered down, yet the Japanese are also desperately looking for nails that will stick up high enough and strong enough to be used as anchors, as beacons, as role models.

During the five years I spent in Japan, I was privileged to meet some of those nails. For example, the young anonymous office worker who decided one day that she would no longer put up with her boss's sexual advances and sued him very publicly, despite the general disgrace, to create a precedent.

Or the journalist who directly triggered the resignation of a powerful and corrupt prime minister and who, in lieu of thanks, has been treated as a pariah ever since, and probably will be to the end of his days.

Or the medical doctor who devotes his life to Koreans living in slums, the very existence of which is denied by the Japanese authorities.

Or the anthropologist who teaches young aboriginal Ainus their own language before it disappears, in order to build a bridge between the last grandmothers and the children yet to be born.

Or the history professor who decides one day that he will no longer teach his students the official curriculum, and who fights the Ministry of Education for the following forty years so that school-children will learn what actually happened during the Second World War.

Or the young sociologist who leaves a promising academic career to go into politics, in the vain hope of changing the old parties from the inside.

Or the angry author who scolds his contemporaries in his books, shames them, accuses them of laziness and weakness, and whose books become best-sellers.

Intellectuals, activists, men and women politicians, creators, they all contribute to shaping Japanese public opinion. Whatever their ideological baggage, they share a deep sense of ambiguity about the past, a sense of urgency about the future, and an intolerable uncertainty as to their identity.

It is through these few "nails that stick out," these Japanese unlike the others, that I tried to understand what is happening in the heart of the other Japanese – those that keep their heads down in silence, being ever so careful never to stick out.

CHAPTER 1

Sexual Harassment

She does not look like the heroine of a Greek tragedy, nor like a martyr, and certainly not like a militant feminist. Yet Kiyomi Kikuchi became a role model, a venerated icon for thousands of young women, the day she sacrificed her career and her private life in order to confront two of the most ancient taboos in Japanese society. Not only did she dare to sue her employers for sexual harassment, but she did it in public, for the whole world to see.

The first time I met Kiyomi Kikuchi, I thought I had come to the wrong place, or that she had knocked on the wrong door.

The occasion was a Tokyo International Feminists meeting, a hybrid gathering of sixty-plus Japanese women who had obviously fought many battles in their lives, and half a dozen energetic young Americans as naive as they were enthusiastic. They had recently arrived in Tokyo to study or to teach English, and they all held the deep conviction that they were accomplishing a basic civic duty by helping their Japanese sisters out of their age-old servitude to males. The way some wear a uniform or an armband as a rallying sign,

6

they all exhibited the recognized symbols of American militants from the 1970s, their mothers' generation: long tightly curled hair as a reminder of their support to Afro-American sisters; skinny T-shirts to confirm there is no bra here; and hairy legs to show their sincerity to the cause.

The cause is to educate Japanese women "and first of all, to raise their consciousness," explains a pleasant redheaded organizer as soon as I come through the door.

They have never heard of the one-hundred-and-forty-year history of socialist activism among Japanese women, their demands, their demonstrations, their political struggles, their times in jail. Having just arrived, they observe that indeed Japanese women are suffering from serious discrimination, draw the conclusion that nothing has ever been done, and, bravely, roll up their sleeves and get down to work. They are the latest of a long line determined to improve the human condition; touching and exasperating all at the same time, they take their mission very seriously.

On that particular day, the young organizers are analyzing a legal text as a preamble to the presentation by their guest speaker. The atmosphere is not unlike a kindergarten: "Who can tell me the meaning of the term 'sexual harassment'? Akiko-san, do you know the answer?"

The tone of voice is way beyond the acceptable level of condescension, but, incredibly, the old Japanese women, their faces leathered by years on the barricades, play along. Docile, they give the answer, like schoolchildren. They are moved by these beautiful passing foreigners, they envy their energy. "We should be careful not to discourage them," one of the Japanese will confide to me later. "They might help us create the critical mass that has always been lacking in the past." So the old militants repeat patiently the difficult words to please the nice Americans, to keep them a while longer. Maybe they will stay long enough to begin to understand, to actually help some day, who knows . . .

In this well-meaning dialogue of the deaf, Kiyomi appears at the door. Like a perfect little *office-lady* (or O.L. for short, the term used to refer to all women office workers), she is wearing her navy blue uniform even though today is Saturday. Her freshly pressed white blouse is held by a blue bow around the neck. Her hair pulled back, a demure smile on her face, her eyes cast down, her moves controlled, she takes off her shoes, steps across the tatami mat, and kneels down in the friendly hairy circle. Her back straight, her hands flat on her knees, she looks like the eternal Japanese woman incarnate.

Can this be the same young woman I have read so much about in the press, who has risked it all, mocked tradition and ancestral values? Can this be the sister in adversity, the young revolutionary, we all came to hear today?

The room becomes silent and, very softly, the honoured guest begins to speak.

What happened to her is painfully banal. She has repeated her story so many times before lawyers, judges, journalists, support groups, that she relates it now in a monotone, with no inflection, no emotion in her voice. That may be the way she has been protecting herself all this time, by maintaining a distance from the sorry events that changed her life.

In 1992, she was working in the service and maintenance section of an office-supplies company. Her job involved visiting client companies with her boss and, as such, she spent a large amount of time with him on the road, he at the wheel, she in the passenger seat.

When you are a new employee, on your very first job, do you have any option but to rush every morning and open the door for your superior, then close it ceremoniously after he has taken a seat? When, his two hands on the wheel in Tokyo dense traffic, the same superior asks you to light him a cigarette, do you have any option but to strike a match and, hands cupped to protect the flame, lean towards him?

It would be a mistake to believe that this deferential attitude arose from the fact that she was a woman and he a man. That earnestness, that deference, every Japanese expects it from his subordinates. It goes without saying. A new employee, male or female, is expected to help his boss with his coat, open the doors for him, carry his brief-case. I once saw a young engineer, who had graduated from one of the better schools in Japan, carry tenderly in his arms a boss who had passed out at the end of a very drunken evening, take him all the way to his room, and tuck him in bed for the night.

These attentions, this consideration, are part of the relations in the workforce, of the unspoken contract between juniors and seniors. The consolation for young executives, as they carry their superior's luggage and do menial tasks for him, is the thought: "One day, it will be my turn."

But what about women? They have practically no hope of ever being promoted to spheres high enough to justify such attentions. They cannot dream of the day when someone will open doors for them, will bring them tea and fuss about their comfort.

Yet, superiors expect to be treated according to their rank, and when Kiyomi was opening doors and lighting cigarettes, she was simply acknowledging the fact that her colleague had more seniority in the company. Sitting at his side in the passenger seat, she was behaving like any other junior employee, male or female, would and should have behaved.

However, it did not take very long before her superior became convinced that she was falling for him. As proof, he would later tell the judge, "You could tell, because she was lighting my cigarettes while I was driving! And she was opening the door for me!"

The day he tried to kiss her against her will, she resisted. "But you could tell from the expression on her face that she wanted to be kissed," he would protest before the tribunal.

When he took her to a *love hotel* (a bleak Japanese institution where couples in a hurry can drive through and rent by the hour), she jumped from the car and ran away in the night. Yet he kept pursuing her. During the inevitable company picnic – dreaded by all women workers because, if you don't want to be seen as lacking of team spirit, you are supposed to get a little drunk and let yourself be pawed – he started a rumour that she was sleeping her way to the top.

When Kiyomi complained to the company's human-resources department, she was told that one does not badmouth one's superior, and that she should be more respectful of a family man. Women colleagues did not provide her with any moral support either. When she tried to raise the issue in the office, she was scolded for making a mountain out of a molehill. Older women were the least sympathetic: "Who do you think you are? We have all been through that kind of thing! It's part of life. Behave like an adult and stop whining!"

"I did not know what to do, or whom to turn to," she recalls. "Soon, my boss was arrogantly grabbing my knee in the car, to remind me that I had no hold against him. When I went home to my parents at the end of the day, I did not dare say anything. One does not talk about such things. Every single night, I cried myself to sleep. I really felt abandoned by all. Then, slowly, I realized that I was not crying tears of despair, but rather tears of rage. I thought, 'If some day I have a daughter and something similar happens to her, what kind of support will I be able to give her? How will I be able to look her in the face, if I don't try to do something against it now?'"

That was when she decided to fight.

All of this was taking place soon after a celebrated trial that had stirred public opinion. For the first time, a woman had sued her employers for sexual harassment, and she had won. The Fukuoka trial attracted a lot of attention in the media, partly because of the dilemma faced by judges: the concept of sexual harassment did not exist in Japanese law, and the term did not exist in the dictionaries. While legal experts were looking for equivalents and precedents in the existing jurisprudence, civil law, labour laws, and in the laws of other countries, the public and the media were looking for a name for this novel and foreign concept. And since it was obviously an imported phenomenon, they did not look for a Japanese word; rather, they took the English term, *sexual harassment*, and shortened it, as the Japanese tend to do with all foreign words longer than three syllables.

It became *sekku hara*. Easy to remember, easy to pronounce, with the added advantage that it kept the foreign flavour of this strange notion that one should not fondle colleagues' breasts at the office.

So then, because of the Fukuoka trial, the Japanese had recently integrated a new word, *sekku hara*, into their vocabulary. Millions of women were discovering with stupefaction that the diffuse discomfort, the furtive unease, the heaviness that caused them to round their shoulders and keep their eyes down at all times, the embarrassment they felt every day in the presence of colleagues and superiors at the office, in meetings, in the cafeteria, everywhere in the workplace, this thing had a name: *sekku hara*. Sexual harassment. And once it had a name, it became possible to talk about it, describe it, question it, protest it, fight it.

That was the task Kiyomi, all of twenty-two years of age, took upon herself, all alone.

The beginning was far from easy.

First of all, she had to face her parents' choking indignation. How could she mention such dirty things? These are not topics for a well-bred young lady to talk about. And how could she be so selfish?

"Now you will never find a husband. That's your problem. But what about your sister? Have you thought about your sister? How will she ever find a good husband under the circumstances? No man will ever want to marry someone whose family has been covered in shame! And what about your brother? He just finished university, was just hired by a major corporation. If they find out, he will never get promoted! Never! His whole career is compromised by your selfishness!"

This line of reasoning was the hardest to confront in a country where the preservation of harmony at all costs is a fundamental rule of good behaviour. It is harder yet when you are the youngest in the family and you are still coming home to Mummy and Daddy for dinner every night.

In fact, as Kiyomi tells her story to the group of young Westerners, the only time when she lets a glimpse of emotion slip from behind her mask is at the mention of her parents' first reaction when they learned of her intention to fight in court.

The obstacles she had to face were many. She had to resign from her job. Then she had to look for a lawyer, which was no easy task. Who would want to defend a young girl with no money, no job, and no political support, in the name of a strange and foreign concept, not mentioned anywhere in legal texts and still suspect in public opinion?

Kiyomi was sent from firm to firm like a hot potato, until a young lawyer, too frightened to represent her, yet sympathetic to her cause, suggested she try Mizuho Fukushima, an activist lawyer known to defend causes that none of her colleagues want to take on. In practice, that reputation has led her to specialize in women rights. Lively, pretty, and articulate, she has become a media darling and is a frequent guest on television shows and at round-table debates and conferences. She has no qualms turning her cases into public events when it seems to be the only way to create a legal precedent.

And that is exactly what she did with the Kikuchi case.

When they met for the first time, Fukushima was impressed by the very simple, straightforward language Kiyomi was using to explain why she wanted to sue her employer. "I want him to understand that his behaviour is not acceptable. I would never forgive myself if I did not try to get men to understand that."

This client who was willing to fight, not for herself but for the common good, despite the fact that she had no job and no money, provided an ideal opportunity for the activist lawyer. She tried to push Kiyomi a bit. Would she be willing to go one step further and carry on her fight in public, for all to see? That meant allowing her name to be mentioned during the trial.

"It was a huge step, yet it took her only five minutes to decide!" the lawyer recalled with admiration. "Despite her shy and meek demeanour, Kikuchi-san has a very strong personality."

Now, addressing the respectful circle of young, affluent feminists, Kiyomi Kikuchi elaborates further: "On that particular day, as I took the decision to let my name be published in the papers, I was hoping to encourage other women to follow suit and start fighting too."

That was a turning point in her life. Overnight, she became famous. Suddenly, her case was on television, on radio, in the newspapers, and the reason for this intense interest was not so much that she was suing her employer, but that she was doing so in public.

In order to measure the magnitude of the undertaking, one must understand the immense reluctance of any Japanese to be first, to be noticed, to be different, to attract attention for whatever reason. Since childhood, they have all been reminded time and again what happens to nails that stick out: they get hammered down. The only way to escape that rule is to stick out so obviously, so outrageously, so relentlessly, so shamelessly, that the norms no longer apply.

This was the route Kiyomi Kikuchi chose, and, indeed, it made her a hero. For, despite the high value placed on the maintenance of harmony, there is also room, in Japanese mythology, for the pure hero, armed only with his sense of justice, who fearlessly confronts the powers that be and defends what is right.

Because of this, Kiyomi went directly from being a source of shame for her family and friends to being an object of adulation in Japanese public opinion. Letters of support poured in by the thousands. Most of them were sent by women between twenty and forty who had lived through similarly trying experiences.

"I felt alone in the world. I thought I was the only one to whom that sort of thing happened. You have given me the strength to talk about it, and now I am going to fight too." Men, too, sent letters of encouragement. From one end of the country to the other, women and men of all ages, touched by her courage, took ten minutes of their time, found a pen, put down on paper words they had never spoken before, searched out an envelope and a stamp, and walked all the way to the mailbox. Each one of these simple acts constituted a small victory against the fear of "what will people think" and a defiance of the hammer.

Multiplied by thousands, it was a revolution.

Kiyomi's mother went with little transition from deepest embarrassment to glorious pride the day she received a letter from

someone her own age, congratulating her for raising such a courageous daughter.

Then, a support group sprung up, as happens sometimes around
a particularly controversial trial. Starting in July 1992, the 150-odd
members of the "Violets Society" published a monthly newsletter,
organized workshops, seminars, and conferences on this new notion
of "sexual harassment," They also arranged to attend, in large
numbers, every single hearing of the tribunal.

Trials drag on for a very long time in Japan. Lawyers and judges
are overworked, tribunals are desperately crowded, and, when I met
her for the first time, Kiyomi Kikuchi estimated that the process
would take about ten years of her life. During the first three years,
she would appear once every two months on the average to face the
same questions over and over: either from her own lawyer, from her
former boss's lawyer, or from the lawyers of the company, which was
also involved in the trial. Meanwhile, the judge retired, and some of
the hearings had to be repeated.

Ten years is a long time for a young woman who is fighting on
her own, and who has to put her life on hold. There was no way she
could think of a career, of getting married and having children. The
Violets Society supported her psychologically to make it through
that difficult period, but its role and function went a lot further.

Are the courts influenced by the existence of the Violets?

"Absolutely!" Mizuho Fukushima replies without hesitation.
"Judges look at these support groups very seriously, and they take
them into account." All the more that, in the area of sexual harassment, judges have no option but to navigate in the dark between civil
law (inspired by the French civil law), custom (inherited from China),
and recent American jurisprudence. Given their reluctance to create
precedents, they tend to trust what emerges as an indication of
acceptable norms for their society at a given time. Therefore, the
spectacle of several dozen little Violets in their navy blue uniforms,
sitting quietly on the public benches, impassive behind a curtain of
black hair, pens in hand, taking notes in their notebooks like so many

disciplined schoolgirls, exerts a pressure and represents a power of persuasion more effective than many speeches.

I met Kiyomi Kikuchi again two years later. It had been three years to the day since she launched into that adventure and decided to sue. The Violets Society had organized a conference to celebrate the anniversary.

From the far end of the room, I watched this slim woman, as bland and shy-looking as ever, recount her tribulations in great detail, and provide her studious audience with practical advice on how to survive in the judiciary system. She was poised and collected, there was no bitterness in her voice nor recrimination in her language. She sounded as if, having identified the enemy and designed a strategy, she had organized and launched into a battle completely detached from her own private tragedy.

The women of all ages who had come to listen to her had the same serious and determined look about them. They were a far cry from the young American feminists of two years before, with their shocked and appalled shrieks. Rather, the atmosphere was that of a headquarters where the strengths and weaknesses of the enemy are examined, one after the other, as well as angles of attack, possible strategies, potential allies . . .

By then it was clearly obvious that whatever the outcome of the trial to which she had sacrificed her private life, Kiyomi Kikuchi had already won the most important battle. In a society where "to lose face" is one of the worst fates imaginable, she had done the impossible: lost face, then found it again, and become stronger.

She had dared fight in public; she had survived; she had broken the taboo.

CHAPTER 2

Justice

Once upon a time, there was a small village in the gardens of the Canadian Embassy, a cluster of wooden huts gathered together under the cherry trees at the far end of the park and dominated by the imposing white building of the official residence.

In this village, there lived a community of Japanese people who were employed by the embassy as gardeners, drivers, electricians, carpenters. People were born there, they married, raised their families, and, when they died, their children inherited very naturally the position of their parents, the way one inherits a privilege.

The village had its own chief, who kept peace and order among the villagers, and solved conflicts as they arose, according to customs. They lived in the relative harmony of a traditional society, where each individual is taught early in life how to respect the rites, codes, and protocols needed for surviving in the community. This world existed practically under the windows of the embassy that provided their livelihood, but there, the rites, codes, and protocols were so different as to be incomprehensible and one had to be content with a peaceful parallel cohabitation.

In the morning, when the driver, the maitre d', the plumber, and the heating mechanic slipped into their uniforms and crossed the park to go to work, they also slipped into another universe, and crossed over to another world.

The trick was to respect the Westerners' rules from eight in the morning to five in the afternoon, and the village rules the rest of the time. This is how the villagers enjoyed a prosperous and ordered life.

One night, there was a rift between two of the villagers. It happened on a Friday evening, during that privileged time when all the workers at the embassy, Canadians and Japanese alike, get together over beer to celebrate the end of the working week. In other words, it happened exactly at the seam between the two universes: in the embassy building, therefore in the Westerners' world, but after working hours. So . . . did the Westerners' rules still apply?

The fight was not a serious one, but there were a few punches, a few injuries, and words exchanged concerning the honour of the wives of the two protagonists.

What was serious, though, was that the rift took place in front of witnesses – worse, *foreign* witnesses.

The village harmony was threatened. The next day, the chief called in all the men, had them sit in a circle according to custom, and invited the two culprits to explain themselves.

I call them "culprits" because they were already guilty of something, before any judgment, before any trial. In Japanese customary law, the victim bears his share of responsibility, whatever the circumstances of the crime. Willingly or not, he has played a part in an incident that troubled the harmony, threatened the peace in the community. That alone is reprehensible.

The fact that his role might have been a passive one is irrelevant. Each individual is considered actively responsible for the avoidance of open conflicts. The implication is that it is not enough to *avoid* aggression against one's neighbour; one must also avoid being the victim of an aggression. In modern parlance, we would say that each

person has the duty to live "defensively." Everyone has the duty to
remain aware of one's surroundings, anticipate the seeds of a rift, and
do all in one's power to avoid a dispute. To be the victim of a crime
constitutes a failure in this basic civic duty. This is the reason why a
victim always carries a certain amount of guilt. This goes a long way
to explain the legendary reluctance of the Japanese to engage in confrontation, as well as the phenomenal attention they pay to avoiding
irritants in all their social interactions.

The question before the villagers that weekend was not simply to
decide who was right and who was wrong, but how much punishment
to impose on the two fighters. The sentence had to come from the
whole community, including the two concerned parties. Then and
only then would order be restored.

No one in the embassy ever found out what actually happened
within the small village that weekend. One does not talk to foreigners about these things. However, on Monday morning, the Japanese
were serenely back at work. Justice had been rendered and the village
was at peace.

Yet, for the Westerners, this was just the beginning. A rift between
two employees during working hours (well, almost during working
hours) is a serious incident. There are rules and regulations to deal
with these things.

The machinery of administration was set in motion. From the
immediate supervisor to the head of personnel, then to the head of
the chancery, the file was getting thicker by the day with "whereases"
and "notwithstandings," so much so that, when it eventually reached
the office of the ambassador, the clash had all the makings of a diplomatic incident.

The ambassador did what he had to do: he imposed administrative
sanctions, according to the rules written by Headquarters. In the corridors of the embassy, people anticipated with dread the reaction of
their Japanese colleagues. Yet, their anxiety was in vain. The sentence
from upstairs was received with total indifference by the two fighters.

"Like water off a duck," remembered a witness.

"As if it had nothing to do with them," remarked another.

And indeed, it *did* have nothing to do with them. The sentence was perceived as one of these calamities that can't be helped, one of these ordeals that one must learn to face in life, in the same way as one must be prepared to expect fog in high mountains, thunder when there is a storm, or a tidal wave after an earthquake. It had nothing to do with justice.

Justice had been dealt with, correctly, in the village.

It would be a mistake to interpret this story as yet another illustration of the misunderstandings that are bound to occur between Japanese and Westerners.

To be sure, irritants are inevitable when two systems of ethics, two different notions of good and evil, two different concepts of law and justice have to exist side by side. But the anecdote from the Canadian Embassy village reflects a lot more. The reason why the two accused were so indifferent to their punishment was not because the boss was a foreigner, but simply because he was the boss.

It is a well-known fact in Japan: one does not turn to official authorities to render justice. Better yet, one does one's utmost to *avoid* the interference of authorities when it comes to solving a conflict between individuals. This idea, deeply ingrained in the Japanese psyche, comes from afar: from sixth-century Imperial China, no less. Since the Middle Ages, generations of country people have had the painful opportunity to check its wisdom, whatever the political regime of the day.

In ancient China, and later in Japan, laws dealt solely with the relations between the Emperor and his subjects: how much tax they had to pay, how many soldiers they had to provide, and the sanctions they faced if they failed in these two obligations.

There was hardly a word about justice.

Chinese lawmakers had no time to waste with what we call the rights between people. The high authorities of the Chinese Empire did not care a fig if a merchant failed in delivering the goods, if a peasant stole a chicken from his neighbour, seduced his wife, or killed his brother.

To be sure, there existed a code of good behaviour (do not kill, do not cheat, etc.), but as to deciding who was right, who was wrong, who was the aggressor, how to redress the wrong made to the victim, it was up to the people to look after these things and apply their own justice. Taxes in their coffers, order in the land, these were the only concerns of the central power.

Such is the system that Japan adopted in the sixth century, a system from which the notion of rights is absent. People do have duties towards their Emperor, their superiors, their ancestors, their parents, but nowhere is there any mention about their rights. They cannot ask for justice, for there is no universal criterion to measure injustice. The law is an instrument of control for the governing bodies and nothing else. It has no relation to justice.

For a Westerner, one of the most difficult things to imagine must surely be a world where law and justice are two unrelated concepts. The reassuring picture of Saint Louis, the French king who sat under an oak tree and administered justice to his subjects, is an icon very close to our hearts, reflecting a deeply ingrained belief: the idea that there will always be a king, a father, a judge, to whom we can run and cry for justice.

This elemental scenario is so fundamental in our Judeo-Christian universe that it is difficult to imagine a world that might be otherwise. And yet . . . Saint Louis's Japanese contemporaries would have found abhorrent the idea of asking for justice from the good king under his oak tree. The prospect of going willingly to a third party to ask for justice would have been perceived as an abomination.

Indeed, if on a daily basis they had to obey the rulers' orders and endure their masters' whims, in return, their private lives were free of any state incursion. There was a totally waterproof separation between the public and the private side of their life.

As for the rulers, they did not consider it their role or responsibility to redress injustices among peasants. Indeed, they did their best to avoid it. Here are two examples:

In feudal times, villages had the option of complaining officially, when they felt the levy on their crops was getting too high. Their complaint was heard, and more often than not, they got redress.

Then, their spokesman was thrown into boiling water. This was considered the normal price to pay for having troubled peace and harmony, regardless of the outcome of the judgment. No wonder, then, that the Japanese developed such a strong preference for amicable mediation over the centuries!

Also in the old days, villages were organized in groups of four or five families. When someone was guilty of a crime, all members of all the families in his group suffered the ultimate punishment. As a result, each individual had a solidly vested interest in the behaviour of everyone else. The mere shadow of a conflict was enough to threaten the whole village. The best way to keep the authorities at bay was to exert a strict internal discipline within the community.

This is the wisdom, refined by fourteen centuries of practice, that was being applied by the inhabitants of the village under the windows of the embassy, on the eve of the twenty-first century. Their reaction illustrates a very common attitude in Japan: better wash your dirty laundry at home.

Obviously, it takes a while to rid society of practices so deeply rooted in customs. Yet, it was more than a century ago that Japan opted for Western law, and since then, the Japanese have enjoyed the notion of fundamental rights. When they suffer an injustice, they can complain; when they are wronged, they can get redress and obtain compensation.

Their courts have a hybrid quality, part European, part Anglo-Saxon; they are desperately slow, but they work. Still, the Japanese do not trust them totally, and they would much rather solve their conflicts the way their ancestors did – between themselves, amicably, to stay away from troubles.

Is this mistrust due to the fact that Japanese courts deal with a legal system that is foreign in spirit? After all, the civil code, the penal code, the commercial code, the procedural codes all used the French or German models as their blueprints. However, it is generally agreed that the two legal experts (one French, one German) who undertook this immense task at the end of the nineteenth century managed to dovetail adequately Japanese common law and European structures.

Rather, the distrust of the courts stems from the ancient wisdom that nothing good ever came from the authorities.

In Tokyo District Court, I have an appointment with a judge who has just been through a very unusual experience: he had just spent three full weeks working as a rookie news reporter for one of the large daily newspapers.

Judge – and reporter – covering the dog-catcher beat!

As proof of his feat, he brandishes the business card that the daily newspaper *Asahi Shimbun* printed for him for the occasion. He shows it victoriously, like a trophy.

As for his real business card, the one that proves that, indeed, he is a judge, he places it perfunctorily on the coffee table in front of me. Nothing new here. Nothing exciting.

And yet!

When a Japanese presents his business card, he expects you to examine it closely, conspicuously, to absorb all the vital information it contains. Then, and only then, will you bow, having measured the angle and the duration of your bow according to the university the person went to, the diplomas he obtained, and his present functions – which are all listed on the card.

A judge is a big deal, and one is expected to bow very low and very long.

A judge is someone who has survived one of the most severe systems of academic triage and elimination. To study law is one thing. But to be admitted to the bar is quite another. Twenty thousand candidates anually write the entrance examination to the Legal Training and Research Institute of Japan. Only 2 per cent make it into the school. The standards are very high, and it is the only way to become a lawyer or a judge. Therefore young would-be lawyers do not hesitate to try again and again. They study night and day for four or even five years, in the hope that they will eventually make it through the institute's narrow door.

A judge is someone who has been through all this, and has had to endure two years of intense training offered by the institute.

A judge is also someone who, at the ripe age of thirty, goes directly from the school benches to the chair of the court. During all these years of study, he has had no choice but to live under his parents' roof, then to board at the institute. Overnight, he abandons his impoverished student status and enters the rarefied world of a privileged élite, without ever having had any experience of practical life.

That is why, from time to time, judges are ordered to do short stints in the private sector, be it at a bank, a manufacturing industry – a newspaper.

Judge Ono had already reached forty, and had been a judge for ten years, when the system caught up with him and he was told to go out there and see how the rest of the world lives.

"I really didn't want to go," he told me, "but it was an order!"

That is how he spent three weeks working for the city desk of a large newsroom, and it was an eye-opener.

"I used to think that reporters can write any damn thing. In fact, they have to check each detail three times before it goes to print. And they work such long hours!"

This experience made him appreciate how privileged he is. Yet, his working environment is Spartan: a very long common room, two rows of four desks facing one another, just like in post offices in the old days. At one end, facing the two rows, the desk of the senior judge. From this vantage point, he can supervise the group, like a teacher in a one-room country school. Everybody can hear every telephone conversation, and see visitors as they come in.

We are introduced in a sitting area, furnished with two tired leather couches and a coffee table.

"Why did you become a judge, rather than a lawyer?" I ask. "They make more money, and they are independent."

"The career of a judge is more stable. But mostly, I was interested in service to the public."

With a small chin movement, Judge Ono draws my attention to two men chatting in a leisurely fashion in the ratty armchairs of another sitting area. Coffee, cigarettes, they talk in low voices, offering the familiar image of two colleagues enjoying their coffee break. "The one on the left is a judge. He is helping a small retailer and his supplier solve a dispute."

After a few minutes, the supplier who cannot get payment leaves the room. The merchant who never got delivery takes his place. More coffee, more cigarettes. Later, the judge will invite the two of them to sit together – by now, the ashtray is overflowing – and he will pronounce his decision, very low-key. Suddenly the two adversaries will be on their feet, bowing to the judge, thanking him, bowing to one another, apologizing, bowing all around, issue closed. Then they will leave the room, and the judge will ask another plaintiff to come in for a coffee and a cigarette.

This is how the judicial system gets closer to the people. The judge's attitude, his tone of voice, his quiet behaviour, totally devoid of any sense of superiority, are cultivated to remind everyone of the village mediator, the one to whom people used to turn in the old days when they had a bone to pick with their neighbour.

"People trust us more," explains Judge Ono. "They are more willing to come and use our services." Then he adds, mysteriously, "There is something else I want to show you."

Off we go through the long corridors to have a look at the courtrooms. There are twenty large ones, forty smaller ones, all laid out in the familiar Western fashion. Then, with a hint of excitement, Judge Ono opens yet another door. Surprise! The room is distinctly smaller than all the others, and there is nothing, absolutely nothing, solemn or intimidating about it. In the middle is a round table in light oak and seven chairs – four for the two parties and their lawyers, one for the public prosecutor, one for the clerk, and one for the judge. The chairs are all rigorously the same – same shape, same size, same colour. All seven of them are equally distributed around the table.

A Japanese male brimming with unbridled enthusiasm is a rare sight, and I feel privileged, at that particular moment, for Judge Ono is almost bouncing.

"This is very recent. The Supreme Court decided to install this format on a trial basis, a few years ago. We built ten of these, but we could use many more. Everybody wants to use these round court-rooms. Judges, lawyers, parties, all those who had the opportunity to try the new courtrooms agree that trials are faster and more effective in there, less adversarial, more likely to send the parties home in peace, having achieved closure. It is an unmitigated success."

What a wonderful irony! For years, Japanese judicial experts went scurrying around the world, looking for a solution to the problem of clogged courtrooms and public mistrust. In the process, they ended up reinventing, from the ground up, the ancient courts that kept the peace in the countryside of the Old Japan.

CHAPTER 3

The White Sorcerer

Tall, lean, and all in black, he moves like a wolf. Supremely at ease in the refined elegance of the New Otani Hotel, he marches through the main lobby like a conqueror, enters the restaurant as if he owned it, spots a table in a corner, and, without asking anyone, takes a seat nonchalantly – with his back turned to the rest of the room. The arrogant wolf dreads the eyes of the public. He is The Foreigner. People think of him as a magician, as a fox in the chicken coop, often as both. He is a constant object of curiosity, of worry and wonderment. What he does and what he says are regularly reported in the financial press as much as in gossip rags; he is admired and hated, envied and venerated, people want to know where he eats, what he drinks, and who he beds. His life is public property.

Philippe Troussier is the coach of the national soccer team. This young Frenchman is a former professional player who developed an international reputation as a coach to call on as a last resort during his years in Africa. For eight years, from the Ivory Coast to South Africa, from Morocco to Nigeria and Burkina Faso, soccer teams competed to woo him throughout the continent. Everywhere he went, he managed to bring less-than-lacklustre teams to a respectable – if not an international – level. They called him the Miracle Maker, the White Sorcerer. The name stayed, so did the reputation.

This is why, in 1998, the Japan Football Association brought him on. Soccer was still a relatively novel sport in Japan, the national league had been created only five years earlier, and Japan had just been chosen as the host of the 2002 World Cup. There was only one hitch: it would share this honour with its hereditary enemy, neighbouring Korea. The sixty-four final matches would take place in ten Korean cities and ten Japanese cities. Such was the verdict of the Federation Internationale de Football Association (FIFA). The Japanese were thrown into an acute case of schizophrenic anguish before this double "first": it would be the first time the World Cup would take place in Asia, and that was an immense source of pride; it would also be the first time the Cup would be hosted by two countries simultaneously. They were close to feeling betrayed.

One thing was clear: the honour of the country was at stake; the national team had to become a team to reckon with, a team that counted in the international world of soccer.

Time was of the essence; the task was urgent. The White Sorcerer was fetched, and it was not long before he started performing his magic. During his first year in Japan, the under-twenty-year-old team made it all the way to the finals in the junior world cup in Nigeria; during his second year, the national team finished in the quarter-finals at the Sydney Olympics, and won the Asian Cup in Lebanon. This Frenchman was obviously a winner.

He was also becoming intensely controversial. When they entrusted him with the task of training their élite players, the Japanese Soccer Federation thought they were hiring a young man in a track suit with a ball. That was a gross underestimation. The minute he arrived, Philippe Troussier toppled traditions, threatened the established order, imposed his methods, pushed, pulled, and coerced, screamed, raged, and demanded, in order to propel the Japanese onto the international field. More than once, the Japanese soccer authorities

wondered whether they had signed a pact with the devil the day they
trusted this shameless adventurer with their national honour, no less.

Yet, Philippe Troussier is taking his mission very seriously. Behind the
nonchalant attitude, the unkempt hair, the arrogant sneers, lurks a
very intense young man eager to talk about his challenge. Ensconced
at the corner table in the New Otani restaurant, he pushes away an
espresso that is getting cold, spreads open a paper napkin, pulls out a
pen, and draws a series of geometric figures to explain how he visu-
alizes the Japanese challenge.

"They asked me to come, because they wanted a foreigner. They
realized that they needed new blood. So, when they tell me, 'Now
that you are in Japan, you have to adapt to our ways,' I reply, 'Sorry,
it's just the opposite. You will have to adapt to mine.'

"My soccer is world soccer. They are too insular. Their soccer is
organized according to their traditions, their island. I don't want to
fight their traditions, but if they actually want to become world-class,
they have to change. The truth is, they are afraid of the outside world."

In his own words, the Parisian street kid echoes generations of
entrepreneurs, diplomats, researchers, and academics who, over the
years, were invited by the Japanese to help the country come out of
isolation and faced similar challenges. In a variety of fields, the
Japanese are desperately eager to become active members of the
international community, yet they fear just as desperately that they
will lose their souls in the process.

Philippe Troussier witnessed this dilemma first-hand: "If they
sincerely want to become international, they must let their players
out of the country. Young people must spend some time abroad, see
how things are done elsewhere, measure themselves against others.
But they don't want to let them go!

"Take the example of Shinji Ono. He is a star in Japan. They
think that if he goes and trains abroad, it will be a loss for the country.
In actual fact, if he doesn't, he will indeed remain a star in Japan and
a nobody in the world."

The French coach has learned one thing: one does not win frontal attacks in Japan. All the same, he can claim a few victories.

"I convinced them to send Hiroshi Nanami, from the Iwata team, to spend a season in Venice. His coaches fought tooth and nail against the project, because his was a first-division team, and I was sending him to a second-division team. They perceived it as an insult. In fact, it was a very positive experience. Nanami went out, he saw new things, new people; until then, he was intimidated by Western women, yet he was a hit with Italian girls. He was cowed by the European players, yet he realized that he was just as good as they were. He grew more assured, he learned to take initiatives on the field, as in life. He came back a new man, his teammates listened to his travel stories, they want to do the same.

"These success stories are still the exception. Most of the time, Japanese coaches manage to keep their players at home. So I told them: 'All right, let us stay at home, train on our home turf, between ourselves, but we still have a World Cup in two years! If we want to become international material, we must work a lot harder!'"

That is Westerner-speak; that got him nowhere.

"To which they answered, 'Yes, indeed, working harder, yes we should, however, right now, you see, it's simply not possible. It's winter, you see, now it's rainy season, you see, now it's sumo season, now it's baseball season. We can't do this, we can't do that, tickets have been sold already, it's too late to change the dates . . .'"

In the elegant New Otani restaurant, Philippe Troussier treats me to a devastating imitation of the federation's administrators – in fact, a devastating imitation of any Japanese trying to say "no": head leaning slightly sideways, the apologetic tone of voice they use to let you know that it is out the question, the sucking of air between the teeth when they are too embarrassed to tell you to your face. . . . This little show lasted only a few seconds, but the message was clear: Japanese soccer is soft. Such is the verdict of the foreign coach.

On the field, Japanese coaches exhibit the same aversion to any kind of risk. Four players in defensive positions, such was the traditional method, taught by the Brazilians who trained the first generation of Japanese players. Today, these men hold senior positions as heads of local teams, or managers of the national federation. When a newcomer fresh off the boat, like Troussier, announces that from now on there will be only three men in defence positions, not only is it perceived as intolerably reckless, but also as a direct affront to a whole generation of pioneers.

Every time Troussier wins a game, the old-timers – they are called "the Brazilians" – lose a bit more credibility. It has come to the point where the old guard cheer and dread all at once their national team victories.

Relations between the young French coach and the soccer powers-that-be are not easy.

To start with, he sacrificed a whole generation of players. They were the best the country had when he arrived; they had played in the 1998 World Cup, and were shaped in the traditional mould. "Powerful physically, headstrong, willing to die on the field rather than accept defeat," Troussier recalls. "But they did not know how to manage a game. They charged without any strategy. I could never make modern players out of them. In order to create what they were asking me to create, I needed more-flexible players, more open, more intelligent on the field, handier with the ball. I would only find them among the next generation."

Ignoring all respect due to age and seniority, he plucked perfect unknowns, one by one, from the sixteen professional teams in the country. "In so doing, I wounded a whole generation in their pride and self-respect. Armed only with a ball, I shook the very foundations of the political, economic, societal system."

Indeed, Philippe Troussier had dared tamper with one of the deepest traditions in Japan: the relationship between *sempai* and *kohai*, which is fundamental to understanding relationships between people.

The *sempai* is someone with more seniority than you. He was in second-year university when you were in first, he joined the company six months before you did, he has been part of the team three months longer than you have. For the rest of his life, the *kohai* or junior, owes respect to his *sempai*, whatever the circumstances.

For instance, it would be deeply embarrassing to be promoted ahead of someone who joined the firm before you did; the *sempai-kohai* relation is often the determining factor, rather than merit. It is true in schools, in the public sector, in large corporations; it is also applies in sports. It is always a shock for foreigners

"When I arrived in Japan to finish my studies, I quite naturally signed up with my university soccer team," a young European told me, still shaken by the experience. "I had been playing soccer since the age of seven, yet they placed me with beginners. I did not touch the ball for a whole year. I would clean the dressing rooms, inflate the balls, rake the field with one of these bamboo rakes used in Zen gardens. I considered it to be regular hazing. The others found it perfectly natural."

That is precisely the sort of attitude the new coach of the national team set out to uproot. Philippe Troussier could not believe his eyes: on the field, a senior player could demand the ball and get it, without a split second of hesitation on the part of his juniors. Troussier would scream and rage when a young player made an extra pass to give his senior the privilege of scoring a goal. He would curse and swear at the exceptionally gifted young dribbler, new to the team, when the kid apologized profusely to the other players, bowing over and over, for moving too fast for them. Other coaches were perplexed. They simply did not understand the Frenchman. They felt that the foreigner was undermining not only their own authority but possibly the foundations of society as a whole.

As for the young players, they were beginning to chuckle in their heart of hearts. These kids, whose only way to rebel against society is to dye their hair yellow, were watching with intense interest the clashes between this coach unlike any other and the authorities in office.

They are called "the Troussier children." They are the new generation of players pulled out of anonymity by the coach of the national team and shaped to his image in order to create the dream team representing Japan in the World Cup. They are totally devoted, and still cannot quite believe what has happened to them.

Tomokazu Miyojin is one of them. Twenty-one years old, with banana-yellow hair like so many boys his age, a sarcastic eye behind a respectful eyelid, the young man recalls the moment that changed the course of his career. When he felt his cellphone vibrate in his parka pocket, he was sitting with a few friends in a Kashiwa coffee shop, without the slightest inkling of what was coming. When the voice at the other end announced that he was now a member of the national team, he couldn't believe his ears.

"I did not have enough seniority to even think about it," he explains. "I was stunned. Suddenly, my whole life changed."

Overnight, Miyojin became a star. People now recognize him in the street, they ask him for autographs, he gives interviews, cameras zoom in on him during games, as experts try to identify in his play the distinctive style of all "Troussier children": fast-moving, strategic, and disciplined.

"With Troussier, our practices are completely different. We repeat the same passes, the same moves, over and over, until they become automatic. As long as the drills are not perfect, he screams at us and we do it again. We are not used to being shouted at. Japanese coaches never shout. In the beginning I could not understand why he got so angry; now I understand that he shouts because he has a deep love of soccer. It's a passion, and he really wants us to be the best."

Voice matters a lot to the young Parisian.

"The biggest difference between him and other coaches is that he forces us to talk! He wants his players to speak, to communicate, to get to know one another, not only on the field but also after practice. He encourages us to talk about the game and also about other things too. No Japanese coach ever asked us such a thing!"

"The Japanese play soccer without any verbal communication," laments Troussier. "During a game, you rarely see them shout a direction, cheer one another, do a high-five. After the game, in the dressing room, they rarely rebuild the world the way soccer players do the world over. They are organized, cerebral, systematic. They play soccer like they would play chess. Yet, soccer is a game of passion, of human relationships!"

As a last resort, he challenges his players and deliberately puts them in situations where they must think for themselves and take initiatives, outside the soccer field.

"Generally, during long training camps, we live together, we share the same restaurants, the same hotels, we go out together during down times, and we get to know one another. But, in Japan, even the down times had to be organized! Players expected it, otherwise they did not go out. It was hard in the beginning. I would tell them, 'Tonight, the evening is free,' They would reply, 'At what time will the bus pick us up to go for dinner?' I would say, 'You are free. Go anywhere you like. The area is full of fun little restaurants.' They would stay and eat in the hotel restaurant.

"I would have the management close the restaurant.

"'Where shall we go for dinner?'

"'Go anywhere you like, you are free!'

"They were lost. They felt I was abandoning them. Then, progressively, they started going out in small groups of three or four. They tried Chinese restaurants, Italian ones, Lebanese ones . . . Now, they love it! They got to know one another, they became friends, and on the field, you can tell the difference!"

"It's not the players who win a match," explains Troussier. "It's the men. My role is to shape these men. I go way beyond teaching them how to move the ball on the field. I need to control what they eat, where they change, how they live, how they sleep . . ."

The national coach does not impose any particular diet on his players, other than frowning on Coca-Cola. He puts them through a physical training designed specifically to increase their power. He was surprised to find a near-total absence of psychological training. In the West, athletes are increasingly relying on methods borrowed from Asian martial arts in order to place themselves in a winning frame of mind. Paradoxically, Japanese players are still content with simply shouting in unison, "We are the best!" before a game.

These things matter, but what matters most is the men. This is one of Troussier's favourite themes. He states without hesitation that the reason the Japanese won the Asia Cup is not because of their specific talent, but because, "it was managed by real men." Then, he adds, almost in the same breath, "I am probably creating a generation of orphans."

Indeed, what will happen to the "Troussier children" after he leaves? At this point, the national coach is running a commando operation, with the World Cup as his horizon. In the process, he sketches what could be the future of Japanese soccer with a modern approach and a long-term strategy. Whether his suggestions are followed or ignored, the "Troussier children" will either become the decision-makers of the next generation or its castaways. It will all depend on whether the present bosses at the federation have the political will and the capacity to internationalize Japanese soccer.

Sergio Echigo moves his massive body heavily. His head is set in his shoulders as if to prevent a blow, and his narrowed eyes suggest a constant mistrust. Before he even opens his mouth, his whole being is already signifying what he thinks of Japan's ability to internationalize.

Echigo belongs to the "Brazilians" generation, but he is an unusual Brazilian: his parents were Japanese, and the blood flowing in his veins is pure Japanese, even though his personality is definitely that of a Latin American.

He came to Japan in 1973, first as a player, then as a coach. He decided to stay permanently, with the idea that his dual heritage – an intimate understanding of Japanese traditions associated with the openness of one of the most multi-ethnic countries in the world – could be of benefit to the land of his ancestors.

Echigo followed with great personal interest Troussier's first tiffs with the soccer authorities. He had gone through the same difficulties and faced the same obstacles – the difference was, however, that at the time his bursts of anger were met with less patience, because, after all, this Brazilian was a Japanese. Sergio Echigo is both amused and exasperated with the Frenchman's grand pronouncements.

"Of course, he is right, if Japanese players are to launch themselves on the international stage, they must get rid of the *sempai-kohai* yoke once and for all, the system must change. Everybody knows that, everybody says that, yet anyone who dares suggest solutions gets hammered down."

And he retracts his head a bit farther into his shoulders.

Sergio Echigo wants to be Japanese, but even after twenty-seven years, he does not find it easy.

"In this country, you are allowed to criticize if you are just passing through, but if you come to stay, you must learn to shut up."

After his career as a player was over, Echigo carved out a role as a soccer commentator. Despite it all, he still believes in the great dream that existed at the beginning of the Japan Soccer League: the dream of a sport unlike the others, not financed by large corporations, but rather rooted in the community, based on the concept of fair play and openness, a sport that would be a prelude to a new society, open to the future and to the world.

In the 1980s, a comic strip called *Captain Tsubasa* struck the imagination of a whole generation of Japanese kids. It told the story of a young boy who plays in the World Cup, bringing victory to his team and glory to his country.

These were the days when the Japanese media were just beginning to broadcast the World Cup games. Japan had no national league yet, but it did not matter. Young people identified with the comic-strip hero, and, through television, they discovered the ecstasy of coming out first in this world event. Thanks to *Captain Tsubasa*, they briefly experienced the feeling of euphoria that comes with knowing that you are a player that counts in the world – a dream that the Japanese have been hoping for and fearing with equal intensity since the nineteenth century.

Captain Tsubasa allowed them to dream their life. The White Sorcerer gives them the opportunity to actually live it. He made only realistic promises: it was out of the question that the Japanese could win the World Cup in 2002. But they could become a team to reckon with. How far would they go? None of the people I talked to dared to mention the quarter-finals, but a win there would obviously have been an immense victory for the whole country. No longer would the Japanese need any comic-strip hero to feed their dreams. They could finally experience that long-awaited feeling of being part of the international community.

Such was the huge responsibility that rested on the shoulders of the White Sorcerer.

CHAPTER 4

Revolution in TV News

" All racists, those Japanese!"
"Xenophobic! They will never change!"
"Ethnic cleansing! We are all victims of ethnic cleansing!"

In the fall of 1994, I spent a week holding court in the back room of a coffee shop off the lobby of one of the large international hotels in town – one of those posh, anonymous coffee shops that look alike the world over, where sleep-deprived Western businessmen talk about contracts, delivery dates, regulations, and non-tariff barriers before heading back to the airport. It was definitely not the kind of coffee shop where television people tend to hang around.

Yet, as I was trying to unravel the root causes of the wrenching crisis that was shaking the world of Japanese TV news, that particular coffee shop turned out to be just about the only place in town where my sources would agree to talk to me without fearing reprisals. Some of them even called back ahead of the interview to make sure that I would pick a table far away from the entrance, as

close as possible to the kitchen doors. They would walk into this
foreign environment looking furtively around them, and take a seat
with their backs to the room. They had all become paranoic. The
daily news show they worked for had just been cancelled, and they
were out of a job, but worse yet, they felt wounded, betrayed, full of
hatred and despair. They saw enemies everywhere, they doubted
their closest friends, toyed with the wildest conspiracy theories, and
were reconsidering some concepts as fundamental as truth, honour,
liberty, and democracy.

There is nothing out of the ordinary about the cancellation of a
television show. It happens every year, before a new season starts. Its
staff may worry about their next assignment, they may indulge in
some nostalgia, but rarely does it justify the emotion I was uncovering
that week in my makeshift confessional. What had been happening?

In September 1994, NHK, the public television network, cancelled one of its daily news shows. Sober, balanced, and serious, *Japan
Business Today* covered business and financial news in a format very
similar to other programs the world over.

Yet, its termination aroused intense feelings in journalistic circles
– feelings way out of proportion to the show's influence and ratings.
For *JBT*, as it was referred to in the corridors of NHK, was a show
unlike any other.

JBT had been a unique experiment, a bold and ambitious venture.
First of all, it was broadcast in a foreign language – English – on
prime time on the national network; few countries would dare do
the same. Secondly, it was produced by an international team of
Americans, Canadians, British, and Australians, working alongside
the Japanese. The fact that foreigners would have any say in the
content of a national information program was per se revolutionary.
Also, *Japan Business Today* was entrusted with a proud and lofty
mission: to make Japan better known to the rest of the world.

The show was rebroadcast every day in Europe and North
America. The idea was to produce a show made in Japan, covering

Japan, with a Japanese perspective, but to do it in a style that would be more appealing to Western audiences than the wooden format the Japanese have to endure from their own network.

Japanese content, Western format: the formula sounded simple enough. Yet it became the greatest adventure of them all.

JBT artisans quickly came to realize that there is nothing simple about separating form and content. Difficulties started at the beginning of the day with the questions that are asked every morning in every newsroom in the world: What are we going to be covering today? What is happening in the world that is worth reporting in our evening newscast? In other words, What is news? That was the first snare.

One of the largest Japanese corporations was suddenly laying off hundreds of employees, for the first time in its history. Should that be in the news? "Obviously," the Westerners would say. Life-long employment was still the norm in Japan in those days, and the announcement was unprecedented. "Absolutely not," the Japanese would protest. "It would draw undue attention to this corporation. Don't you think they are having enough problems as it is?"

At that time, financial scandals were exploding in quick succession, shaking the financial community and the trust the people had in their institutions. Should they be covered by *JBT* reporters? "All right," management would concede. "But be sure not to name the authors of the scandals. They have already been sufficiently humiliated."

What about a series on various sources of energy in Japan? "Interesting," the bosses would muse, "but they would suppress any reference to nuclear energy – always so controversial – even though it is by far the main source of power in the country."

When Westerners wrote, "the Japanese army," they were severely reprimanded. They should know that there is no army in Japan. "The Japanese army" does not exist. One should write, "the self-defence forces." For Westerners, writing "the Japanese army" was saying it like it is. For the Japanese, it was reviving needlessly the most painful of national controversies.

A news item on Taiwan? No problem, provided that the flag did not appear anywhere in the picture. One would not want to hurt mainland Chinese sensitivities and risk a diplomatic incident.

Cherry trees had just started blossoming in Kyoto. Was that news? "Obviously," the Japanese would say. Every newscast includes some reference to the season, such as, "Maple leaves just started turning red in Sendai," "The winter festival is opening today in Sapporo," or "The rainy season has arrived in Tokyo," all of this illustrated with gorgeous footage. These events mark the passage of time and serve as benchmarks. As Christmas and Easter do for us, they suggest a common cultural heritage and give validity to the newscast as a whole. For Westerners, however, blooming branches swinging softly in the breeze for twenty full seconds on the evening news? That is too much!

Every day, *Japan Business Today* staff bumped into that kind of obstacle and discovered yet another facet of the rift between them. Interviewing a public personality was always a particularly trying test. As a matter of course, Japanese reporters submit a list of their questions ahead of an interview. They then ask them in sequence, whatever the answers, without deviating from the approved scenario. To them, it is the most elementary courtesy; one would not want to cause any surprise and embarrassment to the interviewee. Furthermore, a small gift is expected once the interview is over. It sounds like the most natural thing to do in this country, where the most prosaic encounter requires an exchange of presents. Yet, every time, Western reporters did a double take – especially since those "small gifts" often consisted of a thick handful of banknotes in an envelope.

However, of all the sources of misunderstandings between Japanese and Western journalists, the worst, by far, is the existence of press clubs. *Kisha* clubs are the *bête noire* of all foreign correspondents, and one of the worst, yet most permanent, features of Japanese journalism.

Each government ministry has its own *kisha* club. This small group of reporters, each representing his own agency, newspaper, or television station, share the same newsroom in the ministry building, and live off the manna handed down by the said ministry. No effort is spared to facilitate their work: they each have their booth and desk, their computer and telephone line – provided by the ministry. There is even a small dormitory with bunk beds adjoining the newsroom, for those evenings when you might have to miss the final subway because of some breaking news.

The ministry information office is often located on the same floor; as soon as press releases are published, they're placed in each reporter's pigeonhole. Once or twice a day, at a fixed time, *kisha* club members are entitled to a briefing session on the record, before the cameras. Sometimes, the minister himself will attend.

This cushy life has its price: the minister has a say in who can belong to his *kisha* club. One question too many, one aggressive tone in the interview, and you are shown the door. You are sent back to headquarters to face sneers from colleagues, scowls from bosses, a career that starts again from scratch.

It rarely happens. *Kisha* club members watch one another constantly. Even though they are competitors in principle, in practice they all share a vested interest in belonging to a smoothly operating club. Each one of them feels personally responsible for the decorum during the minister's press conferences. They also ensure that these press conferences remain exclusive hunting grounds.

I happened to be in the newsroom of the daily *Asahi Shimbun* one morning when a young reporter full of enthusiasm and ambition pranced back from a press conference given by the minister of transport. When I inquired as to which questions he had asked the minister, he looked at me, stunned.

"Me? Ask a question of the minister? Never!"

"How come?"

"Our newspaper has a reporter assigned on a permanent basis to the Department of Transport kisha club. I would make a mortal enemy out of him if I dared ask a question of *his* minister!"

Only members of the *kisha* club are allowed to ask questions of the minister. This automatically excludes foreign correspondents, because being a *kisha* club member is a full-time activity: over and above their work, reporters take turns to man the station, they organize drinking parties and attend receptions to keep relationships well oiled within the department. It's unthinkable for a foreign correspondent (who is usually alone to cover the whole country) to belong to a *kisha* club and most difficult, therefore, to ever ask a question of a minister!

A Japanese political reporter was telling me one day about the term he had just spent with the *kisha* club at the Tokyo Police Headquarters, as part of an exchange program. This experience took place shortly after the sarin gas attack in the subway by the Aum Shinrikyo sect. That was a complex matter, the incident had been traumatic for Japanese society as a whole, and the public was following with intense interest the actions of the police and the judiciary. As a result, the chief of police was on the news virtually every night.

In Japan, as elsewhere, police officers are rarely keen to confide to reporters, and official statements were few and far between. Yet news seeped through somehow, Japanese-style.

"Every evening after the end of the working day, I would go the chief of police's private residence," this reporter recounted. "I would ring the doorbell to say hello and wish him a good evening. Then I would start pacing slowly around his house. The other members of his *kisha* club were there too. We were circling slowly, sometimes for hours on end. Each one of us was hoping for a chance to get an exclusive interview. From time to time, the door would open, the chief of police would invite one of us to come in for a beer. At one point, late in the evening, he would open the door one last time and announce in a loud voice, to no one in particular, 'I am going to bed!' That was the signal. It was time to go home, and we would all head for the subway station, hoping to get luckier the next day."

This practice has a name. It is called *yoo-mawaru*. Every reporter who has ever covered national politics has lived through it. Reporters assigned to the prime minister's residence do *yoo-mawaru* every day.

Nothing could better illustrate the state of dependence of *kisha* club reporters. How could anyone ever come up with a scoop in that context? When everyone has access to the same information from the same source at the same time, works all day long in the same common room, where no telephone conversation is private, how could anyone ever hope to publish an exclusive story?

I put the question to a Japanese reporter who had invited me to visit his *kisha* club. He smiled with a terribly embarrassed expression on his face, as if I had just uttered a particularly vulgar word in front of his friends. "We do serious journalism here," he said. "We are not looking for sensationalism. We work in depth." He added, "We are not Bronco-chasers here."

With department press releases as the sole source of raw material.

You always get a pained, hurt expression when you mention scoops to Japanese reporters. One the one hand, like reporters anywhere, their prime ambition is to find an exclusive story. On the other hand, the prospect of being the first, the only one, alone out there, is something they have learned to dread deeply since childhood – which places Japanese reporters in an impossible dilemma.

There is a rich pool of anecdotes on the contortions of which they are capable when they stumble on an exclusive story. Take any American correspondent in Japan, sit him in a comfortable chair with a good Scotch in his hand, and within minutes you will be regaled with the well-worn story of the day a Japanese reporter got the scoop on the Crown Prince's upcoming engagement.

To publish such a news item was unthinkable, as it would have shown an intolerable lack of respect for the Imperial Family. There is a tacit agreement on this point between the media and the Emperor. It has partly to do with protecting the privacy of the latter, and partly with distancing Japanese media from British paparazzi. It is a matter of national pride.

On the other hand, the Japanese public was waiting impatiently for their prince to find his princess, so the news item had to come out somehow. The dilemma was solved Japanese-style: the item was slipped to a colleague from the *Washington Post*. The next day, it made the front page of the American daily. From then on, it was quite acceptable for the Japanese media to report that "According to the *Washington Post* . . ."

A similar sleight of hand was used when American President George Bush, Sr., happened to feel sick during an official dinner, and vomited on the Japanese prime minister sitting next to him. An NHK camera shot the whole undignified scene.

To use it or not? The consensus was not to air that footage, but, mysteriously, the tape found its way to the CNN studios across town. Once those sad pictures were seen around the globe, NHK could show them without offending anyone.

At the time of the Kobe earthquake in January 1995, the Japanese media worked with astonishing speed to cover the disaster in all its details and in all its scope. They were the first to acknowledge the stupefying ineptitude of the authorities in the first few hours after the earthquake, but they did not automatically report it. It fell on the *Times* of London to sound the alarm and ask aloud: "Where are the authorities?"

Then and only then did the Japanese media follow suit and undertake to analyze with great diligence their leaders' unforgivable failure.

Self-censorship on a daily basis, deliberate avoidance of exclusives, and the castrating protection of the *kisha* clubs, such were some of the obstacles confronting Western members of the *Japan Business Today* team. "Pack journalism, bureaucratic journalism, fraidy-cat journalism," they grumbled as they went about their daily tasks.

No wonder the *JBT* experiment did not last. "Actually the miracle is that it lasted as long as it did," observed a young American producer, who was more positive than her colleagues. "The very fact that we were able to put a coherent show on the air every weekday during four years is in itself a resounding success." But, at a time when everyone was busy doing a postmortem, her optimism was the exception. From my secluded alcove near the kitchen doors in the large coffee shop that had become my headquarters, I was hearing mostly about failure. The Japanese and the Westerners felt the same exasperation at the outcome they all had so desperately hoped to avoid despite all odds – until the last minute. They called one another toadies and cowboys, yet they had shared the same dream. During four years, they had actually worked in the belief that they would succeed in changing the image of Japan in the world and even, possibly, the geopolitical balance of the planet. And you did not have to push them very far for them to recognize that they saw themselves as the pioneers of a last frontier, which made the failure even more painful.

This television show, which was produced in a windowless room adjoining the generators in the first basement of the immense NHK building, and which had just ended miserably in bitterness and paranoia, had been destined for a great future.

It all started in 1989, with a speech by then-prime minister Toshiki Kaifu to the Japanese Press Club in Tokyo. Those were the euphoric days of "the bubble economy." Japan's economic might was comparable to the United States', every Japanese woke up each morning richer than the day before, and international-management gurus were falling over themselves to offer their analysis of "the Japanese miracle" in academic reviews.

Yet, even then, Japan remained unknown and misunderstood. Misunderstood, isolated, and somewhat irrelevant. Why wasn't Japan taking its place in the world? Why didn't it assume a political leadership in keeping with its economic influence? In short, why wasn't Japan behaving according to its status?

In the country, these reproaches were met with good resolutions: "We must internationalize, we must become international," they would proclaim without anyone knowing or asking what this really meant.

For Prime Minister Kaifu, on that day in 1989, his admonition to reporters was simple: they had to make Japan better known to the world. Those Japanese who had the opportunity to work abroad, be they businesspeople, diplomats, journalists, or students, would regularly come back with stunning anecdotes showing how little the rest of the world knew or even cared about their country, and the prime minister's speech was striking a very sensitive chord.

In the following months, several major Japanese media dutifully undertook to present to the world the human face of Japan.

The daily *Asahi Shimbun* decided to launch a new publication in the United States, *Japan Watch*, which would cover Japanese news but would be written in New York by reporters familiar with the punchy style of American media.

"We expected to draw the same respect and consideration as the British *Independent*," *Asahi*'s publisher told me. "After all, we boast one of the widest networks of correspondents in the world with thirty-six foreign bureaus at this time, and our reporters come from the best universities. But we had underestimated the harsh reality that Americans are rarely interested in what is happening outside of their country, and in any case, they are only interested when the story is told by other Americans."

Japan Watch was a failure.

The world of television, too, was determined to "become international." By coincidence, the winds of change were blowing in the corridors of NHK that year. A new president had been named to the head of the public broadcaster in April 1989. Keiji Shima arrived in his position with fresh ideas, a vast program of reforms, and a lot of enthusiasm. He was determined to do away with old habits, open the windows, and shake out the dust from the grand old house. Inspired and visionary, he anticipated the impact of new technologies on the communication industries long before it became a household concept, and he had little patience with the overly prudent attitude of so many of his countrymen.

The Japanese had to open themselves to the world, do it well, do it fast, and beat the Americans at their own game. To begin with, they had to learn how to produce muscular, punchy television, just like the Americans.

Shima had spent less than a year in the New York bureau. He had acquired admiration and respect for the direct style of American anchors, their dynamism, and the power of pictures. However, Shima's enthusiasm was viewed with suspicion by international reporters, because his knowledge of the Western world was limited to these few months in New York. "His fascination for the outside world is that of a peasant who never came out of his village," one of his best friends explained charitably.

He did not speak any foreign language. "It is because of the war. I never had an opportunity to learn," Shima confessed. His understanding of cultural differences was sketchy at best. Yet, he was the big boss at NHK. He was convinced that, by putting together a team of Japanese-speaking Westerners and English-speaking Japanese, he would produce a very acceptable Japanese version of Walter Cronkite.

This is how *Japan Business Today* was created.

A few months later, he widened the mandate of his pet show. After hearing the prime minister's famous admonition, Shima made his own call to arms: "We cannot count on Western television to cover Asia properly," he fulminated before the Foreign Press Club in Tokyo. "I don't want to criticize Ted Turner, but CNN is forcing international news made in the U.S.A. on the rest of the world." It was time for someone to take over, redress the balance, and offer the world an alternative interpretation of current events. Shima saw himself as the fearless superhero fighting relentlessly for the sake of humanity against the monster of Americanization.

This is what he had in mind: an all-news network that would cover the globe and would be fed in eight-hour segments, alternately from Europe, the United States, and Japan. The project was quickly nicknamed "the perestroika." Its mission was simultaneously to stop CNN's inexorable progress and to promote an alternative, more-Japanese, view of the world. *Japan Business Today*, once conceived of

as a small, experimental project, was suddenly becoming the spear-tip
of an ambitious offensive to give Japan a true international presence.

The global network never came to be, for Keiji Shima's days were
numbered. Even though he had made his whole career at NHK, his
style was not that of the grand old corporation. He was rash and
brutal, he tended to call a spade a spade, he raged openly against
political interference in the editorial process, he managed with a bull-
dozer, terrified everyone around him, and invested little time in
making friends. After two years of this regime, he was expelled the
way a foreign body is expelled from an organism.

The idea of setting up a global network with the Americans and
the Europeans survived for a while, but, ironically, the Japanese were
the ones who withdrew in the end. At NHK, things went back to their
dozing normal, once again a quiet torpor shrouded the maze of corridors . . . and the *Japan Business Today* team found itself orphaned.
Now that their "father" was gone, they became a source of embarrassment, since they owed their existence to someone whose very
name was being erased from the collective memory.

Japan Business Today had lost its raison d'être. Gone was the ambition to take the world by storm. In the following months, NHK pulled
into itself as if healing a wound. The international adventure was
abandoned. Only two programs survived, both equally neutered and
insipid in their depiction of Japanese life for overseas consumption,
and the few foreigners still wandering in the corridors, the studios,
and the cafeteria suddenly looked like interlopers.

But slamming the door is not the way things are done in Japan,
and it took another two years before *Japan Business Today* was allowed
to disappear under a semblance of normalcy.

It is at that time that I held court under the neon lights of my
mysterious and unnamed coffee shop. Now that the whole saga was
actually over, how should it be interpreted?

The Westerners who came to my confessional and opened their
heart were still bristling with indignation, but they were already
turning the page. One was moving, another one was headed to a

faraway beach, a third was leaving Japan and going home; they were all handing out their résumés, and two of them at least would pursue brilliant careers with CNN. They were all busy taking stock, and bracing for the next adventure.

The Japanese staff members of *Japan Business Today*, on the other hand, were suffocating in anguish. More than ever before in their lives and in their careers, they were suddenly alone in the world. They had been misunderstood by their Western colleagues; they were now viewed with suspicion by their Japanese colleagues. They had taken more risk and invested more hope than anyone else in Shima's dream, and their assessment of the project was all the more severe. Shima had sorely bungled his dealings with the bureaucracy. He had been brutal in his personal relations, imprudent in his political friendships, and far too cavalier in general. Mostly, he had shaken the place up, given immense reason for hope, and then let go of the baton before the end of the race.

The Japanese were also accusing their Western colleagues of underestimating cultural obstacles, lacking patience, and abandoning them too soon. The Americans, in particular, had come with the patient condescension of missionaries steeped in their civilizing cause, electronic version. In their enthusiasm, they had underestimated the risks the Japanese were taking when they chose to come and work with them. They had neglected the fact that the terrified junior managers they had pushed around for four years had been their allies and their supporters in the Big House. Alone among this band of adventurers, they were gambling their careers.

Shima's great ambition had been to internationalize NHK, but he had operated so ruthlessly that he accomplished just the opposite, and the Japanese were appalled by the damage he left in his wake.

Indeed, the whole episode confirmed for the traditionalists in the Big House that they had been right all along to be wary of change, any change. Innovations bring nothing but trouble, one must stick to what is familiar, international projects are always rash and venturesome. They would not get caught in that kind of nonsense ever again.

Such was the paradox: *Japan Business Today* had been created to put the country on the map, to turn it into a serious player in the world, to offer an Asian alternative to the CNN vision that was saturating the planet at the time.

Four years later, its disappearance confirmed and reinforced all the worst clichés about Japan: Japan was folding in on itself, Japan was clamming up, Japan was turning its back on the rest of the world. For internationalist Japanese, the disappointment was as bitter as their hopes had been grand.

CHAPTER 5

The Black Sheep of
Japanese Journalism

La Maison du Chat Noir is famous in Tokyo for its unusual architecture as much as for its no-less-unusual inhabitant.

Made of black painted steel, three storeys high, with no windows,
it juts on a narrow angle between two lanes like the prow of a ship –
not one of those elegant cruise ships, but rather a very utilitarian
freighter – sticking out among the low roofs of this working-class
neighbourhood in the east end of Tokyo.

More incongruous yet is the cat, the enormous face of a cat
painted in *trompe l'oeil* over the full height of the building. Two
golden yellow eyes wide open on the third floor, nose and whiskers
on the second, the rest blending into the mat black of the steel wall.

Who on earth could have conceived such a nightmare? And
where is the door? It is four o'clock in the morning, the day is barely
breaking, and suddenly I, too, feel very incongruous, alone in the
sleeping megalopolis, a bag of fresh croissants dangling from my
fingers, looking for an opening in the iron wall of the black fortress,
a giant cat staring darkly over me. However, I came here to meet the
master of the place, and my curiosity gets the better of me.

He is one of the most famous journalists in Japan, and one of the most unusual. He has the reputation of shunning society. He is loved and hated, admired and vilified for what he has done and what he has not done, for what he is and what he is not. At once dour and jovial, a party animal and a reclusive hermit, denounced by all, yet a favoured guest in all forums, he fills a unique niche among Tokyo's pundit élites.

Takeshi Tachibana is one of the most prolific writers of his generation. With voracious curiosity, he has written about topics as varied as the American space program, the agricultural co-op movement, near-death experiences, student uprisings in the 1960s, the philosophy of science, and the brains of large monkeys. A knowledgeable œnologist, he owns a château and a vineyard in Burgundy. A self-taught mathematician, he is taken seriously enough by professionals to be a member of the prestigious Research Centre for Advanced Sciences and Technology. He wants to know everything, do everything, try everything, tell everything. His frenzy fascinates, his appetite is tempting, his enthusiasm is contagious.

Television shows love to invite him as a guest because he talks straight and is afraid of no one. His chubby face and dishevelled hair appeal to the viewers and keep them away from the remote control.

Publishers fight for the privilege of having his name on the front cover of any new publication, because it guarantees a successful launch. The magazine *Bungei Shunju*, to which he is a long-time contributor, published a special issue in November 1996. As thick as a book, as expensive too, it was entirely devoted to Tachibana and his works. Readers were regaled with such treats as a photograph of Takeshi at the age of three, Takeshi at ten, on a beach with his kid brother, Takeshi at twenty, in university. As if he were a rock star, one could learn about his favourite dishes, the brand of cigarettes he chain-smokes day and night, the name of the café he opened on campus while he was in university – Le Snack Gargantua – a picture of his château, naturally, and also a close-up of his fountain pen – a Mont Blanc – his glasses, and even his bed.

Such rock-star treatment for a beer-bellied intellectual in his fifties is indeed surprising. More surprising yet is the fact that he is, simultaneously, the black sheep of the Japanese media – the same media that use his name, his fame, and his *enfant terrible* aura to boost their sales and their ratings.

I did not meet anyone, even among his friends and close colleagues, who had anything clearly positive to say about Tachibana. At best, they mention his tenacity, they envy his easy writing style, they give tribute to his never-ending curiosity – but there is always a "but." He is invited, courted, envied, admired, but Tachibana remains a pariah, alone in the heart of the city.

His sin is this: he can boast having caused, single-handedly, the fall of one of the most powerful postwar prime ministers.

It happened the year of the Watergate affair in the United States. In 1974, Richard Nixon had just resigned in shame, and Americans were still recovering from the shock. The two *Washington Post* reporters who had exposed the scandal were being hailed as avengers of democracy, and the whole journalistic world was bathing in a renewed aura of glory by association.

In Tokyo, young Takeshi Tachibana was toiling obscurely for the *Bungei Shunju*, a weekly with a large circulation and no particular ideology. Writing for a Japanese magazine is a well-paying job, but it is not the most prestigious route for anyone aiming for a journalistic career, and Tachibana was chafing at the bit. Like any young reporter, he was looking for the scoop that would launch him. That is when he decided to emulate Woodward and Bernstein. The two *Washington Post* reporters had just become world famous for triggering the fall of their president. Why not do the same in Japan? It certainly was fertile ground, and there was a story begging to be told.

Political corruption was systemic and institutionalized in the 1960s and 1970s in Japan. Electoral campaigns and major public works went hand in hand, and no one objected. It was considered normal. That period of Japanese politics can be credited for those concrete riverbeds that defile the landscape, those divided highways going nowhere in the countryside, those futuristic bridges linking uninhabited islands, those handsome concert halls built in small towns far removed from any tour circuits. It was called "concrete democracy." The power and influence of a politician were measured according to his post-electoral largesses.

No one had mastered the system better than Prime Minister Kakuei Tanaka. He had started in life as a public-works contractor. He entered politics after the war, in 1947, with a disarmingly simple platform: build enough bridges, roads, tunnels, and railroads to cross the mountains separating Niigata, his native city, from the great metropolis, and drag his countrymen out of their isolation. This program also had the merit of going with the grain of the gigantic reconstruction effort that was galvanizing the country at that time.

His platform touched a particularly sensitive chord in the electors of the Ura Nippon region. The Back of Japan, on the other side of the mountains, the area which faces Korea, China, and Russia, has always been perceived as backward, and its inhabitants as rough peasants whose sole hope for improving their lots in life was to find jobs as chambermaids or day-labourers in Tokyo.

Tanaka's genius was to say, "Let us dig holes through the mountains and join the twentieth century; let us create links between Niigata and the capital, as well as other industrial centres on the Pacific coast."

No sooner was he elected than he launched this vast public-works program.

Success was immediate. Everybody was a winner. The good people from Niigata soon found themselves living only two hours away from Tokyo by train. A divided highway connected them to the capital city, and a nuclear power plant created a number of well-paying jobs in their area. Local contractors were making money, they made sure that electoral coffers also remained handsomely filled, and new contracts kept pouring in.

From general election to general election, Tanaka reinforced his foundations. Success leading to success, he entered the cabinet in 1957, obtained the prestigious Finance portfolio in 1960 and that of Trade and Industry in 1971, before becoming prime minister in 1972.

His influence within the party was such that one could refer to the "Tanaka faction" as a party within the party. Many of his parliamentary colleagues had emulated his technique, and concrete was being poured merrily from one end of the country to the other.

Tanaka was powerful. He controlled his electorate as he controlled his parliamentary colleagues; his party had little ideology other than to stay in power. Tanaka was also a wealthy man, though no one knew exactly how, where, and when he had made his fortune, for he had started with nothing. His father was a cattle merchant, a drinker, and a gambler, who died penniless. Tanaka himself never finished high school – in a country where one expects academic excellence from senior mandarins and other servants of the state.

How could Kakuei Tanaka afford, as early as the 1960s, a private residence in one of the toniest districts of Tokyo, as well as a summer home in the exclusive resort of Karuizawa? How could he spend so much of his own money during electoral campaigns?

The question was asked, whispers abounded, but Tanaka was impervious to all rumours, because it was in no one's interest to dig too deeply into the prime minister's past: not in the interest of the electors, who were expecting their manna; not in the interest of other politicians, who were getting re-elected without fail thanks to the system; and not in the interest of political reporters, muzzled by the *kisha* clubs.

Tachibana was a struggling junior reporter for a general-interest magazine and, as such, he was not a member of any *kisha* club. He had no privileged access to the political élite, no connections to maintain, no source to protect, no IOUs to safeguard. He did not fear being excluded from the press conferences and briefing sessions that are delivered in a trickle daily by ministers and their entourages, because he did not belong to that world. He did not have to worry about what his colleagues might think if he did not play by the rules, because he was not in the game.

He started asking aloud the very simple question that everyone had been asking silently: How did the prime minister become so rich so fast? Tachibana got the go-ahead from his publisher and settled down to the task of finding out.

He started by identifying the prime minister's official income from the amount of income tax he paid every year. That was the easy part, since the information is published by the Revenue Ministry. These documents also provided him with the number of stocks owned by the prime minister; however, they did not identify those stocks.

From then on, Tachibana's task became more complex. He had to establish without the shadow of a doubt where the prime minister invested his money. He remembered that every year big Japanese corporations publish the list of their twenty largest shareholders, together with their annual report. The young reporter hypothesized that, if Tanaka were to invest in a company, he would do it on a grand scale, and he gambled that his name would probably be listed among the twenty largest shareholders.

It was like looking for a needle in a haystack, but it was an inescapable step if he wanted to go beyond rumours and establish evidence. With the help of a team of twenty *Bungei Shunju* junior reporters, Tachibana spent long days in libraries, poring over documents (as Woodward and Bernstein had done before him), and he succeeded in confirming that indeed the prime minister was among the twenty largest shareholders of many Japanese corporations. This was unthinkable on a parliamentary salary, unless one was independently wealthy, which Tanaka was not.

Tachibana then turned to real-estate holdings. There again, it was long and exacting work. From municipal archives to municipal archives, he was eventually able to prove that, through fictional corporations headed by friends of his, Prime Minister Tanaka had systematically speculated on lands destined for those vast public-works projects for which he was both the initiator and the master architect. To say that the Japanese were surprised by these revelations would be an overstatement. They had suspected that much for years. However, for the first time they were confronted not with rumours, but with solid evidence.

Tachibana published his findings in a series of two articles in the *Bungei Shunju*.

"It was like a one-two punch in a boxing match!" remembers Tetsuya Chikushi, who was a correspondent in Washington at the time. By sheer coincidence, the prime minister was scheduled to give a speech to the Foreign Press Club the day the second article was published. That is a rare event. For Japanese politicians, talking to foreign reporters is a low priority, both because it gives them practically no coverage at home and because Western journalists have the unpalatable habit of asking unscripted questions without any concern for the embarrassment they might cause.

On that day, the coincidence was deadly for Prime Minister Tanaka. Foreign reporters did not even pretend to wear – let alone remove – any velvet gloves; they pounced and confronted Tanaka with the accusations published in the *Bungei Shunju*. Exceptionally, the Japanese media were there too, in order to hear their prime minister. They could never confront him directly the way their Western colleagues did. However, once the questions were asked, they had no qualms about publishing the answers.

And the answers were deadly. Never in his worst nightmares had Prime Minister Tanaka anticipated such a barrage of questions. His meek attempts at explanations were shot down one after the other, and he soon had no option but to retreat.

Attracted by the scent of blood, the opposition in the Diet (the Japanese Lower House) took over during the days and weeks that followed. Two months later, the most powerful Japanese prime minister since the Second World War had to resign.

Overnight, Tachibana became a celebrated hero, intrepid fighter of corruption, and virtuous protector of democratic values. He had cut the Gordian knot, he had dared attack the established power. But in so doing, he had also exposed for all to see the glorious incompetence of his colleagues in the national media.

A young stringer, a generalist with no particular expertise or access to political circles, who, to add insult to injury, was writing for a weekly, had dared to tread on a file that was not his. He had had no scoop, no "Deep Throat," no inside information. The documents he had used all belonged in the public domain. In other words, any newsroom in the daily press could have done the same at any time. "It was a public humiliation for all the other reporters," remembers senior journalist Chikushi.

Meanwhile, Tachibana was on a roll. Without missing a beat, he published a book on the Tanaka scandal, then another to explain in great detail how he had led his inquiry, step by step. Two years later, he was once again at the epicentre of another scandal. The Lockheed affair started in Washington, crossed the Pacific, and, like a tidal wave, shook the Japanese political élite to its deepest foundations, starting, one more time, with the former prime minister. Indeed, so powerful was Tanaka, that, even as a fallen prime minister, he still exerted an overwhelming influence on his party, his successor, and Japan political life. In fact, the emergence of the Tanaka faction within the Liberal Democratic Party dates from the period *after* Tanaka's resignation.

"Tachibana had the feeling that he had not totally killed the snake," recalls Chikushi. "He was writing feverishly, publishing everywhere, he was unstoppable." Meanwhile, Chikushi had himself become editor-in-chief of the *Bungei Shunju* magazine.

"I used him often, as I needed good reporters and good writers," he explains. Other reporters were furious: "Why do you allow Tachibana to write in your magazine?" they complained. "Can't you see that he is destroying our image, our reputation?"

Such was the contrast. In the United States, Woodward and Bernstein, Tachibana's role models, were fast becoming legendary heroes; their story would be turned into a successful commercial movie a few years later; during more than a decade, a new generation of students flooded journalism schools, intending to specialize in investigative journalism "just like Woodward and Bernstein." In Japan, however, the reception was quite different. Tachibana had indeed become a hero of sorts, but he was also the man who had disturbed public peace.

Thirty years later, Tachibana was still being treated as a pariah. He lived like a recluse behind the black walls of his iron fortress, slept during the day, wrote during the night, and paid a young lady, as intractable as she was charming, to answer on the phone that "He is not here. He is busy. He cannot receive any visitors. He has no time in his schedule."

"He must occasionally pause for coffee?" I suggest hopefully.

"Indeed, sometimes around four o'clock in the morning," she informs me with a voice that is very much *not* sarcastic, but only because we are in Japan.

I jump at this sliver of an opportunity, do not leave her a chance to backtrack, set an appointment for four o'clock in the morning, roll out of bed in the middle of the night, look for a French pastry so I would not arrive empty-handed, and here I am, standing before dawn in an unfamiliar part of town, tape recorder across my shoulder and bag of croissants in my hand, on the threshold of a narrow black door, a cat hole really, barely ajar in the tall black wall, the giant cat staring high above my head.

"Come in. It's at the top of the stairs," a voice shouts through the interphone. Right behind the door, one of those staircases so common in Japan, extremely narrow and almost as steep as a ladder, leads to the upper floors. The first two steps are obstructed with shoes of all kinds, the next ones with piles of books, newspapers, and magazines.

I tiptoe cautiously to the second floor: several computers on desks littered with papers, books everywhere on the floor, and not a soul. Same thing on the next floor: no windows, hills of files overflowing on the steps of the winding staircase.

On the fourth floor, the landing is blocked with office shelves, loaded with files. There is no way through. How did I get lost?

"Come in, come in," an exhausted voice calls out from the bottom of somewhere.

I manage to squeeze between the shelf and the wall. I am now facing a pile of books taller than I am, then another one, and suddenly, between two computers, I finally spot him.

"Come in, come in," he repeats, without even raising his head.

Now that the goal is in sight, I proceed with more confidence through this obstacle course. I step over cardboard boxes, a suitcase, books scattered across the floor, and finally I am close enough to greet my host.

A big curly head, a round face, chubby like a child's, bags under the eyes, like a man who has lived too much, the shadow of a smile. He briefly remembers his Japanese good manners. I have made my ritual offering of croissants; in turn he must, he absolutely must, offer me tea. Or coffee. Or something.

He gazes hesitantly around him, grabs a half-full mug, empties the contents into a glass pot that sits in a corner, fishes a used teabag out of his own mug, and triumphantly pours some tepid water over it. Mission accomplished.

It quickly appears that he is not interested in talking about the Tanaka affair. He has said everything, written everything; it is ancient history to him.

"Don't tell me that you came all this way to talk about politics?" he asks sarcastically, as if it was the most unlikely of all suggestions. "I am not interested in politics."

Strange, coming from a man who has written two books on communism in Japan in the 1960s, another one on the student movement, on the influence of the agricultural lobby, before destroying the career of the most influential politician in the land, no less, and publishing at least four more books on the topic.

"To try to change the political culture is like watching water falling drop by drop on a stone," he explains.

At this juncture, there is a hiatus in our conversation. A sincere misunderstanding. I understand him to say that he is disappointed, discouraged, exasperated by the fact that things have hardly changed in the last twenty years. That he would have expected to be more influential. That he despairs to see how slowly ideas, attitudes, behaviours evolve in his country.

Am I ever wrong!

As I invite him to elaborate on the slowness of change in Japan, he practically pounces out of his chair.

"What would you like? A revolution? Is that what you would want?" His tone is withering.

I suddenly take a measure of the cultural immensity that divides us. In an instant, East and West face each other in disbelief among the mountains of books. The West, always ready to change the world for better or for worse, to turn the page, to clear the table, to start afresh and hope to do better next time. And the East, for whom the history of humanity is measured in five-thousand-year-old sighs.

"I am not interested in politics."

"What are you interested in then?"

"Everything!" he purrs. At that moment, he looks like an old cat given a cup of warm milk.

A friend of his who hosts a show at NHK had warned me, "Tachibana's appetite for life is insatiable."

In order to explain his immense appetite, he quotes the opening sentence in Aristotle's *Metaphysics*: "All men naturally want to know."

"I am interested in everything. I want to know the world. It is an instinct for me, as strong as a religious feeling."

One look at his surroundings is enough to convince me. Shelves, covering all the walls from floor to ceiling, are crammed with the most mind-boggling array of titles. From Wittgenstein to the medieval mystics, from Lao-Tseu to Renaissance art, from the brain of primates to the mathematical universe, from a French geography textbook to anthropic cosmology, he has books in French,

English, German, Japanese and Chinese. It looks as though no topic has been left uncovered.

"Thirty-five thousand!" he announces proudly. And he obviously knows where each one of them is located, despite the apparent mess of the room.

His interests are anything but superficial. He spent three years poring over biology, neurology, and cybernetic reviews to research the functioning of the brain of primates. When he turned his interest to the space program, he convinced NASA to let him go through the same tests in weightlessness as astronauts do. "Don't ever plan to travel with him in rural France," sighed one of his friends. "Before he orders anything in a restaurant, he demands to know everything about every single dish on the menu: its geographic, ethnic, historic origin; where the ingredients come from and how they are grown. Then he wants to watch the chef in the kitchen; sometimes he even wants to help . . ."

Insatiable, and in a hurry. When you want to learn so much about so many things, every minute counts. In a corner of the room, a jacket is hanging from a nail in the wall, and on the floor, a mattress, inevitably littered with more books. That is his home. Or at least, this is where he lies down from time to time, when sleep gets the better of him.

He does have a family that lives a few doors down on the same street: two daughters (he does not remember their ages) and a son from an earlier marriage (he does not remember what the son is studying). The Maison du Chat Noir is his office, his territory, his den, his retreat, and he does not get out of it much. He designed it himself in order to house him and his books, so he could work in peace.

By now, we have talked about everything. He has proudly shown me the three Web sites he created at Tokyo University, where he teaches Applied Ethics and Changes in Paradigms. Somewhere in the conversation, I must have passed successfully some mysterious test, for he has become almost civil, and offers to give me a grand tour of his territory. We climb down the winding staircase to the main floor, where the exquisite watchdog spends her days accomplishing a monumental research task and protecting her master against the intrusions of the outside world.

The visit is not over. Tachibana has kept the best for last. He leads me towards a vertical ladder and into the basement.

A wine cave! A superb collection of great French crus, meticulously classified according to year and region, in an atmosphere electronically regulated for temperature and humidity.

"When I come down here to open a bottle, I choose it according to the personality of the friend I am going to share it with." In an elementary-school notebook, with blue lines and red margins, he has written down on each page the date, the friend's name, the wine, and the topic of conversation that day. On March 20, 1996, he opened a Château Latour 1979 with a Mr. Udagana. For Hiroko Kuniya, he uncorked a Chassagne-Montrachet Cru Caillerets 1989. Mr. Pitt scored a Château Mouton-Rothschild 1981, on a dark evening in December 1995.

At the risk of sounding vain, I ask heedlessly, "What kind of wine would you open for me?" to which he answers, with transparent simplicity, "I can't tell you. I don't know you well enough yet."

The guided tour is over. Or is it? At the far end of the cave, Tachibana is now moving a heavy cardboard box to clear a trap in a floor. Yet another ladder. Shorter, this time. He climbs down ahead of me. He has stopped talking. When in turn I set foot on the ground, he simply gestures with a wide-open hand and an expression that seems to say: "Here it is!"

Here it is, indeed! The ceiling is too low to stand upright, yet the room is vast. Along the walls, cardboard boxes, dozens of cardboard boxes carefully aligned (what a contrast with the upper floors!), meticulously labelled, dated and identified: The Tanaka affair, The Lockheed affair. All the documents that were instrumental in "killing the snake." Lists of shareholders, income-tax returns, land registries, real-estate contracts, interviews, parliamentary debates in Tokyo, Senate committee debates in Washington. It is all there.

We are in the Holy of Holies, two storeys below street level. My host is now speaking in a whisper, the way one does in church. He informs me that here, too, the humidity and temperature are carefully monitored. And that the steel beams supporting the ceiling are earth-quake-proof.

So there we are. These boxes in front of us have been aligned there for posterity. They constitute what must remain (if the city were to be flattened some day) to remind future generations of the strength of relations between power and money.

In the Maison du Chat Noir, the black sheep is waiting for his time to come.

Seven o'clock in the morning, it is full daylight, and it is time to go to sleep. Tiny old ladies clean the sidewalk in front of their porches with delicate sweeps of their brooms. As I walk back towards the subway station, I am struck by the idea that there is something quin-tessentially Japanese in this hermit in the heart of the city. His insa-tiable appetite for everything the West has ever written, thought, and accomplished echoes Japan's voracious curiosity about the same Western civilization. An acquisitive curiosity, together with a deep-seated indifference. As I was asking him why so few of his books have been translated in English, in French, or in German, he answered simply, "What for?"

Some of his books have been translated and distributed in China and Korea. Beyond, the world is nothing but a vast and wonderful playground.

Like Japan, he is in the world, but he is not from the world. He belongs to no group, no one owes him anything. He is famous but misunderstood, rich but useless, sometimes admired but always kept apart; one marvels over his prodigious energy and deplores his lack of sense of mission.

Like Japan, he suffers from his isolation, yet he plays it to his advantage. He desperately wants to be understood. "I want my books to be accessible to all," he says. Yet he savours his opacity, as did another Japanese intellectual who told me one day, "Deep down, we, the Japanese, don't like to be understood."

CHAPTER 6

The Most Beautiful Girls

The third day of the third month of the year is little girls' day. Everybody knows that in Japan. On that day, every family exhibits its doll collection, enriched with each generation, from the hieratic miniature that belonged to the great-great-grandmother to the latest Barbie. Friends are invited to come and admire the family heirlooms. Little girls, wearing their first kimono, parade proudly before the dewy-eyed assembly.

The fifth day of the fifth month is little boys' day. Everybody knows that too. On a high pole erected next to the house, every family flies a kite in the shape of a carp (symbol of good fortune) for each one of its sons. The more carps the better. For several days, the carps fly proudly in the wind for all to see.

The fourth day of the fourth month . . . what about the fourth day of the fourth month? And who is it for? It is for those in-between, for people in the grey zone. Everybody knows that in Kabuki-cho. Kabuki-cho, a neighbourhood in central Tokyo, is definitely not the kind of place where you want to take your mother. It is the district of nude dancers – they exist in all cities the world over. In Kabuki-cho, there are often signs at the doors: *No gaijins*. No foreigners. "It is because of Americans; they want to touch, it always creates troubles," I am told. Bawdy houses post their services and the price on the sidewalk, the way restaurants post their menus: "Massage: 3,000 yen"; "with soap-down: 4,000"; "blow job, plain: 5,000"; "swallowed: 7,000"; "the works: 100,000." Passersby stroll leisurely from one to the other, compare prices, inquire about the quality of services and merchandise with the doorman.

Most of all, Kabuki-cho is the neighbourhood of the ambiguous. There are homo clubs, for the activists and for the surreptitious; sado-maso clubs and intellectual ones; clubs for weekend transvestites and for confirmed ones; transsexual clubs; peeping-Tom clubs; exhibitionist clubs . . . and pizza-delivery boys who zoom through the narrow lanes, bringing an air of normalcy to this kingdom of the equivocal.

In this effervescent jungle, vulgar and good-natured, the Black Swan Lake distinguishes itself as a temple of good taste and sophistication. Access is severely restricted: a doorman in a bright red uniform carefully checks your entry ticket before letting you into the private elevator. Two storeys below the street, the door opens into an elegant bar with a British flavour, shaped in a crescent around a small circular stage.

The friend who dared take us to this place quivers with anticipation. "Soon, you will see," he announces, "very modern, very daring. Like the Folies-Bergère, except . . ." Except that the girls are men, most of them immigrants from the Philippines. Some went through a sex change, others cross-dress for fun, but when the curtain rises and they romp on stage, these details seem irrelevant, such is the vitality and energy they bring to the show.

The choreography lies somewhere between postmodern disco, the theatre of the absurd, and sheer adolescent silliness, hilarious and nonsensical. Is there a subliminal message behind the spectacle of this white rabbit, suspiciously long-tailed, bouncing between two rows of Second World War pilots in their blue uniforms?

Which audience do they hope to shock with these three pious nuns, dancing a devilish French cancan together with three blonde striptease queens? What is the meaning of the feverish disco dance, bringing together Saddam Hussein dressed as a drag queen, Bill Clinton wearing Ray-Ban glasses like CIA agents in spy movies, and Ronald McDonald, the famous red-headed clown from McDonald's restaurants throughout the world?

Our familiar icons meet briefly on stage, do a few pirouettes, show a bit of cheek, bat their eyelashes, and are gone. The show is well done, the rhythm fast, the lighting sophisticated, the dancers excellent, the costumes dazzling, leather, laces, and ostrich feathers all at once.

A fun and inconsequential evening in the grey zone of Kabuki-cho.

Life is but a stage, all good things come to an end, let us enjoy the day and be merry. Such is the theme of this light, silly, sparkling show.

In the next scene, the dancers are clad in surgeons' tunics, splashed with blood. As for the head surgeon, the blood on his white uniform spells clearly: Abe. The audience does a double-take.

Abe is the name of the senior official at the centre of an infected-blood scandal that cost the lives of hundreds of hemophiliacs and has recently shaken the whole political world.

The scenario unravels in a flash: a patient lies down in a magician's box – the sort of box used to saw beautiful women in half – and is spun in a centrifugal machine until the last drop of his blood is extracted. The stage is copiously splashed. Circling around him, hilarious doctors dance a few steps, looking like cannibals from some crude comic strip.

Political satire in a transvestite club? Unexpected, but why not?

For the next scene, three women wearing Okinawa traditional costume dance, in slow motion, one of the traditional dances of this remote southern island. The suggestion is that of a bucolic and eternal Asia.

In the foreground, three mini-scenarios in rapid succession: first, the rape of a little girl in a white dress by two American GIs wearing

Ray-Ban sunglasses – "like CIA-agents-in-spy-movies"; next, the collective suicide of several young virgins in their military uniforms – referring to an actual incident, familiar to all the Japanese, which symbolizes all that was horrific in the battle of Okinawa in 1945; and finally, a pitiful cortege of wounded soldiers, bandaged from head to toe. While they limp miserably across the stage on their crutches, the traditional dancers are still swaying softly in the background as if to suggest that, even through the worst adversity, the spirit survives.

I am stupefied. The whole Okinawa tragedy has been revived before our eyes, in less than four minutes, by the choreographer of this decidedly unusual Cage aux Folles. Okinawa, ancient kingdom of the southern seas, was brutally annexed by the Japanese. Its inhabitants were ruthlessly used as sausage meat in a fierce battle against the Americans, a battle that did not concern them, yet for which they are still paying the price today. Indeed, it is on this tiny island that most American military bases have been located since the war, with the unspoken blessing of the Japanese government. At the time when the Black Swan Lake was producing this show, mainland Japanese had just been reminded of the tragic fate of this remote territory, because of the rape of a local schoolgirl by two American marines. In Tokyo, the national government had taken advantage of the incident to charge more money to the Americans for the maintenance of their military bases. Nowhere, however, was there any suggestion to lighten the load of the island of Okinawa and move some of the U.S. bases elsewhere on the Japanese territory.

The political satire is strong, focused, and unforgiving. The message is aimed at the audience, made up mostly of Japanese, as much as at the leading decision-makers. In the room, spectators take it in stride and have the grace to laugh but . . . didn't they come here tonight to have fun, see some flesh, and forget about politics?

Indeed they did, and it is time to retreat to the safe and familiar terrain of more-traditional cabaret shows.

A cute "little girl" with a ponytail bounces on stage and waltzes with Mickey Mouse to the theme music of a popular children's television show. From time to time, she lifts her pink skirt all the way to her navel, looking innocent and childish. We all applaud.

More "little girls" join her on stage and do the same. We applaud some more.

The stage is now crowded with familiar cartoon characters, twirling with little girls who look the way little girls are supposed to look on television: blonde braids, pastel dresses, thumbs in their mouths – except that, from time to time, they turn their backs to the audience, lift their skirts, and show their bums.

It surely is not in the best of taste, but what to expect in that kind of burlesque show? This is what people came for tonight: to see beautiful girls kick their legs. In actual fact, this show might be considered conservative, even prudish, in terms of the amount of flesh shown. In a Paris cabaret such as the Folies-Bergère, dancers would wear the tiniest string, if anything, while here, they are wearing regular underwear.

Suddenly, a double-take. Something is wrong. Very wrong. Where are the ostrich feathers, the tantalizing black lace, the titillating garter belts? Stop everything! That is real children's underwear the dancers are showing! Practical, durable, 100-per-cent cotton, won't fade, won't shrink in the wash . . . All at once, the audience realizes with horror that what they have been applauding heartily is a direct reference to child-porn magazines, which are available freely in kiosks everywhere.

There are dozens of these magazines. They are published every week and lie for all to see in waiting rooms and hotel lobbies. Men leaf through them distractedly in the subway on their way to work. Periodically, some protest groups voice their concern, but the general attitude is one of indifference, and these publications remain a flourishing industry.

Routinely, these magazines show on their cover five- to twelve-year-olds, exposing their genitals, expressions of profound boredom on their faces. The pictures are all the more shocking because of the many details from daily life, such as no-nonsense cotton underwear, which suggest complete availability.

A sense of deep embarrassment and confusion falls on the audience in the Black Swan Lake. On the one hand, the audience members would like to cheer the pretty dancers, their funny costumes, the irreverent choreography. On the other hand, they cannot be seen to belong to the shameful category of pedophiles. Yet, that is exactly what the show has just done. All together, in the semi-darkness of this upscale bar, we realize with horror that we have just been pushed into a trap. We have been drawn, unsuspecting, into an area that was not on our agenda. We came here for light, inconsequential entertainment, we have been treated to a sharp and brutal political satire. Worse yet, we are the ones being singled out! We are all voyeurs. And pedophiles too, when the circumstances are right. And accomplices to crimes of power, blind and deaf witnesses to injustices in the world. That, too, is us.

Such is the message slowly sinking in, as dancers of all sexes whirl gaily on stage for a spectacular finale.

Our consciences have just been rudely shaken up. We thought we would come out of this evening with a mild case of guilt, as is *de rigueur* when you go to a striptease show.

In fact, we have just been called to order, to the most fundamental moral order, by a band of individuals of indeterminate gender, religion, nationality, and skin colour.

"Sheepish" would be too weak a word to describe the atmosphere in the bar. Horror-stricken would be closer to the way we feel, horror-stricken by the brief reflection we have glimpsed in the mirror held perfidiously in front of us.

Fortunately, the show is over. The lights come back on in the bar, this fleeting vision of our darkest gardens evaporates magically, waiters are already circulating from table to table and refilling our drinks.

There has been no time to put our perceptions in order. Did we really see what we think we saw? Did others see the same thing? Or did we all project a bit of ourselves on what we thought we should be seeing?

As when watching Chinese shadows or a Japanese puppet show, our Western insistence on separating illusion from reality turns out to be more cumbersome than helpful: the impressions we felt during the show were real, and that is the only thing that counts. It matters little whether these impressions were provoked by a living body or by its shadow. And it matters little whether the body was that of man or of a woman.

As if to add to our confusion, the dancers are now coming into the bar to pay a courtesy visit to the customers. They are all agonizingly beautiful, smooth and light, transparent, luminous, innocent . . . the illusion is complete.

The bar owner goes from table to table and informs us that "this one has had the operation," "that one will have it next month," "this other one is only a transvestite," and there is even a girl who was born that way! The poor thing seems a second-class citizen in this strange universe.

Two of them sit at our table with great grace and poise. They explain cheerfully that they were born in the Philippines, that they came to Japan because that is where you make the most money. Like most migrant workers in the world, they support whole families in some remote mountain village.

"What do your parents think of your profession?" I ask stupidly.

"They are very pleased that I make so much money, and they are proud of me because I am the best!"

Castratos or economic refugees, who cares? The fact is that, even up close, they are gorgeous – pale blonde, of course, with long slim legs, long thick lashes, long red nails, smooth oval faces . . . One is not sure whether to admire the beauty of the woman or the perfection of the illusion. We are all a bit confused. The men in our group are drooling, despite themselves. The women feel bland and grey. I find myself wishing I had such a smooth skin, such a bright lipstick . . .

Everything about them is fake, except the smile. These young people enjoy their success, their low-cut gowns, and the expression of ravished confusion that flickers on men's faces when they come and sit on their laps.

The confusion is multi-layered. Westerners are struggling to explain and rationalize: "Did you see those hands? Those muscles? You couldn't mistake them for women's hands." The fact is, you do.

The Japanese, on the contrary, enjoy the violence that has just been done to their senses and relish the ambiguity.

CHAPTER 7

The Perfect Lover

I met the most beautiful women in a transvestite burlesque show. And I met the most seductive men in a musical comedy in which all the characters are played by women.

The Takarazuka is a strange phenomenon indeed. This fairly recent form of theatre appeared at the turn of the twentieth century, as if to provide an ironic counterbalance to the classic Kabuki theatre, where all the characters are played by men. Through the ages, men took it upon themselves to define what constitutes femininity: dainty little steps, elegant moves of the wrist, impervious smiles, and artful angles of the neck should be all a real lady needs to express the gamut of human emotions. The most venerated Kabuki actors are often overweight sexagenarians who are celebrated and admired for the exquisite precision with which they play eighteen-year-old ingenues.

In Takarazuka theatre, the tables are turned. Women get even and create their own version of what a perfect man should look like. However, the comparison between these two art forms ends there. Indeed, while Kabuki theatre is relished for its refinement, the Takarazuka does not trade in subtlety. Rather, it models itself on

American musical comedies. The themes and costumes are resolutely Western, and men look like all men should: tall, dark, and handsome, pure Valentinos, romantic and chivalrous to boot. Enough to make one fall in love at first sight.

I went alone to the Takarazuka one fine summer afternoon – alone because, curiously, no one in the circle of Japanese friends who were usually so eager to introduce me to their country and culture seemed to be available that day.

"So sorry . . . I would have loved to . . . you must understand . . . so busy . . . maybe some other time . . ."

The truth is that Takarazuka is shunned by the cultural élite. Takarazuka is vulgar. Takarazuka is lowbrow. Takarazuka is a form of Japanese culture that one does not boast about. And yet . . .

On that particular Wednesday afternoon, there was a full house. Eight hundred seats, eight hundred women coming to enjoy their favourite show at a time of the day when husbands are at work and children are in school.

In this novel form of gynaeceum, I am greeted like family. In a different context, these women would never talk to a stranger without having been properly introduced. Here, they come to me spontaneously, strike up a conversation, and create in an instant a protective and intensely curious cocoon around me. Apparently, it is a rare event to see a foreigner at the Takarazuka. They all want to know what I am doing here, and why, and who is my favourite actress, and "Have you seen the previous shows?" and "Will you be able to understand everything?" and "Would you like me to explain it to you during the play?" I feel crowded, overwhelmed, submerged with kindness. This is the first time strangers have struck up a conversation without starting with my husband's station in life and my children's ages and course of studies. In this temple of illusion, husbands and children have been left in the cloakroom.

The curtain rises on a set representing a street in Chicago, gangster-movie version. I am soon reassured: despite my very limited knowledge of the language, I will probably be able to understand the story. Bad guys wear black hats, the hero is dressed all in white, the pure heroine wears pink ball gowns with sparkles, just like the good fairy in Walt Disney movies, and the traitor stomps around in tall, black-leather boots. One cannot miss it.

Part French operetta, part American musical comedy, the show is fast-moving and energetic, the contralto voices of the male characters are warm and surprisingly powerful.

On stage, the young heroine is now in dire straits. She has just been taken hostage by the enemy gang, and one would not want to bet on her honour – all the more since the only man who could save her was left for dead with a knife in his back at the end of the previous act. Suddenly, the door bursts open, and in he walks, carrying a submachine gun and peppering the bad guys until they are all dead on the floor. Then he bends with infinite tenderness towards the sobbing young virgin, who, despite being tied up in her dungeon, has somehow managed to keep her pink ball gown immaculate. The audience applauds in relief, as children do at a puppet show.

For the finale, the hero and heroine, both dressed in white, treat us to a languorous waltz, while, inexplicably, snowflakes fall all around them. It is all quite beautiful. People cry openly in the room. The lady in the seat next to me, teary-eyed, asks me kindly whether I understood everything.

All these ladies are a little bit in love with the hero. Not only is he impossibly handsome, with his slick black hair, narrow waist, and velvet eyes, but also he is always there when you need him. He is courageous, audacious, daring, and, furthermore, he knows how to talk about love. He says words like "true love" and "absolute" and "forever" and "eternal" . . .

To Japanese women, this is all very exotic. No man has ever spoken to them that way. It is simply not done, it is ridiculous, laughable, and vaguely vulgar to talk about love. "If my husband came home one night and told me he loves me, I would immediately conclude he has a mistress," a young Japanese friend confided one day.

"I know he loves me, but he never declared his love," a newlywed told me with wonderment in her eyes. "We understand each other without speaking."

A fifty-year-old man explained to me one day that "my wife is part of my life like the water I drink and the air I breathe. It would be meaningless to tell her I love her!"

And both men and women mention the "communication from the stomach," a famous concept, so totally enigmatic to a Westerner, that allows them, they say, to understand one another without the support of that imperfect and rudimentary means of communication that is the spoken word. However, hundreds of devoted wives and mothers pay good money to come and cry like young girls in the afternoon, watching these Princes Charming kneeling before their Princesses, these Princes who are so handsome, so kind, and, most of all, who talk so beautifully about love.

In Takarazuka theatre, the stars are the ones who play male roles. They are immensely famous, everybody recognizes them in the street, their names on the credits guarantees a full room, they have their fan clubs, and when they step on the stage the audience cheers. Women dream of their faces as they fall asleep.

And when they decide to leave the stage and make a career change, they do not have to deal with the same dilemmas as other actresses. Having spent their life playing male roles, they are taken more seriously than their colleagues who specialize in female characters. The Takarazuka training taught them how to look like a leader, walk like a leader, talk like a leader, and they find it easier than most to go into business or politics.

This is the route followed by Akira Matsu. From the stage to the senate via television studios, she has been a public personality all her adult life.

Even before meeting her, one cannot ignore that here is someone used to being in the spotlight. In the lobby of her senate office, her cheerful face greets you on giant posters everywhere. There are posters from her last electoral campaign, her famous smile next to her husband (he is a member of the Lower House, she is a member of the Upper House). Her stage name is printed in large letters under her married name. There are also twenty-year-old posters for *La Rose de Versailles* to remind everyone that this is no ordinary senator. Everything in the manner and behaviour of her staff shows that their boss is somebody special – and not because she is a representative of the people! Her small office is cluttered with white orchids like a star's dressing room on opening night.

Soon, the star walks in. Tall and slim, impeccably made up, an orchid on the lapel of a white tailored suit that has certainly not spent much time on the benches of parliamentary committees, she exudes both assurance and femininity – an unlikely combination in a Japanese woman.

She was twelve years old when she saw her first Takarazuka show.

"I was immediately fascinated," she recalls. "From then on, every day in the school bus, I dreamed up scenarios to do a show. I was in the theatre club in school, and because I was taller than the other girls, they started a rumour that I wanted to become a Takarazuka actress. It was a Catholic school, and I was immediately summoned to see the Mother Superior, who talked to me severely and called my parents. I was good for another stern talking to. In order to definitely convince me of the error of my ways, my father introduced me to one of his friends, whose wife had been a Takarazuka actress. His hope was that his friend would discourage me, but instead, he took one look at me and exclaimed, 'You were made for Takarazuka!' Eventually, my parents were convinced, and after one year I was accepted in Takarazuka school."

There, she learned classical ballet, jazz, and modern dance, tap-dancing, and traditional Japanese dances. She took singing lessons, piano lessons, and had to master traditional Japanese string instruments, such as the *shamisen*, the *koto*, as well as the *taiko* (Japanese gong). All the while, she was also covering the regular compulsory high-school curriculum.

"We had classes six days a week. We studied very hard, because it was drilled into us that good marks were not enough. Some of the girls passed all their exams, and yet they never made it on stage. You must be very good, and then you must have something extra."

Akira Matsu obviously had this extra something. Soon, she was targeted to play male characters, thanks to her height and contralto voice. This was the beginning of a brilliant career. And once she added *La Rose de Versailles* to her repertory, she reached the summit of her fame.

I watch this beautiful, poised, and self-assured woman, whose warm voice has seduced so many of her contemporaries. She became the Prince Charming incarnate to a whole generation, and her ownership of the character is such that, even now, women feel a warm, ambiguous feeling in their heart when they meet the private Akira.

Akira Matsu created for her admirers a man more perfect than real men – a man as strong, masculine, and handsome as the transsexual dancers from the Black Swan Lake were soft and feminine.

CHAPTER 8

The Innocence Imperative

I woke up very early that morning, to ascend Kompirasan, one of the most celebrated shrines on Shikoku Island. I had arrived the previous evening in the pretty little town of Kotohira, built on canals, like Venice, and I wanted to climb the sacred mountain like the pilgrims: slowly, gravely, in the stillness of dawn, hours before the tour buses arrive.

The delight is in the details of the progression: an ancient, paved street winds up the hill, lined with souvenir shops for tourists and pilgrims alike. As it climbs, the tea shops and boutiques become fewer and farther between, the slope gets steeper, and the lane narrows to a path of long low stone steps.

Soon, there is nothing around, save the earth and the sky.

It was before sunrise, the birds were singing in the forest across the valley, and it felt, very simply, like the first day after Creation. The physical exertion added to the perfection of the moment, and the religiosity of the place.

Suddenly, a city! At the top of the hill, a vast complex of temples, shrines, inner courtyards, and covered passages spread out under

century-old cypress trees as tall as cathedrals. Another world exists up
here, busy, but silent and peaceful.

The very last echoes of a gong are still vibrating through the air,
some priests in their red and gold habits are quietly getting ready for
the next service, an attendant hangs his colourful wash of temple orna-
ments out to dry, a young priestess in a red robe walks across the courtyard, her black wooden *getas* clicking noisily on the paving stones.

Slightly intimidated, I make my way through the complex to the
last of the shrines, which is reserved for men of the sea. Strange as it
may seem, this Shinto shrine, located far inland, on top of a mountain,
is indeed dedicated to sailors and fishermen. On the walls, hundreds
of votive offerings, brought here by generations of seafarers, recount
their terrifying adventures. The paintings may be naïve, yet the nightmares they depict are frighteningly realistic: fishing boats threatened
by gigantic green waves, battleships dwarfed in the storm; tall ships
surrounded by sharp-toothed sea monsters; naval battles; nightmarish
shipwrecks; pink cadavers emerging from white sea foam. Each one of
these pictures suggest the horror of death and the eternal gratitude of
survivors. And, surveying it all, is Audrey Hepburn.

Pure and serene Audrey Hepburn, forgiving Audrey Hepburn,
understanding Audrey Hepburn, Audrey Hepburn whom some cast-
away must have asked one day to intercede for his safety, and who
quite obviously obliged. She appears in an oil painting, executed by
someone as inexperienced as he was devoted. The portrait hangs in
the place of honour, among dozens of other seafarers' offerings. I
look again in disbelief, but there is no doubt possible, it is indeed
Audrey Hepburn in *Sabrina*, except that her smile has acquired an
ineffable beatitude about it. Like a Madonna, or a Buddha.

Or probably both! For syncretism comes easily to the Japanese.
They have no difficulty amalgamating elements of various religions.
For instance, it is not unusual to discover a Buddhist deity represent-
ing a Shinto spirit – or the reverse – and no one seems to be offended.

In the far south, Christian sects that survived underground for
centuries, despite a ban from the authorities, developed a cult for a

strange deity known as Maria Kannon, part Virgin Mary, legacy of
the missionaries, and part Kannon, the (male) Buddha emanation of
compassion.

So, Saint Audrey, patron of purity and innocence, reigning in a
Shinto shrine and interceding with Our Father who art in Heaven in
a gesture of Buddhist compassion for the salvation of seamen . . .
Why not?

Audrey Hepburn is the object of a quasi-religious veneration throughout Japan. In this country where tragic princesses have been peopling
the tales and legends since ancient times, this pure foreigner finds
herself right at home in the popular iconography.

Her picture is everywhere: in Ferragamo boutiques, posing with
her favourite shoemaker; in department stores, blown up in huge
posters in the teenagers' section; on soap and body-lotion packages;
in French-style cafés where aging intellectuals seek refuge; and even
on the walls of a student brasserie in a small provincial town where,
one autumn evening, I sampled – accidentally – the specialty of the
house: octopus sauerkraut with Coca-Cola.

Whatever the context, Audrey creates an atmosphere, Audrey
sets the tone, Audrey sells and, most of all, Audrey inspires dreams.
Exotic yet approachable, foreign yet familiar, Audrey is a rare breed:
a Western woman imbued with Eastern virtues. Slim and poised,
always immaculately groomed, even when she is being chased by
killers or when the house is on fire, she speaks with an even voice, and
her face registers only four expressions: happiness, sadness, fear, and
– mostly – innocence.

This is familiar ground for Japanese women. They are *Breakfast
at Tiffany's* humble heroine, hiding her real self to survive in the big-
city jungle; they are *Roman Holiday's* young princess, who gives up
love in the name of duty and country; and how they would love to be
Sabrina's penniless young lady, whose sincerity seduces the wealthy
Prince Charming!

Like a magic mirror, Audrey sends Japanese women a Western

version of their own image. As for Japanese men, they are all a little bit in love with her, for she exudes the most valued of all qualities for a woman: purity in body, in soul, and in spirit.

There is a word in their language, which is particularly dear to the Japanese: *kirei* means "clean, straight, pure, smooth"; it refers to a perfectly washed laundry, as well as to a white lily, a spotless melon, or an honest politician. It is also the word used to describe a beautiful woman. In other words, to be attractive, a Japanese women must be pure, virginal, and innocent like a child. Or look as if she is.

Adult women cannot escape this innocence imperative. The challenge is woven through their daily life, whatever their age and station in life. The task is easier for *office-ladies*, for whom the look of innocence goes with the territory, since their regulation blue uniform is not unlike that of schoolgirls. The challenge is more daunting for women executives: how can they exude authority and professionalism, yet suggest the naïveté of childhood? They often resort to a compromise solution: a severely tailored suit, cut in tender light colours, sometimes with a frilly collar for added innocence.

Their public behaviour requires the same calculations and precise dosages. This is why Japanese women learn to cultivate two voice registers: the voice they use in private and the voice they use in public and when a man is present. At home, between themselves, among friends, they speak in warm, colourful voices, determined and even imperious; a group of Japanese women alone on an outing is noisy, earthy, and even Rabelaisian. However, let one man into the room or even close to the group, and instantly the voices jump one octave, the discourse is punctuated with the silliest little laughs, straight affirmative statements are banned, and sentences end on a trailing high note, almost a question, as if to reassure all around that these nubile young ladies have no idea of what they are talking about. The contrast is brutal, and incomprehensible to Westerners.

My surprise must have shown during one of these elegant receptions where people flow from group to group, as do the conversations, and where women's voices were oscillating from one octave to another as men were moving about. A kind and observant lady took me aside. "We may look weak, but, in fact, we are very strong, you know!" She uttered this explanation from the corner of her mouth, almost without looking at me, as if it were a dark, hidden secret. She had a Ph.D. in chemistry, spoke several languages, and belonged to an all-women mountain-climbing team; her husband was very proud of her, yet he would have been horribly embarrassed if her public behaviour had been anything other than that of a charming and innocent little girl, light as a cloud and transparent as an early morning.

It took an incursion into the washroom of a theatre in Tokyo for me to realize the extent of the innocence imperative. The circumstances were banal: intermission, a short social drink, a quick run to the washroom before the show started again.

I entered the cubicle, closed the door behind me, pulled from a dispenser the paper shape designed to cover the seat and guarantee an antiseptic experience, I sat, or rather I almost sat where I should . . . and at the precise moment when my bottom was about to touch, a split second before contact was made and the inevitable followed, I was startled by the sound of a small creek gurgling on river stones.

I froze in a halfway position. Could it be the lady next door who . . . no, there was not anyone next door. In the cabin to my right, a mountain stream was cascading down a hill, though. A bit farther, waves came lapping softly on a sandy beach. Elsewhere, they were crashing against a cliff. Each cabin was equipped with an electronic eye and a tape of various sounds of water in the wild, as a means to cover the sounds of water in this place!

I learned later that my theatre experience was definitely a class act. In other circumstances, I triggered a mechanical "Für Elise," with apologies to Beethoven. One day, in a provincial train station, I laughed aloud all by myself as a metallic "Happy Birthday to You" played again and again in seven crazed loops, as cohorts of hurried travellers made quick stops in the seven cubicles. Some institutions, less versed in high art, are content with installing in their washrooms the taped sound . . . of a toilet flushing. Anything to cover the sound of what actually happens in a washroom.

It is for the same sort of reason that it is often difficult to find tampons in Japan. They are usually hidden at the far end of the drugstore, on the lowest shelves, far from eye level. At the checkout counter, they will be wrapped separately in a brown opaque anonymous paper bag. No one should ever be led to believe that this particular customer has passed the age of puberty!

I knew a twelve-year-old Kyoko who jumped out of bed at the last minute every morning, splashed some cold water on her face, shook her hair in place without even taking the time to brush it, and jumped into the pleated skirt and blazer the colour of her school. After which, she devoted ten long minutes to spreading white glue ever so carefully on her legs – a special glue available only in teenagers' stores. Delicately, she would then slip on fat, thick white woollen socks, soccer players' socks, way too large for her, and position them at half-calf. The trick was for the socks to look ill-fitting, bunched up in the wrong places, for them to sag heavily on her pretty patent shoes.

Once she was satisfied with the result, Kyoko could then leave for school, where that artfully provocative look was *de rigueur* for all the girls. No school regulation ever succeeded in getting rid of the craze for big, white socks that was taking over the country at the time.

In Japan as elsewhere (starting with Victorian England), schoolgirls in uniform are an object of fetishism. Stories abound in the media of collectors waiting at school gates in order to purchase regulation cotton panties – provided their owners have worn them for two or three days.

Teenagers are perfectly aware of the kind of attention they attract in their military-style blazers and convent-girls collars. By adding the ugly, sagging socks to their uniforms, they manage to suggest all at once that they do not care a fig about their physical appearance, and that they just lifted the socks from some rugby-player lover, thus bringing a subtle refinement to the traditional erotic panoply of college Lolitas.

Those nostalgic for the good old days during the bubble economy still remember with fervour the Juliana, a club now defunct, famous for its dance floors: set high above the tables, made of translucent Plexiglas, they allowed customers a leisurely look up under the dancers' skirts as they sipped a beer with their buddies.

What made the Juliana so special was that there was something for everyone. *Office-ladies* came there to relax after a long, tedious day at work. They would not even take the time to change from their severe office uniform; however, they did remove their underwear for better dancing. Everybody loved the Juliana.

Up on the transparent platform they would dance, legs slightly apart, their faces expressionless, as if lost in their thoughts, like children when they play, concentrated on their game, oblivious to their surroundings.

Men enjoyed the spectacle. Most of all they relished the fact that the ladies seemed perfectly unaware of the trouble they caused. The attraction came not only from what could be glimpsed under the skirts, but from the innocent look on the faces.

In their own way, Juliana customers were all looking for their Sabrina.

CHAPTER 9

Two Women

A Canadian friend was asking me one day what would happen to my daughter if she were Japanese. I answered with no hesitation that she would probably hold a number of prestigious degrees from the better Japanese and American universities, she would be overworked in some office job with no challenge and no future, she would be doomed to marry sooner or later, and resigned to that inescapable outcome.

The fate of Japanese women is not an easy one, even for those who have been privileged by life and enjoy the luxury of making their own choices. What do young women dream about? They all have the same vacuous look about them. Yet, the golden rule in Japan is never to judge people on appearances. I was given many opportunities to confirm that those candy-pink outfits, those adolescent giggles, those high-pitched squeals of wonderment about nothing and every-thing, those ecstatic yet empty expressions on their faces, are all screens, masks, shields, and should never be taken at face value.

These masks are imposed by society, obviously. However, they also provide an effective protection for exceptionally vulnerable people who face the threat of being eaten alive every day.

In the same week, I met two young women about the same age, with similar family backgrounds and education. They could have been sisters, yet they ended up making radically different life choices.

Mari has a Ph.D. in nuclear physics and does fundamental research at the prestigious Tokyo University. Michiyo left her job recently to make an arranged marriage.

I met the newlywed first. For Westerners, there is something endlessly fascinating about an arranged marriage. In our imagination, it is only one step removed from a forced marriage. It carries with it a whiff of tragedy, and conjures up images of disconsolate lovers torn apart by family interests, lives dictated by fathers and husbands, quasi-commercial transactions in societies where peace and family interests matter infinitely more than individual happiness. An exotic remnant from the past, this is how we perceive the institution.

Once, at a large wedding reception attended by Tokyo who's who, I was surprised by the presence of two matchmakers, a man and a woman, sitting at the head table between the newlyweds, while the four parents were relegated to a faraway table, right by the kitchen doors. My surprise stemmed from the fact that I knew, as did the other five hundred guests, that these two young people, in their thirties, had met at the Harvard Business School, were partners in a business they created together, had been sharing the same New York loft for two years. In other words, they had proven abundantly to the world that they did not depend on anyone for introductions.

What, then, was the significance of this masquerade? Why were these two old people enthroned on stage as if they should be given credit for this happy gathering? Their function was, in fact, comparable to that of our witnesses, who sign the marriage register together with the two newlyweds. Left over from times past, they still provide the real function of widening the circle and establishing new links. Often, they are friends of both families, and their presence affirms publicly the alliance of two families.

For most younger Japanese, however, their presence during the wedding ceremony is nothing more than a formality.

That is why I was particularly intrigued to hear about a twenty-seven-year-old woman, graduated from a good university, who grew up in the United States, and who had deliberately called upon intermediaries to help her find a husband.

I am eager to meet this young dinosaur. I imagine her as a poor little rich and ugly girl, and I am bracing for a strained interview. To make things easier, we decided to meet in a quiet restaurant overlooking a peaceful garden, and the staff has been instructed to respect our privacy.

The dinosaur walks in, radiant in a bright-orange maternity dress, carrying three thick photo albums under her arm, delighted to have the opportunity to tell her story. Without being stunningly beautiful, she is a far cry from the ugly duckling I expected, and our conversation will soon reveal that this young lady is certainly smart enough to find the man of her dreams by herself – had she wanted to.

I make these mental notes as we exchange business cards and small talk to break the ice. I will have to catch myself a number of times during this encounter, because this candid young woman will keep knocking down my ready-made ideas, my half-baked conclusions, my facile parallels, and will time and again force me to readjust my Western perspective about arranged marriages.

We take a table, and she immediately pulls out of her purse a thin file with my name on it. When one has been put in charge of educating a *gaijin* (a foreigner), one must start with the fundamentals!

An arranged marriage is called *mi-ai*, and the etymology of the Chinese character paints a telling picture: *mi* means "to look" and *ai* means "to join." In other words, an arranged marriage is a marriage where two people look, observe, eyes wide open, before they create links and tie knots. The underlying implication is that, in other marriages, people don't look before they commit.

Michiyo explains patiently: when two people meet in university, at work, or through friends, fall in love, and get married, they are making a chance marriage. The Japanese language has a specific term for it: *renai*. The concept of marrying for love is relatively recent.

"It is a marriage based on a chance encounter," explains Michiyo. "In my case, on the contrary, I knew everything about my future husband, even before we met. I had a picture, his résumé, I knew what he studied in university, how much money he made, what his interests and aspirations were, how many children he wanted. I also knew his family history: whether he had a normal, happy childhood, whether his parents get along, I knew all of this even before I saw him for the first time."

I am searching her face for either some trace of contempt for those adventurers who marry out of love, or, on the contrary, some trace of regret. Nothing. She remains perfectly serene.

"Are you in love with your husband?"

"Of course! I wouldn't have married him otherwise."

Pause. I am confused. One can make an arranged marriage and yet marry out of love? She realizes the extent of my preconceived ideas and explains, very simply, "You know, it is not like before. In the old days, young people were married off and were told that love would come later. But me, I am a modern girl. I was certainly not going to marry without love. And neither was he. Before me, he had been introduced to twenty-odd girls from good families, with a good education, and I understand that some of them were quite pretty, but it never clicked. His mother's friends were trying very hard to find him a good match, and blamed him for being too difficult. He was just waiting to fall in love."

She then tells me how it happened.

"The first time, we met in the coffee shop of an international hotel downtown. My mother and his mother were there, plus the two friends who had organized the encounter. Five women and one man, that was not an auspicious beginning! Fortunately they had the good sense to leave us alone after the introductions. We drank a cup of tea, we made small talk, I remember that at some point we talked about football. I noted that he had a nice voice. It was relaxed and comfortable.

"We made a dinner date for a few days later. We went out

together four or five times in the following weeks. 'If I am not in love within a month, I will not marry him,' I was telling myself. He was doing the same thing. Yet there was no pressure. It was very relaxed."

There is something very serious and deliberate about the way she is telling her story. I try to imagine this man and this woman, sitting face to face in a situation where there is no room for playing games, since all the cards are on the table. They do not need to tell their life story, brag about their prowess in sport, their achievements in school or at work. It is all already on paper before them. They both did their homework, studied their files; the only thing left is to discover whether there is room for any physical attraction. Personal affinity is the only missing piece in an otherwise perfect puzzle.

Here they are then, sipping their green tea, planning their schedule to allow for any potential physical attraction to develop. These things cannot be stage-managed, and there will be no loss of face if it does not work. It is all terribly pragmatic, with no obligation. In that game, cheating is not in anybody's interest.

When and how did they know?

"One evening, we were on the beach at dusk. It was very romantic, and I realized that I wanted him to hold my hand. I concluded that I loved him. It was so simple! Yet he did not hold my hand that evening. In fact, he never even touched me before he asked me to marry him. I said yes, of course, and it is only then that we actually fell in love."

Then came the engagement – a very formal affair organized by the two families – the wedding and the beginning of married life.

The time has come to look at the photo albums. In every single picture, private moments or official portraits, the young husband displays a hard, sullen expression on his closed face.

I recognize that face. It is the same one one meets by the thousands every morning in the subway, late at night in the business district; it is the interchangeable face of the *salarimen*, those sad office workers, hardened before their time, distrustful, weary, unhappy, and desperately overworked.

There is not a hint of a smile on his engagement day, nor on his wedding day. No tenderness in his eyes, nothing to indicate that it is supposed to be the most beautiful day of his life. I feel sorry for Michiyo, so fresh, open, made for happiness.

Then we open the third album. The honeymoon album. The pictures are uniformly bad, over- or underexposed, out of focus, haphazardly framed, obviously taken in haste by some passerby who was asked to please push the red button on the camera, thank you very much.

But what a spectacular transformation in the subject!

Standing at the side of Michiyo is a very young man, almost a boy, a charming, tender smile on his face, slim, almost fragile-looking in his jeans and sports jacket, hair tousled like a child's. The distance between his public and private persona is stunning – but, sadly, it is not unusual.

Without his samurai mask, this Japanese man is objectively very vulnerable. Like so many of his contemporaries, he grew up without really knowing his father, who was always at work or on business trips. Raised among his mother, his aunts, and his grandmothers, he has had no male role models. When in doubt, the samurai model, even the caricature model from a television series, seems like a safe bet. This is indeed the mask he has been wearing to give himself a countenance in work and in life.

I no longer worry about Michiyo. The man she married is not an uncaring monster but a very nice young man who happens to be shy.

This new couple, smiling for the camera, page after page, when did they . . . how did they . . . as I am struggling to find the proper way to ask, Michiyo answers ahead of me. "We waited until after we were married to make love for the first time. We wanted to start everything together, from scratch." Then she adds, on a curiously flat tone of voice, "It went well."

The conversation turns to other topics, the trip to Italy that was cancelled because of the baby that came too soon, her husband's work that often keeps him in the office until one or two in the morning, the apartment block where they live together with other junior company executives, the long hours she spends alone at home.

Then, suddenly: "I am going to tell you something my husband does not know: for the longest time, I went out with an office colleague. We were madly in love; we had an intense physical relationship. I will never experience that again. But it was difficult. He came from a different social background, his parents were divorced, he felt he could not commit, because a childhood friend was expecting him to come back home to his village. I often did not understand him. I cried a lot, he did too; eventually, I left him because it was simply too much work. I still think of him as my lover, but I have no regret, my present life is so comfortable!"

She often uses the word "comfortable," and it occurs to me that the English word is not quite adapted to what she is trying to express. Once more, Chinese characters are called to the rescue.

The equivalent of her "comfortable" is represented by a woman under a roof. A woman in a sitting position, not in a kneeling one. A woman not at work, but at rest, suggesting an atmosphere of quiet normalcy. That is what is suggested by the ideogram, and that is what Michiyo appreciates in her new life.

She will again use the word "comfortable" when she talks about her university days.

She wanted a career in advertising. But that program was not offered in her school, and she did not want to change schools and leave her friends. "It was so comfortable. We had all known one another since kindergarten. We came from the same social class, we spoke the same language . . ."

Instead of advertising, she studied political science. Once she graduated, no advertising agency would hire her, and she ended up at Mitsui, one of the largest trading companies in Japan.

"In the beginning, I found my colleagues boring; then I realized that they always behaved like gentlemen, there were no dirty jokes, no embarrassing behaviour as happens so often in the workplace.

They were all polite, we all came from the same social class, we were together like one big family. It was comfortable."

That word again!

Is Michiyo obsessed with an exceptional need for "quiet normalcy"? Or is this young woman using very simple, everyday words to suggest a societal phenomenon?

The answer will come a bit later, as conversation turns to her girlfriends. They all plan to get married some day, but they are in no hurry.

"They are wary. They are protecting themselves. They are extremely prudent, maybe too prudent."

"Are they considering a *mi-ai*, an arranged marriage, the way you did?"

I sense a brief hesitation. She looks slightly embarrassed.

"You know, there is a negative side to *mi-ai*. But people don't like to talk about it."

"Please tell me."

"In order to get into an arranged marriage, one must first write this profile, this biography, which is then handed to the go-between. One must answer all the questions. It is easy for people who have the right background, who attended the right schools and have a great career ahead of them, but what about the others? It is no easy thing to put to paper the story of one's life when that story is less than perfect."

Here we are: the *mi-ai* are reserved for people who were born with a silver spoon in their mouth. For most Japanese, *mi-ai* has become an antiquated institution, which survives only in its formal aspects. But for the privileged ones, *mi-ai* represents the ultimate bastion, the last protection to guarantee good breeding, despite the intermingling of the classes in modern society.

Michiyo is not naïve, nor does she suffer from the fear of the unknown that paralyzes so many Japanese. Her parents did not trap her into constraining codes of behaviour. She travelled, lived abroad, had normal loves and friendships. Yet, every time she had important life choices to make, whether in her studies, her career, or her marriage, she reflected carefully, weighed her options, and every time, with her eyes wide open, she chose the most "comfortable" option in the sense of "quiet normalcy": the quiet, the familiar, the predictable, the no-surprise.

With her eyes just as open, Mari, deliberately, made diametrically different life choices.

Mari could be Michiyo's older sister: she had the same privileged background, the same open-minded parents, a similar childhood spent in the United States, the same transparency in her eyes, the same quiet certainty that she took the right decisions. There end the similarities.

Mari holds a Ph.D. in nuclear physics. A graduate of Stanford and MIT, she has a brilliant research career at the prestigious Institute for Industrial Science at Tokyo University. She is also a bit of a pioneer in a field where few women venture, in Japan as elsewhere.

"Mari, as in Marie Curie," she announced proudly when we were first introduced, warm smile on her face and hand extended for a deliberately Western handshake.

Mari, as in Marie Curie, because that was the most beautiful name her father could think of when his daughter was born. He himself was a professor of nuclear physics, and today he is obviously very proud of her accomplishments.

"Yet he never pushed me," says Mari. "I decided to study physics because I was interested, not because of my father. The more I got into it, the more I was fascinated."

Indeed, I can almost feel the passion in her voice as she regales me with magneto-hydro-dynamic phenomena and flux distortions caused by magnetic fields in nuclear-fusion reactors. For the time being, her goal is to be part of an international project to build one of these reactors. The best and brightest researchers from Japan, Europe, the United States, and Russia will work together on this project into the new century. The ultimate party!

Until this wonderful project comes to life, Mari pursues her research at the institute, with the twin anxieties common to all

Japanese researchers. The first one is to find financing: "Will the private sector manna keep coming, so that I can pursue my research for another season?" The second one – and the more serious – is not to lose face: "Will my results be conclusive?" If they are not, you are disgraced, vilified by your own colleagues, and your project is put on ice by your university.

A Japanese researcher is allowed to explore, but not to make mistakes. "It is the very antithesis of the scientific approach," Mari fulminates. "That's what kills creativity!"

While Mari "as in Marie Curie" rants and raves softly, I note the pink linen dress with matching jacket, the short pearl necklace: subtle yet non-equivocal signs that I am dealing with a professional woman in a senior position of authority. Otherwise, she would rate the eternal navy-blue suit with high-neck white blouse. Mari wears no pantyhose; in the heavy, humid heat of midsummer, it might seem like the normal thing to do. Yet, for someone in her position, in Tokyo, to go bare-legged constitutes a formidable declaration of independence.

Recently, Mari has affirmed her independence in yet another way: at the age of thirty-three, she left her parents' home for the first time. She confesses that she had to push herself. "Their house is very close to the institute, it was very convenient, they charged me an affordable rent, we get along very nicely . . . but at my age, it is time to get my own place, don't you think?"

The adjustment was hard. She wanted to remain downtown, and, on her budget, she had to be content with a studio the size of an average North American bathroom. In order to move in, she had to pay four months' rent ahead of time, plus agency fees. Buying a car is out of the question: parking spots downtown are simply not affordable.

"It is ridiculous! I make as much as my European and American colleagues, yet one-third of my income goes into taxes, and I am reduced to having to live like a student! Everything is too expensive, and there is no good reason for that. It really makes you want to run away and live elsewhere!"

Why doesn't she? One of her sisters is an architect in Paris, another one is a senior executive in a large Japanese company in New York. Daughters in this family aim high, and they aim far. Has she ever been tempted to follow her younger sisters and go to live abroad?

Instead of an answer, I am treated to a very Japanese expression: a kind of embarrassed half-smile, almost guilty in its quality, which usually precedes an admission of success or of some ambition likely to cause admiration and respect.

"Well . . . you see . . . I was thinking . . . possibly . . . I might contribute to society . . . very pretentious on my part . . . but if girls had more role models in high school, they might get more interested in science."

I learn that Mari devotes part of her time to giving presentations in public schools; she convinced the institute to have an open house for high-school students twice a year in order to attract them to scientific careers. She aims at girls in particular.

"For an academic career, what counts is your brain, not what you have between your legs," she says softly. When there is a critical mass of women in research positions, they will no longer be considered as oddities, they won't have to face the same obstacles I did in order to be taken seriously."

To be taken seriously means to assure that colleagues and superiors think about her as a physicist, a researcher, a magneto-hydro-dynamic expert, before they think of her as a woman. She succeeded, but she paid a high price: there has been no *boyfriend* in her life, not in university, not in adulthood. "I think about it, but I don't have anyone in sight. It is not easy to meet people, and I am always so busy . . ."

Yes, she would like to get married and have children, but in practice, the system will not allow it. She explains with controlled but deep exasperation, "With children at home, I would need domestic help, like professional couples in Europe and North America. It is expensive, but the real problem would be where to house her? Tokyo apartments are so small, even the most expensive ones!"

Then there is the matter of kindergarten, a constant source of anguish for parents. Their regulations are ironclad. If the kindergarten closes its doors at six o'clock, pity the poor parents who show up at the door at two minutes past six to pick up their child. They will be severely reprimanded, and will be shamed publicly during the next parent-teacher meeting. They will also receive a warning by mail: "Do not let this happen again, or your child is out!" This is the worst threat of all. Waiting lists are long, so long in fact that some children are put on the waiting list at birth.

Kindergarten tyranny is a very concrete obstacle for women pursuing a professional career. Whether they run a research lab or an operating room, whether they sit in the Diet or defend a case before the tribunal, at one minute before six o'clock they must be at the school gate. "No exception will be tolerated!"

Mari is making a list of all the reasons Japanese women have not to get married, whether or not they are nuclear physicists. She then extends her diatribe to the education system: "The whole system has to be overhauled. It is killing creativity. It is very serious!"

The comment in itself is banal. It is the topic of endless editorial, television round tables, and parliamentary white papers. To say that Japanese education kills creativity is stating the obvious. However, that statement takes on a whole new meaning coming from someone who is devoting her career to research.

"The Japanese do not have the right to err, and that includes scientists. In traditional society, to err is to destroy harmony, it is an unforgivable sin, the most serious of them all. However, in scientific research, it is fundamental to have the right to err! How can we explore uncharted areas if we must simultaneously be certain not to err? How can we verify a hypothesis if we must first ascertain it is correct? It is nonsensical. Did you ever wonder why there are so few Nobel Prizes in Japan? That's the reason, right there."

Mari is glowing in righteous anger, and her indignation has the tone of sincerity. As she speaks, I am reminded of a Japanese chemist, who, every year, taught in an American university for one semester.

That period outside the walls allowed him to run his experiments. If he did not get the results expected, he simply went on to test the next hypothesis, as any scientist should, without being penalized. If, on the other hand, his hypothesis panned out, he was able to go home bathed in glory.

I am also reminded of comments made by an engineer who specialized in industrial ceramics. He, too, was exasperated by the obstacles set in the way of Japanese research: "My colleagues are so afraid of failure that they are testing and testing again and again, even when they have established evidence. Meanwhile, American researchers are the ones raking in the Nobel Prizes!" He was not expressing any jealousy or envy towards Western researchers. Quite the opposite, he was railing against the timorous and diffident attitude of his countrymen.

Today, Mari is making the same damning analysis. She is now drawing a bleak scenario in which all the Japanese with initiative, imagination, and creativity would be leaving their country like rats leave a sinking ship. "It would be a catastrophe!"

Then she adds in anguish, "Yet, that's exactly what is happening now."

So, she stays. From a distance, she watches her two adventurous sisters with a pinch of envy. Yet she stays. If she keeps up-to-date and pursues her research in magneto-hydro-dynamics, if she keeps receiving private-sector financing, if she is offered a permanent chair at the institute, within fifteen years she will have acquired enough influence to change things.

Perhaps.

Meanwhile, she lives a monkish life between her minuscule six-tatami-mat apartment and her lab, she makes her regular high-school rounds in her pastel suits, and she dreams about that nuclear-fusion reactor – with a little something in her heart every time she happens to walk by a kindergarten.

CHAPTER 10

Hiroshima Today

The year of the fiftieth anniversary of the end of the Second World War, a popular Japanese weekly magazine polled eighteen- to twenty-five-year-olds. The purpose was to measure their civic sense and also, between the lines, to test whether militaristic aggressiveness is part of the Japanese genes, as some people like to claim.

The wording of the questions was silky-smooth. Until the last one: "How would you react if there was another world conflict and your country were threatened?"

To which a majority of the young Japanese polled answered immediately, "I would take the next flight to Zurich."

One would like to believe that this answer reflected a deep-seated wisdom, or at least an enlightened pacifism inculcated in them since childhood. In actual fact, it simply reflects a royal indifference to public life. War as politics belongs to another world and does not concern them in the least.

"I knew practically nothing about the war until this year, when a number of articles were published on the subject." The man who is making this surprising confession is in his fifties. He is the senior editor of a large publishing house. Sitting on the floor, flopped against the wall of a traditional restaurant, he has been philosophizing in a leisurely way with his dinner companions.

The time is a few days before the fiftieth anniversary of the end of the war. The occasion is the preview of a play by Hisashi Inoue, a famous contemporary playwright, which will be presented later tonight in a small experimental theatre located in a working-class neighbourhood of Tokyo. The meal is almost over, the low table is littered with sake cups, half-empty beer bottles, and half-full ashtrays.

"Until this year, nobody ever talked about those things."

Approving nods around the table. They are all about the same age. Together, they represent no fewer than six of the best-known Japanese publishing houses. Graduated from the better universities, they belong to an educated élite. They are more informed than the average Japanese, their hearts are in the right place, and they have a sense of mission: to educate and inform the Japanese public.

Yet, here they are, slightly embarrassed, confessing that, until recently, they knew precious little about the war years and the role played by their country during that dark period of its history.

They did learn in school that Japan had colonized Korea and invaded other Asian countries, but they were taught that the purpose was chiefly to build railroads and improve the standards of living of the local populations. They also learned about Pearl Harbor, Hiroshima, and Nagasaki. They are not entirely naive. They are aware of the fact that the Education Ministry keeps a close watch on what is being taught in history textbooks. Yet the atrocities committed by the Imperial Army in Southeast Asia, the Nanjing massacre, the research labs in Manchuria, where war prisoners were used as guinea pigs for new weapons of bacteriological warfare, all these things were only vague, unconfirmed rumours until recently.

"We Japanese know nothing," they sigh, as the atmosphere gets heavier with cigarette smoke. Then, with a little help from beer and sake, it soon becomes: "We Japanese want to know nothing."

This is the tragedy of memory in which Japan has been trapped for a half-century. War criminals, as well as victims of Hiroshima and Nagasaki, spent all these years alone with their nightmares, unable to share them with anyone, paralyzed in their silence. And this is the theme of the play these well-meaning intellectuals are about to see tonight.

The story takes place in Hiroshima, four years after the bomb. The set shows the backyard side of a Japanese house. This detail is relevant as, in Japanese tradition, a lot of attention is paid to the contrast between the back and the front, the inside and the outside, what one says and what one thinks, what one expresses and what one feels.

Therefore, as soon as the curtain rises, showing the backyard, we are given to understand that the play is going to be about the "inside," the "behind the mask," the deep feelings and emotions, as opposed to what one says out of formality.

The main character is a young woman who feels profoundly guilty because, alone in her family, she survived the hecatomb. Someone has just brought to the local museum where she works several pieces of memorabilia: melted bottles distorted by the intense heat of the atomic explosion, kitchen utensils bent grotesquely, the half-burnt bust of a *kami* (one of those local divinities one sees everywhere in the countryside), a clock whose hands are forever frozen at 8:15, the time when the bomb was dropped on the city.

These objects are familiar to the audience, indeed to the Japanese public in general, because they are exhibited in the Peace Museum in Hiroshima, which thousands of people visit every year. However, the play takes place in 1950. No one is thinking of museums just yet, and, for the city authorities, the disparate collection is only garbage to be disposed of.

The young woman, assailed by doubts, volunteers to store them in her own backyard, but she soon finds that the proximity of these remains from a too-recent past is intolerable. Having to see them every day, lying outside her window, revives her sense of guilt. "They are dead, I am alive. How could I ever again dare enjoy life?"

She realizes that she will never be able to lead a normal life as long as these grotesque mementos remain with her. Yet she cannot get rid of them, she cannot deny history and condemn to oblivion all the people who lost their lives on that fateful summer day of 1945. Caught between the need to forget and the fear of forgetting, she is paralyzed, frozen, incapable of any decision and any feeling.

The parallel with Japan's state of mind since the war is obvious. In the play, the young woman's dilemma is resolved when her father visits her from the Kingdom of the Dead to explain that her duty is both to keep these keepsakes and to enjoy life, to laugh, to love, to move ahead.

The symbolism is heavy but efficient. Everyone is crying in the small theatre. My companion, a Japanese woman in her forties, whispers to me that this play is the best possible way to commemorate the end of the war.

I am struck by the fact that she is talking as if the war had just ended. As if, until that particular moment (it is 1995), the Japanese had not been quite certain what to do with their own mental mementos. As if they had been living in a state of suspended animation for fifty years, hypnotized and paralyzed by this collective memory that they do not know how to handle, waiting for a father to visit and help them pick up the thread of their history – a father who never came.

Foreign visitors to Hiroshima all have the same purpose: they want to see traces of a place marked by fate, some confirmation of the unique vocation of the city, even a new post-humanist wisdom in its inhabitants. In actual fact, apart from the museum and the famous dome that is now a World Heritage site, they discover that Hiroshima looks disappointingly similar to other Japanese cities. Brand new – for obvious reasons – entirely rebuilt around the inevitable castle (each town seems to have its castle), parks and green spaces along the river, this could fit the description of many other cities in the archipelago. As for the inhabitants, they rather enjoy the attention they get from the international community, although they occasionally find it tiresome to be pegged forever as victims.

I am with my husband on one of his official visits. We pay a courtesy call to the governor and to the mayor; we meet businesspeople, the president of one of the universities, the director of the Peace Museum. It is a two-day intensive immersion. We learn a lot about the circumstances of the August 6, 1945, tragedy, the reconstruction, the "survivors" traumas (a special word was coined in Japanese to distinguish Hiroshima and Nagasaki survivors from those of other tragedies), and the existence of a number of people whose bodies, fifty years later, are still rotting slowly in the city hospitals from the effects of radiation.

When one visits Hiroshima, one must also go and admire the world-famous Miyajima Shrine, built in the water, its tall vermilion gate springing out of the sea. "One of Japan's most beautiful sites," claim tourist brochures.

We drive a few kilometres to a nearby village and embark on the ferry that will take us to the legendary island. Leaning on the railing, I gaze across the immense bay as we move away from shore. The city of Hiroshima lies right behind the cape, and I muse aloud, to no one in particular, "People who live here in this bay must have been at the best vantage point to see the mushroom cloud rising above Hiroshima."

The guide, who has been with us for the last two days, draws mournfully on his cigarette: "Yes, indeed, we saw it very clearly."

I jump, startled. "You were there? Did you see it?"

"Yes. This is home for me. I was born in this village."

I am bewildered, confounded, astounded. For the last two days, this man has been guiding us in our peregrinations, he has been piloting these foreigners who ask so many questions. He was present for all the conversations, all the briefings, he had ample time to measure the extent of our curiosity, he heard our wish to meet with eyewitnesses to the tragedy . . . And yet, at no time up until now did he ever volunteer that he himself is one of these "survivors." It is only as a coincidence, because smoking is forbidden under deck, because we both climbed upstairs at the same time to light a cigarette, that I accidentally stumbled on this confidence. Maybe, out of a natural reserve,

he would not take the initiative to talk about himself to strangers? I
try to prompt him a bit:

"How old were you?"

"I was eight."

"What were you doing when it happened?"

"I was just about to leave for school. In the morning, all children
would go all together from school to work in a factory."

"What did you do when you saw the mushroom rise in the sky,
above Hiroshima, from behind the cape?"

"I turned around and went back home."

"Why?"

"Because it did not look like any of the bombs we had seen until
then. Right away, I realized that this was something different."

"Your mother was at home?"

"Yes. She, too, had left work to come back home. All the windows
in the village had imploded."

"And then?"

I have a hard time hiding my impatience. He has been answering
my questions without hesitation, but he does not volunteer anything,
he does not offer any more than the minimum amount of information. I have to beg for every detail.

"We spent the morning boiling water and ripping cotton material into long strips for the wounded."

"The wounded?"

"They started arriving around one o'clock in the afternoon. We
saw them from afar, on the road from Hiroshima. Their skin was
coming undone in strands. We had never seen anything like it. We
spent the rest of the day and the following night looking after them.
Everybody in the village was helping. We had nothing but hot water
and these cotton strips to help them. And they kept coming and
coming. There was so little we could do . . ."

The whole thing is delivered in a bland, lifeless voice, as he keeps
pulling on his cigarette and gazing at the horizon. The Hiroshima
nightmare as seen by an eight-year-old schoolboy. He does speak

about it when pushed, but these are not the kind of memories one brings back more often than necessary.

It suddenly dawns on me that I have been more than a little ruthless. I look towards the Miyajima coastline, which is getting nearer, and our conversation turns to the long history of that shrine on the sea, the deer who roam freely on the island, the wind and the sunset.

I encountered a similar resistance with a charming young woman who is in charge of public relations with a large Hiroshima corporation. In her thirties, she was born in this city, she could be the daughter of the man on the ferry. She has travelled the world, she is resolutely Western in her manners, international in her approach, and I feel I will not be out of line if I ask her, very plainly, how was it to grow up in Hiroshima?

With exquisite politeness, she answers that it was the same as growing up anywhere else. I pretend to ignore this demurral. There has to be more. Her mother was born in Hiroshima five years before the bomb, she herself was raised between her mother and her grandmother. With these two "survivors" living under the same roof, the little girl must have heard a lot of stories?

"No. We never talked about it at home."

"Why wouldn't you?"

"My mother was too young to remember. My grandmother did not talk about it. Me, I never thought about it when I was a kid."

Third scene: the story takes place in an all-girls junior college in Hiroshima. A group of students have just come back from a three months' stay in a Vancouver high school. It was the first time they had left their country, and they are still bubbling about their trip, their daily life in a Canadian family ("Sometimes, it was the father who cooked dinner!"), the friends they made at school.

In the reports they write for their college, though, the leitmotif is this: "Canadians kept asking us questions about Japan, and I realized I knew very little. Most of all, I knew almost nothing about my own city, nothing about Hiroshima, nothing about the bomb."

Such was the situation fifty years after the end of the war. Between those who did not want to talk, those who wanted to forget, and the monumental blanks in the school curriculum, there was this void in the collective memory, as, in the old days, the blank spot left on a doctored group photo.

The root causes of this deliberate amnesia are understandable. In the years following the end of the war, Hiroshima and Nagasaki "survivors" were treated as if they had the plague. The notion of radiation was a novel one, people thought it might be contagious, and "survivors" were turned away when they went looking for a job or an apartment to rent, or were simply shopping for groceries. Eventually they learned to hide their "survivor" status in order . . . to survive!

The Japanese suffered also, as do all witnesses to armed conflicts, from the fact that some experiences are too traumatic to be shared. The president of a large Japanese corporation told me one day, with no apparent emotion in his voice, how, during one of the bombings of Tokyo, his father had handed him the only bicycle in the household, "because I pedalled the fastest," and had ordered him imperiously to pedal as fast as he could heading north, without stopping and without looking behind him, or else. This is the last memory he has of his father. All the members of his family disappeared in the incendiary bombs that annihilated one million people in Tokyo in 1945. Now, he is recalling the event in a detached tone of voice, simply because an ill-mannered, nosey foreigner is pressing him with questions. But he has never told the story to his children.

"Why should I bother them with ancient history?"

A young Japanese woman, married to a Canadian, recently discovered that she is related to the High Priest of the Meiji Shrine. It is almost as if the Pope were her cousin! Her mother mentioned this illustrious kinship in passing, during a casual conversation about something else. Kyoko is quite excited by the news, and very proud. Yet, she is puzzled. "How come I never knew about this?"

For the first time in her life, she realizes that she knows precious little about her family history; nothing about her ancestors, her parents' childhood, the circumstances in which they met, nothing that precedes her own memory. It is obvious for all to see that Kyoko does come from a very good family. You can tell from the ever-smiling mask on her face, from the way she walks in measured little steps ("six steps to one tatami length," her grandmother taught her), and the aborted bows, which a Western education never totally erased from her demeanour.

Yet, she suddenly compares herself to her Québécois husband, who knows his family history over several centuries, and who draws from his long lineage a reassuring sense of belonging, a solid weft over which he weaves his life experiences. By comparison, Kyoko feels almost like an abandoned child. Since her discovery, she has been questioning her parents, with little success. To talk about the past reminds them of the magnificence of a world that is no more, the grand family mansion, summers in the countryside, trips in horse-drawn carriages, private tutors . . . Rather than sink back into nostalgia, they did their best to erase it all from their memories. Kyoko is condemned to living without a past.

For the civilian population, the war years were hell years: nothing to eat – whatever rice was left went to soldiers – children in factories, boys drafted at an earlier and earlier age, tuberculosis, the "thought police" roaming the streets, and, from 1943 on, the incendiary bombs that destroyed everything. And, to top it all off, once the nightmare was finally over, they learned they had been on the wrong side of the conflict, that they were the shame of humanity. In an instant, civilians as well as soldiers saw their memories, adventures, tribulations, their fears and sacrifices, lose all legitimacy the day their country lost the war.

The traditional aura of glory that surrounds the soldier coming back to his village was out of the question: rather, soldiers were spit on by civilians when they returned home.

Grandmothers could not regale their grandchildren with the sacrifices they made during the war, because they could not tell them in the name of what such sacrifices were made.

There was no background, no context. The Japanese had lost their own history. There was nothing they could tell their children.

That may explain the unprecedented success of the elephants' story. In 1951, a primer entitled *The Loyal Elephants* was published in Japan. Its popularity was such that it was soon added to the list of manuals approved by elementary schools throughout the country.

Once upon a time, nice friendly elephants lived in the Tokyo zoo. Children liked them a lot and paid them a visit every Sunday. Then, war came. There was nothing left to eat. The zoo-keeper had no money to buy food for the elephants. He cried a lot, and then he decided to add some poison in the grass he fed them every day. The elephants fell sick, children found them weaker and weaker when they visited. Finally, one fateful Sunday, when the children arrived at the zoo, they discovered that their elephant friends had died. Therefore, war is bad.

This inept little tale went through ninety-two printings. Totally detached from real life (elephants are a far cry from the Japanese daily life!), indecent in its purpose (was it really the time to feel sorry for elephants when so many people were mourning their dead?), impertinent in its conclusion (would war be more acceptable had the elephants survived?), this inane story appeared, to my Western eyes, as an intolerable insult to children's intelligence.

The Japanese, however, see this fable as a coded story with two hidden messages, and the keys are as follows:

Why elephants? One can only see them in a zoo, that is, in captivity. They are huge, one can sense that they have an enormous inner strength, yet they cannot make use of it, because they are locked in a cage. Their power remains virtual. And when one looks at their eyes under the heavy lids, one is struck by their sad and resigned expression. This is how the Japanese see themselves, or rather, this is how they saw themselves in 1951 when the book was published.

The second hidden message of the story has to do with the elephants' death. If they must die, why inflict on them this slow death, this poisoning spread out over several weeks? Because all forms of life, even the most insignificant, is divine in nature. Every instant of life is as precious as an eternity.

The message may seem passing strange, so soon after a conflict during which the Imperial Army had distinguished itself with the most violent massacres, inhumane treatments of prisoners of war, suicide missions imposed on fourteen-year-olds . . . yet, in 1951, this elephant story was all the Japanese could muster to tell schoolchildren about the war.

Extraordinary about this country is the fact that, for two generations, children have been deprived of an experience common to children the world over: listening to elders recount stories of times past, stories that usually start with: "In my day . . ."

Only in the weeks preceding the fiftieth anniversary of the end of the war did the old-timers start to talk. Faced with the imminence of death, their reserve began to pale, compared with the urgency of passing their memories on to the next generations. The final push was provided by the voracious appetite of media and historians alike for "survivors'" testimonies during that year. In Hiroshima, particularly, it seemed as if the whole world had descended on the city: 95 foreign television networks, 316 journalists from 21 countries, together with at least a thousand Japanese journalists and reporters, all came down on Hiroshima like locusts to cover the fiftieth-anniversary remembrances.

Many others came too, including academics, researchers, historians, pacifists, politicians, educators, and simple people of goodwill. For them, to be there on that particular day in that particular place, was a modest way of becoming themselves witnesses of history.

They were all equipped with cameras and tape recorders. And all these microphones were looking for "survivors" to talk to.

That is when the little old ladies came out. They settled under the cherry trees that grow in Peace Park, kneeled Japanese-style, and started talking, for hours on end, surrounded by people from all over the world – young people mostly, who were listening with immense respect. To find themselves suddenly, finally, the centre of attention, what an astounding experience! Encouraged by the attentive faces and the cameras, they let words and memories pour out. For the first time they were hearing the sound of their own voices recalling those events, they were living them all over again, kept talking through their tears, the cameras zooming in. They saw themselves on the seven o'clock evening news, and finally, after so many years, they were able to achieve closure.

A group of teenagers from a Third World country are visiting Tokyo, thanks to some NGO's mission to promote understanding between people. For the first time in their short lives, they have left their small South Pacific island, and the experience is pure wonder: the crowded thoroughfares, those automatic machines that distribute cold drinks in the streets, the lights, the city, the subway . . .

They are travelling on the Yamanote line, which circles around Tokyo. Kneeling on their seats, brand-new baseball caps pulled down over their ears and worn backwards to look *cool*, noses on the window, they are watching the immense megalopolis, when a very old man calls upon them: "Hey, kids! Where are you from?"

"Yap! We come from Yap!" They shout all together, delighted with the attention.

Upon which, the old man starts to cry, right there, in the middle of the subway car. The children are stupefied.

"I know about Yap. I flew over your island many times. I was coming to throw bombs over you." Now he is sobbing openly. "But I swear, I never dropped my bombs on your island. I always dropped them over the sea! When I returned, I would tell my superiors I missed because of the wind. I did not want to hurt you. But it was the war. I was against the war. I didn't want to kill anybody, I swear! My bombs, I always dropped them in the water!" Words and tears are pouring in a torrent. It is the first time in fifty years that he talks about the war, that he hears himself talk about the war. He is crying, crying, crying.

With the help of an interpreter, the children are beginning to understand. Rather, they understand the words, because for them the war is ancient – very ancient – history. Their priority is to console this old man who seems so sad!

"Don't cry, Mister. So your bombs fell in the sea. So you didn't kill anyone!"

"But I said nothing! I did nothing! I should have done something to prevent the war . . ."

Whether they were civilians or military, the Japanese who lived through the rise of fascism in the 1930s often express a similar remorse, the feeling they could have done something, they should have done something when there was still time . . .

Naoko Mizutani is a young historian who specializes in modern China. She was on a study trip in Shanghai when she received an urgent call from her father. "Your great-uncle is very ill. He is demanding to talk to you before he dies."

Naoko returned to be at his bedside, and learned with horror and stupefaction that her dear uncle, who spent his adult life selling fish in Tsukiji market, had been a war criminal.

He was attached to one of those medical-research units, in which new bacteriological weapons were tested on prisoners of war. He never told anyone about this sorry part of his life. However, he devoted the later years of his existence to writing his memoirs, based on his old diaries.

It is all there: names of places and people, dates, everything that can help historical research. He hands the whole thing to his grand-niece in lieu of extreme unction, and dies three days later with a clean conscience.

The young historian has her career path laid out ahead of her. She will devote the rest of her life to looking for the individuals mentioned in the manuscript, and shed all the light possible on these medical-research centres whose very existence was denied for many years, and about which very little is known to this day.

The path is clear, too, for Sadamitsu Ushijima. In 1945, his grandfather, who was the commanding officer during the battle of Okinawa, refused against all evidence to surrender to the Americans, and committed *seppuku* after having given orders for his men to fight to the death. The gesture came straight from the samurai code of honour, but it triggered an unprecedented confusion that lasted five days and cost the life of thousands of civilians – without any purpose whatsoever, since the battle was over.

The young Ushijima teaches in a Tokyo elementary school. He cannot erase the past, but he can ensure that the past does not fade conveniently in a collective oblivion.

The Imperial Army left bitter memories in Okinawa. It requisitioned the whole civilian population, even children, yet it treated them like enemies in captivity. During the three-month-long battle, the locals learned that it was a far better fate to be captured by the Americans, who handed food and medicine to their prisoners, than by the Japanese, who killed them like dogs for a sin as harmless as speaking in their own dialect.

This aspect of the war has been kept under wraps in mainland Japan, but it left a deep, burning memory among the inhabitants of the remote southern island, and a bitter resentment, an extinguishable anger, which does not abate with time.

Ushijima took his pupils on a study tour in Okinawa. "I felt my grandfather's fateful decision weighing on my shoulders," he commented then. He discovered a book, a biography written by a woman who recounts how, at the age of eight, she found herself alone in the world in a cave, surrounded by decomposing bodies, only to be kicked out by Japanese soldiers, themselves looking for shelter against the relentless rain of American bombs. Ushijima undertook to have this book distributed in the whole country, in order to amend what is taught in history textbooks, and to redress within his own limited capacity the unmeasurable wrongs caused by his grandfather.

With him, a new generation of teachers, tired of waiting for Ministry of Education directives, started calling on Second World War survivors to address their students about war, peace, and peacekeeping.

That is how, three generations later, very young Japanese are finally beginning to learn about their country's recent history.

CHAPTER 11

The Textbook Cases

Mention "the textbook case" to a Japanese, and you are sure to see him roll his eyes in exasperation and let out a deep, frustrated sigh.

This lawsuit was the longest in Japanese legal history; it was in the eye of the media for more than thirty years, triggered memorable demonstrations in the streets of Tokyo, caused ministers to resign, shortened a judge's career, provoked diplomatic incidents between Japan and its neighbours, mobilized public opinion, and crystallized the postwar paradoxes of Japanese society.

In the eye of this storm was an old and stubborn history teacher, Saburo Ienaga, who wanted to force the Japanese to face their past, recognize the horrors committed by the Imperial Army during the Second World War, and educate the next generations to ensure that history did not repeat itself.

I had just arrived in Japan in 1993 when the textbook case – in other words, the lawsuit brought by Ienaga – was going through one of its many rebounds. Dumbfounded, I witnessed one of the wrenching crises that periodically seize Japanese society.

Day after day, on the front page of the major dailies, in editorials, commentaries, and televised debates, the same question was being repeated over and over: What *really* happened during the Second World War?

I would later learn that, in Japan, hardly a week goes by without a news item, a special report, or a testimony fuelling the same debate: Were we, the Japanese, the aggressors or the victims? What are our memories? Who gets to write history?

For foreigners, the whole controversy sounds surreal.

Whether in school, at the movies, or in our comic strips, we all learned as fact that the Empire of the Rising Sun was on the wrong side of the world conflict. For Americans, the proof was in the attack on Pearl Harbor. For Europeans, the proof was in the alliance between Japan and Nazi Germany. For Asians, the proof was in the invasion of China, the Nanjing massacre, the brutal occupation of the Philippines, Malaysia, and the rest of southeast Asia.

Where is the debate? The Japanese were on the side of evil. They lost. End of story. For us all, there is no controversy.

For the Japanese, however, things are far from being that simple.

The older ones, who grew up under the military regime, were taught in school that Japan's mission was to liberate Asia from Western domination, and, whether one cares to admit it or not, things learned in early childhood tend to stay with one for life.

The intermediate generation, born during the war, endured militaristic propaganda, then American propaganda, and learned to be wary of both and sceptical of all.

Finally, the younger generation know hardly anything about their country's past, precisely because their elders cannot agree on what to tell them.

This explains why, more than fifty years after the end of a conflict that set the whole planet ablaze, the Japanese are still wondering how the history of the Second World War should be interpreted, whether they can reconcile national pride and national guilt, and how they can deal with their past.

Westerners may guffaw at the qualms of conscience, the accusations, the convolutions, the rehashing, and the doubts – mostly the doubts – that clutter the pages of newspapers almost daily.

But for the Japanese, young and old, it is a morass from which they cannot extricate themselves and in which leftist and rightist ideologies, modernity and tradition, conflicts of generations, and also various visions of reality are hopelessly entangled.

At the end of the war, Saburo Ienaga was already a scholar of some renown for his work on the history of ideas. A professor emeritus from Tokyo University of Education, he had won the Japan Academy Prize in 1948. He then undertook to write *The Pacific War*, a book that was published in 1950 and translated into several languages.

Ienaga was no great friend of the military regime, yet he was astounded with what he discovered as he was doing his research. That prompted him to write a high-school history textbook, including less palatable episodes, such as the colonization of Korea, the massacre of Nanjing, and the existence of research labs on chemical and bacteriological weapons in Manchuria and Singapore, where prisoners of war were used for experiments.

For the first few years, Ienaga's textbook did well. It was widely used in secondary schools and went into reprint four years in a row. The Japanese had just inherited a brand-new constitution, courtesy of the Americans, and for the first time in their history they enjoyed what we call fundamental liberties, including freedom of expression. Those were the days when the whole country was enthusiastically learning about this still-foreign concept of "democracy." Socialists were coming out of the woodwork and won a respectable number of seats in the new Diet.

However, after the euphoria of the early years, the winds began to turn. As the Allied occupation forces withdrew, the Japanese settled back into the driver's seat, and it did not take long for old habits to return.

In the Ministry of Education in particular, public servants soon recovered their proprietary attitude towards curriculum and textbook content. Teachers were given precise blueprints of what to teach for each grade, and all textbooks had to be screened before publication. In history, it soon became clear that the priority was to give young Japanese a positive image of their country, rather than a truthful account of events, with words like "sacred mission," "sacrifice," and "abnegation" creeping back into the vocabulary.

That spelled trouble for Saburo Ienaga. The manuscript of his fifth edition was sent back with a number of corrections. For instance, where he mentioned "Japanese aggression in China during the thirties," inspectors stalled on the word "aggression." Such a negative-sounding word! Why not use the term "military advance," they suggested helpfully.

They explained their concern with candour: "In the education of citizens of the next generation, it is not desirable to use a term with negative ethical connotations to describe the acts of their own country."

According to the same principle, they asked the historian to soft pedal what happened in Nanjing in 1936. Regarding the Nanjing massacre, Ienaga had written, "Many Japanese soldiers and officers violated Chinese women."

The ministry's response was as follows: "As it is common throughout the world for troops to rape women during war, it is not appropriate to single out the acts of the Japanese Army. Too much emphasis is placed on specific incidents."

Inspectors balked at the pacifist flavour of Ienaga's textbook. For instance, one of the illustrations in the manual showed the picture of a very young soldier who lost an arm in battle. The accompanying caption read: "The horrors of war: Even though war came to an end, the arms and legs of soldiers lost in battle will never return." And he quoted Article 9 of the new constitution, in which Japan renounces war forever.

Despite this constitutional reference, the text was rejected by the ministry because "it conveys an excessively negative impression of war."

At first, Ienaga tried to play along. He would provide corrections, soften his words, and occasionally haggle for shreds of truth, as in: "If you let me mention the Nanjing massacre, in return I will reduce the official number of civilian victims."

But this was wearing thin on the professional historian and, after nine years of bargaining, he decided to take his fight before the courts. The year was 1965, and it was the first of three lawsuits that would occupy the limelight in Japanese public life for more than three decades.

Ienaga was fighting on two fronts: he wanted young Japanese to know what happened during the war; he also wanted to establish that, under the new constitution, the Ministry of Education had no right meddling with the content of textbooks.

In the spring of 1993, the Supreme Court was about to render its decision on the first of the three lawsuits, and public opinion was in a state of high excitement. For twenty-eight years, the case had been before the courts; for twenty-eight years, Japanese children had been taught an expurgated, honeyed version of their country's history; but for twenty-eight years, too, the textbook issue had rebounded with metronome regularity onto the front page of newspapers.

Indeed, Ienaga had launched two more lawsuits, one in 1967, the other in 1984. There had been appeals every step of the way and, as a result, the textbook-screening case had been back in the headlines at least ten times. And each time Ienaga appeared before the tribunal, each time the Ministry of Education counsels addressed the courts, each time a famous witness was heard, each time a judge rendered a decision, the media went into another frenzy.

For weeks at a time, editorials, commentaries, letters to the editor, round tables, televised debates, and open-line shows were focused on the Nanjing massacre – How many dead? How many rapes? Was it aggression? Who was telling the truth? And also, were we to believe those survivors who were now rising everywhere: these old soldiers who, on their deathbeds, were making the most frightening confessions to save their souls and these women landing on our

shores from all over Asia to tell appalling tales of being sexual slaves
to the Imperial Army.

It mattered little any more whether these topics were or were not
part of the high-school curriculum. Every Japanese was hearing
about Nanjing, and the comfort women, and Unit 731 (the research
unit on bacteriological warfare in Manchuria) as they read their
newspaper in the subway or listened to the radio in their car.

Old Ienaga was educating the Japanese despite themselves. He
was losing all the battles before the courts, yet he was winning his war
before the public.

I wanted to meet the man who had taken it upon himself to become
Japan's living conscience. Perhaps a letter, written in English just in
case, asking very humbly for an interview by a foreign journalist,
might eventually find its way to the desk of the famous author.

That same evening, the phone rang. To my surprise, the great
man himself was on the other end of the line. His voice was broken
with age, and his mastery of English was as uncertain as my Japanese,
yet there was no doubt: the famous professor was inviting me to his
home, the sooner the better.

A nondescript suburb, a maze of dull little lanes, a narrow house
like any other, the professor opening the door himself, apologizing
profusely as any good Japanese should, confused, hurried, embarrassed.

He is a very old man, looking exceptionally frail, with a bald skull,
round and pink, which, paradoxically, makes him look like a child. He
welcomes me into his living room, crammed with books from floor
to ceiling, and we sit around a low table where a tray has been prepared for tea.

I will not be given a chance to recite the civil niceties I practised
so dutifully for the occasion. Ienaga has little patience for preambles.
The embarrassed old man of a minute ago has already made way for
the crusading militant. From his years of fighting the administration,
he has learned that courts are very sensitive to international public
opinion; a foreign journalist is perceived as an opportunity to advance

his cause. I am in his living room, and therefore there is not a minute to waste. (He will even forget to pour the sacrosanct cup of green tea, for which I will get a panicked phone call the next day, and another stream of apologies.)

Ienaga pulls out a fragile little book and opens it carefully to the first page. It is a 1922 history textbook. The paper, yellowed and dry, is as brittle as straw. The first chapter deals with Creation. It explains how Jimmu, Japan's first Emperor, was the great-grandson of the first man, himself born from the Sun Goddess Amaterasu. This is an eighth-century legend with which all Japanese are familiar, as its theme appears frequently in literature and iconography.

"But in 1922, it was presented as a true historical fact," explains Ienaga, shaking his head in disgust. "And things got worse as time went by. With the rise of fascism [in 1926], legend took precedence over history," he adds.

By way of demonstration, he opens another textbook, dating from 1944, which states as an unquestionable fact that the first Emperor came down from heaven and landed right in the middle of Japan in order to reign over the world.

"This is what we were teaching eleven-year-olds! And authors had no qualms mixing reality with legend when it fit their purpose. Look." He chooses a chapter dealing with the Russo-Japanese war in 1905 and draws my attention to two old photographs: a Japanese battleship and a portrait of Admiral Togo.

Very important, this Admiral Togo. He beat the Russians at sea, and, thanks to him, Japan became overnight a player to be reckoned with on the international stage. Forty years later, during the world conflict, he was seen as one of those icons that allowed leaders to justify their expansionist policies in the Pacific.

As any good historian, Ienaga is exhaustive and systematic.

He still has one demonstration to make, in order to prove the extent of history books' distortions under the fascist regime. He opens the chapter about the colonization of Korea in 1910. By all accounts, that was a particularly harsh and repressive process. To this day, Koreans remember that period with deep bitterness. Yet, in 1944, Japanese children were taught that "the Korean people and the Korean Emperor himself wished to tie their fate to that of Japan." They were told that "everybody in Korea wished for Japan and Korea to become one."

The old professor has finished his diatribe. He closes the book and hangs his head in shame. "That's what I was teaching my pupils. I was a historian, yet I was propagating this nonsense. I did like the others; I didn't say anything."

Then he sits erect and looks at me straight in the eye: "That's why I decided to fight, when I saw the same attitudes rise again after the war. I had been too ashamed for too long."

He is also embarrassed by comparisons between Japan and Germany. Even during the war years, there was a resistance movement in Germany, while Japan never had anything like it.

After the war, the Germans launched into a vigorous national *mea culpa*, together with a history curriculum aimed at avoiding a repetition of past mistakes. By contrast, fifty years after the end of the war, the Japanese were still wondering whether a *mea culpa* was in order. "Our great misfortune is that the ruling classes survived the war. After the end of the conflict, they resumed their positions, and it was business as usual. Deep down, their way of thinking never changed."

I will hear similar reflections from Ienaga's publishers, and from his lawyers (of which there were about thirty donating their time to the textbook case over the years): The Japanese's misfortune is that they never had to fight for democracy. It was imposed from outside, at the end of the war. This novel-but-foreign concept was embraced without having been yearned for.

The Japanese inherited a new constitution (modelled on the American constitution), but it was not an easy fit. In the judicial process, for instance, form is scrupulously respected, yet cases drag on for so long that one might argue that justice is denied; citizens' right to dissent is recognized, yet no one takes offence when a judge is seen sleeping and even snoring during hearings – as happened during one of Ienaga's trials; and no one raised an eyebrow when a judge from the Tokyo District Court saw his career frozen for having ruled, in 1970, that schoolbook screening was unconstitutional.

Despite all this, Ienaga's efforts were not in vain. Quite the contrary.

As years went by, the content of textbooks softened progressively. One has to wonder, however, whether this reflects a greater respect for fundamental rights, or whether it was simply to avoid diplomatic spats with neighbouring countries.

In the early 1980s, during one of the many appeals of this case, Ienaga's manuscript was approved on condition that the word "aggression" not be used, that the word "invasion" be replaced by "advance" of the Japanese army in China and Korea, and that he refrain from referring to any rape at all when talking about the Nanjing massacre.

Upon which, the Beijing and Seoul governments made official protests in 1982.

At the risk of putting into jeopardy the whole North-East Pacific geopolitical balance, the Minister of Education remained intractable. There was no way Japanese children were going to be taught that their country had invaded Korea in 1910 and China in 1930. Diplomatic relations between Tokyo and its neighbours hardened dangerously during the following months. Eventually, the Japanese government caved in, but it did so very grudgingly, and the required amendments were added to the history textbooks two long years later.

It is the last Friday of August 1997. The heat is crushing, yet there is a feeling in the air that the end of summer is near. For the thousands of demonstrators massed in front of the Supreme Court, it is also the end of an era. In a few minutes, the Supreme Court is going to render its decision on the third and last of the cases brought by Saburo Ienaga against the Ministry of Education. In the courtroom, there are forty-one seats set aside for the public. They were assigned by lot early in the afternoon, and the happy few have already gone inside. Everybody else has spent the last three hours marching around the vast concrete building with its futuristic architecture, waiting for the verdict under the supervision of police officers stationed every sixty feet.

Now the time is near, they are all standing, silent and motionless, in front of the door – not the building's formal entrance, the very official-looking door that faces the Imperial Palace moat, but a service door located in the back, opening on one of those narrow lanes that wind through downtown Tokyo. The well-behaved crowd has gathered obediently on the sidewalks, for municipal regulations require that streets must remain clear at all times, so traffic can get through.

As it turns out, traffic, on that particular day at that particular location, consists exclusively of the sinister black vans of the radical right. They circle ever so slowly around the building, again and again, Rising Sun flag flying, as their loudspeakers broadcast military music and nationalistic exhortations from dark men with severe faces.

"You are all bad Japanese!" they accuse the silent crowd.

"If you don't like your country, go live in North Korea!"

"You are all victims of Chinese propaganda!"

On a large banner stretched across the wide avenue leading up to the Imperial Palace, a slogan proclaims: "There was no Nanjing massacre. It is an invention of Japan's enemies."

And another one: "Comfort women were not slaves but business-women."

The crowd of Ienaga supporters remains impassive before these provocations. At most, one can feel a rustling under the most murderous accusations coming from the black vans. The people who came here today are long-time militants, and obviously, they are used to this sort of thing. They keep their cool. This crowd, waiting patiently, eyes rivetted on the small door, represents the range of successive strata of the Japanese left since the end of the war. It makes for a peculiar mix: older intellectuals, wearing black berets, French-style, as in the good old days of Sartre and Saint-Germain-des-Prés; greying survivors of the 1960s, still in flowing long hair, as in the good old days of Haight-Ashbury; intense young lawyers, standing stiff in their navy-blue suits; and women, lots of women, innocuous-looking, white cotton sun hats pulled over their ears, and shielded behind the perpetual dim-witted smile that Japanese women wear as the most efficient of protective masks.

"I am only a housewife," one apologizes, "but I am against the war. Any war." It turns out that she has been a militant for thirty years against Japanese rearmament and the presence of American bases on Japanese territory. I try to push her a bit: "Even to save democracy? Even to protect your country?"

"No cause in the world justifies killing people, whether they are civilian or military," she shoots back without a hint of hesitation.

Her friend adds, "In 1945, Japan committed itself to become a pacifist country. We must respect our commitment."

A schoolteacher intervenes, "During the Gulf War, Japan sent some minesweepers. Nothing else. Yet, that was enough to alarm our Asian neighbours. They all dread to see Japan militarism rise again."

One often hears that the Japanese are shy, that they do not like to speak in public and take part in a debate. However, today, a small cluster – mostly made up of women – gathers spontaneously around me. They all want to talk, as if it was of the utmost urgency to let the foreigner know that there is more to Japan than meek politicians and faceless public servants.

Their pacifism is of the ferocious kind. Here, I will not hear the usual lamentations about Hiroshima and Nagasaki. For this group of militants, that would be facile "anecdotism." Their reasoning is crystal clear in its simplicity: war is a calamity. Everybody knows that. It brings suffering, in all places and at all times. Yet each generation finds a new reason, a new injustice, a new cause, and people start fighting again. It is a vicious circle that has to be broken. Who better than Japan to show the way? We have been the worst of aggressors and the worst of victims. We committed the worst horrors and we suffered the worst suffering. We know what war is; we lived it, we don't want to see it again, ever, under any circumstances.

That is, roughly, what these women are telling me. I am facing the hard core of the Japanese pacifist movement, a rock-solid block of the electorate, which, to the Americans' bafflement, took to the letter the famous Article 9 of the constitution, imposed at the end of the war by those same Americans: "The Japanese people forever renounce war as a sovereign right of the nation and the threat or use of force as a means of settling international disputes."

With Article 9, Japan became effectively the first conscientious-objector country in history. For many Japanese – and not only for militant pacifists – it is a source of pride, a responsibility, the world mission their country has taken on.

On that point, they are intractable, and politicians know it. Let Japan launch into any military venture, whatever the circumstances, and the government in place is sure to lose the next election. The picture of a Japanese soldier abroad under the flag is unacceptable, whatever the flag. Even the flag of the United Nations.

In 1996, a Japanese police officer was killed accidentally during a surveillance operation of elections in Cambodia. It was the first time since the Second World War that a Japanese in uniform lost his life in an armed conflict.

The reaction in public opinion was like one single enormous collective attack of revulsion.

The picture was intolerable, unthinkable, unacceptable. The scandal of death, the anguish, the torment, all the traumas of war were coming back to the surface with unbearable violence. It was as if each Japanese family had just lost a son – once again.

At the time, I had been surprised and intrigued by the magnitude and intensity of the general reaction. Today, surrounded by these women of steel in their paisley blouses, I am beginning to understand. Their pacifism is no passing fancy. They have been fighting for thirty years, and the Supreme Court decision coming down in a few minutes represents the final denouement of their long crusade.

A man with an engaging smile joins the group and whispers something I do not catch.

Suddenly, all hell breaks loose.

A stocky schoolteacher hurls insults at him at the top of her voice, spitting in his face; the man shouts in return, still smiling – the shouts are all the more unexpected since, only a second ago, all conversations were murmured. They exchange another string of insults. The man is still smiling, the woman tries to jump on him . . .

And then, they back away from each other, shaking their heads, looking confused, and silence falls again just as suddenly. The other women speak softly to their colleague; they stroke her shoulder, the way you do to calm a nervous horse. She is still grumbling, gazing at the tips of her shoes, trying to control her fury.

The man has vanished in the crowd.

"*Agent provocateur*," someone says, in lieu of explanation.

I am puzzled. What did he say, this man appearing from nowhere? What could he have said to trigger such a violent reaction?

Here are the incendiary words: "Japan must be proud. Shouldn't we be proud of our country?"

There you have it. With this short sentence, you can enrage the most seasoned pacifist, cause a street fight, start a riot.

I glance around me. The police officer on guard a few steps away has not flinched. Stiffened a bit, possibly. People in the crowd are still standing motionless, silent, impassive, their gazes straight ahead of them, their faces stone, as if nothing had happened. Yet everybody heard, everybody witnessed this altercation, as loud as it was short.

And suddenly I understand that the surrounding calm is in fact an exercise in control and discipline of every moment. I measure the intensity of the fire that burns in the heart of this crowd standing on guard in front of the Supreme Court.

In the end, it will be a day of victory for Ienaga and his supporters, but a bittersweet victory. By a majority of three against two, the Supreme Court will come down on his side and recognize that Ienaga should have been allowed to mention the existence of the sinister centre for biological research in Manchuria.

This is a paltry victory. The case dragged on for so long that, meanwhile, the existence of the centre has been confirmed by a number of experts. It is no longer an issue, everybody knows about it, and already some other authors have mentioned it with impunity in recent textbooks.

It is a paltry victory too, since, in the same decision the Supreme Court comes down in favour of the ministry for suppressing seven other paragraphs, including details on the Nanjing massacre and the battle of Okinawa.

It is a paltry victory also because nowhere does the court affirm that it is illegal, simply illegal, to censor textbooks. Without any irony, judges simply suggest the Ministry of Education should "censor as little as possible."

The ministry will later reply gravely that "it takes the decision of the court very seriously and that it will continue ensuring that the content of textbooks is appropriate."

In other words, nothing has changed, and I know that, in their hearts, Ienaga's lawyers feel they have lost.

All his supporters are celebrating, though. Indeed, for the first time in history, the Supreme Court has recognized explicitly that there is a limit to the power of censorship from the Ministry of Education.

For me, a Westerner raised in square Cartesian logic, it is impossible to be both legal and illegal. If censorship is illegal, how can the judges tell the censors, "Don't go too far?" The contradiction is gross, flagrant, evident, gloriously scandalous.

But in this country, people can live with this formidable ambiguity. They do not see it as a contradiction, but simply as an obstacle along the way. Victories are won in small increments, one small step at a time, and, at each modest stage, one celebrates what can be celebrated.

In a public hall crawling with cables and cameras, Saburo Ienaga gives one last press conference, which sounds rather like one last call to arms. He thanks the audience for their support during all those years, apologizes very Japanesely for this mitigated victory, begs for forgiveness from the people from Okinawa for the fact that their version of history is decidedly not gaining many adherents in Tokyo.

He bows very deeply, enjoys for one last time the ovation of the crowd, bows again, steps cautiously down from the stage. These are the very last moments of his public life. He looks older and more frail than ever as he proceeds slowly towards the end of the room, towards his new life – a life where, for the first time in thirty-two years, he will no longer have to fight.

All eyes follow him, cheers accompany him as he walks. He steps out the door and into history.

I wish I could conclude that Saburo Ienaga was a hero in modern Japanese history, and, more than anyone else, he applied himself to put his country back on the right track of history.

I wish I could conclude that, if his struggle was so epic and lasted so long, it was simply because the aftermath is hard for the vanquished country. Some time had to pass, and Ienaga's heroism was that he held the fort until the next generation could take over.

However, only in fairy tales do stories end so well. During the last few years of the textbook cases, while the daily news was catching up with history, while newspapers were confirming every day what Ienaga had written three decades earlier, and while ancient controversies were melting one after the other before the evidence, a new generation of historians was rising.

They were young and sharp, armed with diplomas from the best universities in the land, and ready to rewrite history – yet again!

Theirs was a history that would not be "masochist" and that would give children a more "positive" image of their country. "Since the end of the Second World War, we have been told that we were the bad guys. That's why we have lost the ability to make decisions for ourselves," Nobukatsu Fujioka was saying one year before the Supreme Court's final decision on the textbook cases.

Fujioka is a professor at Tokyo University. He wrote a new text-book, in which he describes the Japanese myths, the creation of the world, the Goddess of the Sun . . .

"Japanese children must know their legends," he explains. "Just because they were used by military regimes does not mean that they have to be eradicated forever from our collective memory." The academic argues with the authorities that the more controversial incidents from modern history should be pulled out of the next batch of textbooks. "Our young must be proud of their country."

Senior officials, who are approaching retirement, cannot remain indifferent to this message. It is like an echo of what they were learning in primary school. New pressure groups are being created to promote national pride in textbooks. And the unfortunate publishers, who have been busy integrating the newly authorized paragraphs into Ienaga's textbooks, find themselves caught between the old left, which took thirty years to raise the conscience of the country, and this new right, seductive and provocative, arisen from who knows where like a dark phoenix.

CHAPTER 12

Shinto

A gigantic penis bobs like a cork above traffic on this rainy morning.

The town of Tagata is similar to so many other provincial Japanese towns: low, stone grey roofs, except for the concrete box of city hall, a main street as devoid of any grace as its mid-American equivalents, used-car lots and fast-food joints, a jumble of electric wires hooked haphazardly, a dense traffic of small trucks and white delivery vans, the familiar McDonald's arches overlooking the whole thing, this sorry urban landscape could be found just about anywhere in Japan.

Except that, on this particular March morning, in the icing rain and the exhaust fumes, there is indeed a giant penis proceeding slowly along Main Street. This is the day of the Fertility Festival, which has been marking the beginning of the seeding season, and the season for love, since ancient times.

Sixteen feet long, shocking pink, a most realistic phallic symbol is emerging from a portable shrine carried by two dozen young men dressed in white, soaking wet, exhausted, giddy, and drunk as skunks. Walking a few steps ahead of them, the Great Priest, in purple robe and high black bonnet, proceeds with great majesty as he throws salt by the handful ahead of him to purify the path.

More portable shrines follow, carrying other phalluses, big and small, black and white, grey and pink, all pointing straight to the sky.

Alongside the procession, more priests in bright-coloured robes, young priestesses dressed in red, their wet hair down, each carrying a penis in her arms lovingly, the way a mother carries her newborn baby.

Still farther behind, the familiar figure of the Tengu walks alone, imposing a respectful distance around him. This equivocal ogre eats little children, yet protects them against curses too. Easily recognizable, with his long dishevelled white hair, bright red mask, and nose as long as Pinocchio's, he is part of all the festivals. On Fertility Festival day, though, Tengu's famous nose takes on an aggressively phallic profile to mark the occasion.

Finally, ending the procession, a tall banner flapping in the rain offers an anatomically precise illustration of the theme of the day, including foreskin, pubic hair, blood vessels, and other details belonging to a medical manual rather than a popular country festival.

It is a long way from the female shrine, where the procession set off early in the morning, to the male shrine, where it is headed. The tall hardwood phallus, the size of a large tree trunk, weighs several tons. For the bearers of the fertility shrine, this procession represents an astonishing physical performance. Horizontal beams resting on one shoulder, they move in strange, slow motion, skipping all together from one foot to the other. Every two seconds, they let out a rough guttural cry, in unison, to the rhythm of the gongs and the team leader's double-whistle. And every ten minutes, they pause and are cheerfully handed another paper cup full of sake.

It is barely ten o'clock in the morning, and, from the shrine-bearers to the Great Priest and the well-wishers trotting alongside, everyone has had at least five rounds of that strong rice alcohol.

Meanwhile, in the paved courtyard of the male shrine, the crowd is getting denser by the minute, as pilgrims arrive from the station.

There are now thousands of people waiting patiently in the pelting rain. Some of them take that opportunity to do some devotions to the huge granite phallus sitting in a small temple at the far end of the garden, where one would normally expect to see a statue of Buddha.

Young couples pull the chord and ring a bell (shaped like male genitalia) to call for the gods' attention, before they recite a short prayer. An older man, all by himself, pensively strokes one of the massive testicles. Is he hoping to regain some of his past vigour? A pregnant woman is standing motionless, her right hand lying flat on the stone head. She is probably hoping for a boy.

In the garden, fence pickets are shaped as penis heads, decorative rocks look like testicles. In the merchants' alley, street vendors sell hot sausages and chocolate-coated bananas with the tip dipped in some bright pink confection; for children, lollipops of all colours and size, all shaped like a penis, all with an appetizing pink head for the first lick. Phalluses of all sizes are lined up by the hundreds in souvenir shops. Two old ladies are pondering whether to buy the marble or ebony version to decorate their home.

From the temple, one can now hear the gongs and whistles. The shrine-bearers are getting closer. The procession has reached the last crossing on Main Street and, in the courtyard, the atmosphere is electrified. People are now packed densely together, stretching their necks to see "them" arrive. A loud group of American marines, visiting from their nearby base, are making vulgar jokes. Old Japanese fall into prayer. Young fathers lift their children on their shoulders so they can see. And everybody is brandishing a camera.

When the Great Priest finally enters the temple courtyard, followed by his forest of phalluses, it's a pandemonium. In an ultimate burst of energy, the bearers charge into the crowd, using the giant phallus as a ram. People scream with excitement. They charge and charge again all around for a few minutes, then, with infinite ceremony, they go and lay down their burden in its final resting place, on a white silk sheet spread out in the Fertility temple. They kneel around it in a respectful circle, and strike up a chanted prayer to the shrill notes of bamboo flutes.

The American marines are no longer guffawing. They came here with their buddies to see the "big prick," and they suddenly realize they are attending mass, after a fashion.

The day ends with one last outburst of frenzy. Two dozen priests climb on a balcony high above the ground and pelt the crowd with balls of cooked rice, as big as a fist and as hard as rock. It is a veritable stampede. People jump up, dive, tackle one another as in a rugby game to catch one of these essential fertility symbols.

The party is over, everyone goes home taking their treasures with them: a ball of cooked rice, a branch of sacred bamboo, a plaster phallus . . . The crowd strings out slowly towards the small station to catch the local train that will take them back to the twenty-first century.

The Fertility Festival is pure Shinto. Related to the soil, agriculture, and the cycle of the seasons, this ancient celebration is entirely ritual. The giant phallus that is transported throughout the city is neither a god nor a cult object. Anthropologists would tell you that it is a sign designed to attract the attention of the gods. The reason it is so big, so long, so shiny, is that, as in ancient Greece, the gods are often busy elsewhere and do not always pay much attention to what is happening here below.

For the participants in the festivities, it is also a rallying symbol, a way of gathering the community, to mark the beginning of the seeding season, to express all together and explicitly the worries and anguishes that each one carries in his heart: I hope we will have a good crop this year, that there will be no hail, that I will be able to pay off my debts, that my daughter will find a good husband; I hope I will become pregnant, that it will be a boy, that he will be born healthy . . . On Festival day, you say these things out loud, you share them with others, you air them and feel less alone. The rest of the year, you dress in drab colours, you go through life with downcast eyes, you measure each one of your moves, each one of your words.

On Festival day, you can wear the brightest colours, the most gaudy outfits, the craziest masks. You are allowed to shout, to cry, to laugh, to get drunk all together. It is an outlet. For one day, daily life is suspended.

This contrast between the daily and the exceptional is also one of the founding principles of the Shinto religion. The more numerous the codes, norms, and imperatives structuring everyday life, the more a great exploding release is needed from time to time.

There are festivals throughout the year: to mark the change of seasons, to celebrate the beginning and the end of the harvest, to keep away calamities, to implore the gods, to purify the bodies. Some festivals are losing their original significance as people leave the country for the city. Still, festivals survive as rallying points, and play a very beneficial role in a country where, too often, people have lost a sense of belonging and do not know which way to turn to validate their life.

The firmament of Shinto gods is complex, incongruous, and arbitrary. As with the ancient Celts, there are gods in each tree, in each mountain, in each rock. There are gods in streams, in the hearth, and in the wind. Most of them show only a slight interest in what humans might do or not do; however, wisdom suggests they should be treated with respect, because they have the capacity to cause you trouble.

Some are powerful, others less so; and it is always advisable to see a *kami* (small local deity) settle in your village, because he can protect you against natural calamities and intercede with more important gods.

It would be a mistake to believe that these are historical oddities, ancient beliefs that have accidentally survived into the twenty-first century.

During the 1950s, a number of new cities were created throughout the archipelago, as industrialization was spreading. For sociologists, it was a rare opportunity to observe how strangers, coming from various parts of the country, learn to live together.

Most new cities knew a fate similar to those of European and North American cities during the same period: atomized families, isolation, sadness, alienation, delinquency, and the associated litany of familiar social problems.

However, in some of these new cities, residents demanded a *kami*, and would not rest until Shinto high authorities assigned them one of these all-purpose little gods. The *kami*, sent directly from Ise (the senior Shinto shrine), was welcomed in a solemn ceremony; a shrine was built to make him feel at home; local lay priests were named to look after his well-being. The only thing left to do was to graft onto this the usual celebrations: festivals, offerings, dances, and other seasonal rites, in order to recreate a structure to the life of the community, and a sense of belonging for the inhabitants.

One generation later, sociologists were marvelling: the new towns with a *kami* had taken root, inhabitants were proud of their city, they felt at home, and when a social problem arose (no society is exempt), there was no compelling reason to trace its root cause back to a deep sense of global alienation.

Such is the strength of what is called "Shrine Shinto," which serves as background to the daily life of all the Japanese, without exception – even Buddhists, even Christians.

The Shinto religion has a sulphureous side too: State Shinto is the cult of the Emperor-Living God, which provided the ideological support to the rise of militarist nationalism in the 1920s, the fascist authoritarian regime of the 1930s and 1940s, and Japan expansionist imperialism in the Pacific.

The picture of the ruthless Japanese officer, standing stiff in his shiny boots, popularized by Pacific War movies made in Hollywood, that is State Shinto. Prisoner camps from which no one came out alive, research labs on bacteriological warfare where experiments were run on humans, Pearl Harbor, the battle of Okinawa, this is all State Shinto.

That Shinto is arrogant, imperious, contemptuous, xenophobic. It lost its status of official religion at the end of the war, but it would be a mistake to believe that its spirit has disappeared from today's Japan. Quite the contrary.

"What are you doing here? Who are you?"

It is lashed at me, hard and cutting like a whip. Accustomed as I am to sweet salutations, to the never-ending string of polite, submissive formulas with which honourable visitors are overwhelmed, I turn around all at once, surprised.

Did I walk on a forbidden lawn? Did I set foot on some sacred space by mistake?

The man who just addressed me, in quite passable English, is staring at me severely. In his thirties, with exceptionally handsome features on a totally unfriendly face, he is standing straight, too straight, as in a military parody.

"Where do you come from? Why are you here?"

Around us is an apparently good-natured crowd of families on outings, couples dragging children and cameras, good sons pushing old ladies in their wheelchairs, old men, many wearing ancient military uniforms . . . An eighty-year-old parades in army boots in surprisingly good shape, fresh from a recent morning shine; another old man sports a leather bomber jacket with cap, pilot's goggles on his forehead, looking like some ancient Red Baron, ears covered despite the sweltering heat . . .

"Who are you? Why are you here? Today?"

Here, it is the Yasukuni Shrine. Today, it is August 15.

Here, today, you don't come without a good reason. Here, today, to be a visiting tourist is no acceptable explanation. I need an answer, fast, to avoid insults and abuse.

"Here, today, it's important for Japan," I answer.

Whew! That was the right response. I am allowed a short respite. My questioner's face relaxes slightly. Still no smile, but a hint of pride lightens his stone face.

"It is a very important place. It is a very important day," he declares formally.

The truth is he would like to see me disappear, me and all the other foreigners who, looking idle and inoffensive, are here this morning, ambling leisurely in the hope to catch pieces of history.

History indeed! My questioner has an acute sense that it was stolen from him on that infamous day in 1945 when the Emperor surrendered to the Allied forces. Since then, foreigners of all stripes have had a fine time writing and rewriting history as they see fit. It is a constant humiliation, but on this anniversary date, within the precincts of Yasukuni to boot, it borders on the intolerable.

"This is a very important place. This is a very important day," he repeats with vengeful defiance. Whereupon, satisfied he has accomplished some sort of duty, he turns his back on me and walks away.

Located in the centre of Tokyo, a stone's throw from the Imperial Palace moat, Yasukuni Shrine is without contest the most controversial place in the country.

Erected in the nineteenth century in memory of all the soldiers who died for the empire, it acquired a sulphureous image after 1945, because it is dedicated equally to the two and a half million common soldiers who lost their lives during the last world conflict and to those war criminals who were judged and condemned by the International Military Tribunal after the war.

Nowadays, Yasukuni is still identified with the militarist and nationalist extreme right. Here, people don't talk about the Second World War or even the Pacific War, but rather about the War for the Liberation of Asia.

Every time a Japanese politician dares set foot at Yasukuni, he triggers a diplomatic incident that sends shock waves all the way to Seoul and Beijing. For the Koreans and the Chinese suffered so much from Japanese colonization and occupation that, to this day, they watch suspiciously for the slightest signs of nationalist resurgence in Japan. As if to give credence to their misgivings, every year on August 15 some senior politician or other makes their way to Yasukuni and fan the flame of revenge in the hearts of right-wing extremists.

On that particular day, Yasukuni Shrine is the scene of events that manage to be alarming and pathetic all at once. Since dawn, an impressive display of police force has been put in place in the entire surrounding area, ostensibly to direct traffic. Huge tourist buses have been arriving by the dozen from remote parts of the country. Waves of provincials, coming to honour their dead, are pouring out, dazed with exhaustion from a night on the road, the wilting early-morning heat, and, drowning out the cicadas, the deafening slogans from relentless loudspeakers.

The big black vans of the extreme right are parked all around in large numbers, carrying bright banners, broadcasting tragic martial music and muscular messages, reminding everyone that those who are lying here died for the glory of the empire, that the Japanese constitution is a treason imposed by American imperialism, that the Kurile Islands must be snatched back from Russia at whatever cost, that it is time for the Japanese to find again the purity of their culture sullied by contacts with the West . . .

Under a white canopy stretched across the long alley leading to the shrine, several hundred people are attending an unusual funeral service, for the two-and-a-half-million Japanese who died "for the liberation of Asia."

With a voice choked with emotion, his romantic face framed with long white locks, a famous ultra-nationalist composer affirms that Asia is and has always been the core of world civilization, that it was humiliated by Western hegemony for five hundred years, that in 1941 Japan took it upon itself to liberate the continent from the yoke of colonialism, that in fact it succeeded, since today, the West is on its deathbed . . .

Television cameras scan the audience – average age: seventy-seven – and zoom in on furtive tears, old arthritic hands clasping white handkerchiefs.

A little farther along, in front of the shrine itself, TV news cameramen delight in yet another scene: a tall and majestic old man, draped in long, white robes, his face streaming with sweat and tears, prostrates himself as he does every year and begs forgiveness from all the men who gave their life for the Emperor, and for the fact that the said Emperor, year after year, refuses steadfastly to set foot at Yasukuni.

Along the main path, in the shade of the cherry trees, young men, all dressed in black, earplugs in their ears, right hands too close to their inside pockets, are keeping watch, looking grave and severe.

Six men in white uniforms with gold stripes, wobbly on their old legs, yet trying to stand very straight for the picture, are posing in front of the flag of the Rising Sun, the navy flag with the sixteen sunrays.

Between the extreme right, thirsty for vengeance, and the prowling mafia that has been put in charge of security, veterans come here looking for memories. Naive oil paintings are exposed under the cherry trees, where it is cooler. They illustrate the cruelty of war: a group of kamikaze drinking their last cup of sake at dawn, before leaving for their ultimate mission; a very young kamikaze with a tender face, hugging a puppy "before leaving for his ultimate mission"; a child pilot writing his last letter to his mother, "before leaving for his ultimate mission . . ."

Passersby gaze for a long while. Some of them have brought magnifying glasses to get a better look at each detail. They nod approvingly; they recognize themselves – as do veterans the world over. As do those who commemorate every November 11 at our war memorials, they come to remember their youth, to check that their comrades are still there – each year, the group photo gets thinner – to wear their medals and march one more time – some sporting their infantry caps, some their pilot goggles, some the sailor's white jacket.

To march in step becomes a challenge with arthritis, and the bugle player has hardly enough breath to get a sound out of his instrument. All the same, small shreds of regiments manage to parade over a few hundred feet to arrive almost all at the same time in front of the shrine, to shout almost all together a ferocious and quivering *Banzai!* before retreating to the shade of the cherry trees, reminiscing over the bridge on the river Kwai, and licking a well-deserved ice-cream cone.

All these scenes, pell-mell, are State Shinto.

Shinto is also the Emperor, sowing with his own hand a highly symbolic rice field within the walls of the Palace on the first day of spring. It is the neighbourhood festivals, earthy and brawling, where beer flows like water from early morning. It is the inauguration ceremony of a major construction project, a surprising sight! Twenty-odd developers, financiers, heads of corporations, and ministers, all clad in the uniform of success, navy-blue suit and gold-rimmed glasses, prostrated on their knees before a plain wooden altar, in the open, in the downtown core of the megalopolis, while a young virgin priestess in a long red robe, hair flowing in the wind, throws four grains of salt to the four cardinal points and purifies the site of some futuristic glass tower before the shovels can start digging.

Shinto is Japan. Japan is Shinto. From a simple and primitive pantheism, this religion, original to the archipelago, integrated ideas imported from elsewhere over the centuries, without ever losing its fundamental identity.

For instance, Japanese Buddhism is unlike any other in Asia. It is Buddhism Shinto-style. Confucianism came from China and was also "shintoïzed" before it could fuse with Japanese customs. And, if Christianity never took a strong hold in Japan, it is because, despite the valiant efforts of some intellectuals in the nineteenth century, it is hardly "shintoïzable."

The Shinto spirit is everywhere in Japan, it is the very weft of Japanese life, and yet, nothing is more difficult than trying to describe what makes it what it is.

The reason is simple: the essence of Shinto is not to talk.

"Do not trust words." Such is its fundamental principle.

Purists will tell you that Shinto is a state of mind, a way of seeing the world, of seeing oneself in the universe, and that, if you need explanations, you probably don't deserve them.

As for me, I had made noble resolutions, I was determined not to fall into the trap of ethnocentrism. Yet there comes a point when the rational Western mind stalls: "No explanations. Okay, fine. But please explain why! And if Shinto is a state of mind, please describe it for me!"

I harassed my Japanese friends with questions they didn't understand, since there is nothing to explain. I harassed them so much that, eventually, somebody suggested that I should meet the Great Guji himself.

The Reverend Toyama is the highest-ranking priest in the Shinto hierarchy. Close to the Imperial Family, very influential, he is also one of the masters of the doctrine. To obtain an interview is no easy thing. After lengthy and protracted proceedings, the Great Guji receives me in his oak-panelled office on a cold winter afternoon. Outside, shreds of fog are hanging from the tall cypress trees in the dark forest that surrounds us. It is hard to believe that we are in the centre of Tokyo. My host, draped in sumptuous white silk robes, offers a charming yet inscrutable smile, and begins.

"We do not need a written doctrine. Our doctrine is a certain manner of living, which we transmit from generation to generation."

That's an unexpected beginning from the master of doctrine!

"Shinto considers that man is fundamentally good. The breath of life we pass on to our children is something we got from our own parents, who themselves got it from their own parents and so forth, all the way to original gods. Therefore, each one of us becomes an ancestor, a divinity, when he dies."

The Reverend Toyama then undertakes to demonstrate the superiority of Shinto over Christianity:

"All cultures celebrate their dead. See the Lincoln Memorial in the United States! The difference is that you don't revere them as divinity. Your own gods have been created in a vacuum. While in Japan our gods come from ourselves."

He leans forward and asks, in a conspiratorial tone, "May I ask you a question? How many gods do you Christians worship?"

It is a trap, quite obviously, but I feel that, just as obviously, I am expected to fall into it, which I do with good grace: "But . . . as you probably know . . . we worship one single god!"

He is delighted.

"Ha ha! That's what you say! But I went to Europe. I visited your cathedrals. There were statues of Christ, and the apostles, and the saints, and the Virgin Mary. See! You, too, worship several gods!" He has the triumphant voice one uses to declare "checkmate!"

The Great Guji then takes on Christians' moral fibre. The main difference between Shinto and Christianity, he says, is the attitude of people towards work.

"For you, it is a sin not to work. You will be punished if you don't work. One day a week, you rest and you go to church to get closer to your god. Then, you go back to work. For the Japanese, it is the opposite. Our gods, our ancestors, used to work. Therefore, for us, to work is to imitate the gods. Christians work to avoid punishment. Japanese work to please the gods. That's the Japanese mentality."

Next, he is on to the inconsistencies in Christian doctrine:

"Look for instance at Darwin's theory of evolution: it was always rejected by the Pope. Yet recently the Vatican recognized it as a scientific fact. You see, your doctrines do change. Your religion is inconsistent. While we remain loyal to ourselves, we don't change, since we don't have any doctrine."

All the same, over the centuries, Shinto ended up having to explain itself in order to confront verbalized ideologies coming from outside.

From the sixth century, when monks started landing in Japan and spreading Buddhism, Shinto beliefs and rites were progressively formalized. The local religion had to have its own written texts and body of doctrine if it was to survive. Yet, Shinto does not fit easily into structured shapes. Contrary to what we commonly call the "great" religions, there is no creating entity in the Shinto religion, no myth to explain the creation of man, or of the universe.

There is only a legend, which appeared rather late and explains how Japan was created, how the Emperor is a direct descendent from the Sun Goddess. For anyone raised in the Judeo-Christian tradition, it is most difficult, even impossible, to envisage the history of the world without a beginning and an end. Shinto Japanese, on the other hand, move easily in a universe with four tattered dimensions. No creator, therefore no dichotomy between the creator and his creatures, no distinction in nature between god and humans.

"There is a continuum between all living things" explains the Great Guji. "The most important is the present. Life is constantly being transferred from one living thing to another. For instance, when we eat rice, we take life. When we sow rice, we give it. Our rites mark these passages, they remind us we are part of an unbroken line. Time is of little relevance."

The Ise Shrine is the perfect illustration of this continuum. It is the most important of all Shinto shrines, because it is the place where, according to the legend, the Sun Goddess decided to settle, in the origins of time. Nowadays, still, its grand priest is always a member of the Imperial Family.

For the Japanese, Ise is the ultimate pilgrimage destination. For the foreign visitor, it causes stunned surprise. For this most venerable shrine, the history of which is inextricably linked with that of Japan and stands proof of its antiquity, this holy of holies that can only be reached after a long walk under cypress trees some of them a thousand years old, this most venerable, most antique shrine . . . is spanking new!

According to a tradition going back to the sixth century, Ise Shrine is levelled every twenty years and rebuilt from scratch with new materials, following the same blueprint and using the same techniques as generations before, without any changes whatsoever.

Why twenty years? Because that is the time it takes for a child to reach adulthood. In their twenties, young carpenters build Ise with their fathers as masters. Fathers, in their maturity, teach their sons what they themselves learned from the previous generation. Nowhere is there any room for innovation, improvement, rationalization of the process. Each gesture must be made exactly as the ancestors made it.

Of course, the result is that visitors, be they pilgrims or tourists, see with their eyes the very same thing as did visitors fifteen hundred years ago. The patina of time that we cherish in our cathedrals, our monasteries, even in our simple country churches, is erased systematically every twenty years. Time is annihilated. The shrine is always new. Religion is always new. Such is the message.

In the clearing, deep into the dark forest, the main building of the Ise Shrine is surrounded with a high fence that smells of fresh wood. The monumental gate is closed; you cannot go any farther. That's all there is to see.

Japanese visitors, distraught with the religiosity of the place, fall into prayer. Foreigners can barely hide their disappointment. We came that far to see the holy of holies; we want to see it. Yet, it is no secret that there is nothing, absolutely nothing, in the shrine core. A wooden construction built on the same design as ancient rice granaries in the centre of a pebbled courtyard, such is the place where the cult of the Sun Goddess is perpetuated.

The Great Guji was explicit: there is no doctrine. It's all in the rites.

Same thing here: the centre is empty. Everything resides in the symbolism attached to the place, and in the rites performed here: the consecration of the new rice crop in October; incantations to ensure a good crop in the spring; offerings to the Sun Goddess; rice cooked in an earthenware pot, which is then broken, for it should only be used once, the fire started by rubbing together two pieces of cypress wood; it is all very beautiful and very poetic. Such ancient agrarian rites, still alive at the heart of the second-largest industrial power in the world, what a treat for an amateur anthropologist! Yet the fact is that here I am, facing the solidly shut wooden gate, with nothing to see. I bring my nose closer to the wooden wall, hoping for the impossible: maybe the carpenter who built this wall will have had a lapse, a slip, a split second of inattention, maybe I will find a small sliver of a crack, a minuscule interstice, I will put my eye against it, and I will finally be able to see what is beyond, even if it is only a corner of this square courtyard in which I know there is nothing to see, nothing but round grey pebbles.

Alas! Ise Shrine carpenters are infallible. No gap, no crack, no slit, nothing. In any case, I am called to order by a peremptory voice, totally incongruous with the overall serenity of the place.

"Move away! Don't come close! This is a holy place!"

The man is in his fifties. He is wearing an impeccable navy-blue suit, gold-rimmed glasses, precise short haircut, a stone-hard expression on his exceptionally handsome face.

The feeling of déjà vu is overwhelming. I know this cutting voice, this icy look. The same as the man from Yasukuni!

"And no pictures! It's forbidden!"

His outrage is similar to that of a good Catholic discovering a group of foreign tourists in skimpy shorts horsing around the altar of his cathedral. There is something more too: this man hates me – or, rather, he hates what I represent. I am someone from another country, another culture, another religion, I have not been showing enough respect in this holy place. But I am also more than that.

I am foreign.

And in this place where, of all places, the Shinto religion and the Japanese identity are perfectly entwined, foreign is, necessarily, foe.

CHAPTER 13

The Drama of the Koreans

The hundreds of tourists who disembark at Kyoto station every day all leave from the North exit. They walk through the brand-new glass-and-concrete hall, using the Kyoto tower as their beacon, and, guidebook in hand, they scatter to visit some of the hundreds of ineffable and mysterious temples, the rich pavilions and their exquisite gardens, the palace, the castle, the ancient lanes, which all serve as witnesses of the long urbanity of this most refined Old Capital, whose history is so intricately woven with the history of Japan.

The South exit is used mostly by businessmen who have scheduled short meetings in the café of the Shin Miyako Hotel, across from the station, before they go on to Osaka, where, people will tell you, true business is conducted. South of the train station, there is nothing for visitors.

Old Kyotoites might mention a temple that played an important role in history and where the best flea market in the city is held once a month. But, truly, the southern quarter is not for tourists. It is the backside of Kyoto. On this hot July morning of 1997, that is where I am meeting my tour guide for the day, a law professor who offered to give me a glimpse of what he calls Japan's hidden face.

Leaving behind the opulent Shin Miyako Hotel, we soon enter another world. Low houses, narrow lanes devoid of any charm, small, ugly convenience stores with half-empty shelves, where old people congregate for company once they have accomplished their chores for the day: sweeping the sidewalk in front of their door, watering the geraniums, feeding the cat . . .

Walls and electric posts are plastered with the greasy smiles of local politicians, neon-pink leftovers from the last electoral campaign.

We arrive at Dr. Yamamoto's clinic. It looks as insignificant as the neighbouring buildings, which also means that it is not intimidating. This is a place where no appointment is needed, where no receptionist will bar the access with one of those dreaded questionnaires that are so difficult to fill out. Anyone can walk in, at any time, and get to confide in the good doctor.

Yuhji Yamamoto is an institution in lower town. He has devoted his whole life to the forgotten of society, and today he has invited me to accompany him on his house calls, together with our mutual lawyer friend. He shows us his territory on a large wall map of the neighbourhood. Red and black stickers are pasted in clusters, spread out between the train station and the river.

Each black sticker represents a Burakumin family. This cast of untouchables was considered impure in ancient Japan. Its members were assigned to all the professions relating to dead flesh: cemeteries, abattoirs, leather work, and, later, butchers.

Theoretically, there is no longer any discrimination against Burakumins in modern Japan. It was eradicated in the 1946 constitution. Burakumins now enjoy full civil rights, and the Japanese hasten to add that they are now citizens like any others. In practice, though, it is another matter: they are shunned as employees, as tenants, as students. Most of all, one does not want them as in-laws. When in doubt, one can resort to agencies that specialize in genealogical searches, to check the ancestry of the future son-in-law, the future employee. The

name, and sometimes the street address, tells of a Burakumin's ancestry. As a result, they still tend to live all together, in ghettos, and avoid
interactions with authorities and public services.

This de facto discrimination means that poverty is perpetuated
from one generation to the next. Burakumin families are the black
dots on Dr. Yamamoto's map.

The red dots are the Koreans. They represent one-third of the
inhabitants in this part of lower town. Even more than the
Burakumins, they suffer from poverty and exclusion. They have no
Japanese nationality, no right to vote, no politicians to defend their
interests and speak on their behalf. Some of the families have been
here for nearly a century.

Korea was a Japanese colony from 1910 to 1945. Japanese was the
official language, and many Koreans would cross the sea, some willingly, some unwillingly, to find work in Japan and provide a cheap
labour force for the dominating power. They stayed, so did their children and grandchildren, and to this day they are reminded at every
turn that they are not at home.

They are not all poor, quite the opposite. But their rights are
limited, and they are excluded from some of the more prestigious
careers.

A competent young interpreter who had been assigned to assist me
during a factory visit told me with great simplicity that, yes indeed, she
worked eight hours a day, six days a week, for that company, but that,
no, she was not a permanent employee, she had no job security. This
was quite understandable, since she was Korean. She was born in Japan,
so were her parents; no one spoke a word of Korean in her family. Yet,
in the eyes of the Japanese, she remained a Korean, therefore a threat,
and no one seemed offended by this overt discrimination.

In the immense chaos in Kobe following the great earthquake of
winter 1995, some Japanese victims of the disaster had to turn to the
local Korean community centre for a bowl of soup. The event made
the national TV newscast that night:

"How did it feel, to eat with Koreans?"

"I was very surprised. In fact, they eat almost like us."

"It didn't smell bad. In fact, it smelled rather good."

"They were very polite with us. Not mean at all."

"They lived practically next door all these years, but it is the first time we actually talked to them."

Watching the news item, it was hard to decide what was more shocking: the surprise of the Japanese as they discovered that their neighbours did not have horns or hooves, or the fact that their experience was deemed worthy of an item on the national evening newscast.

Japanese and Koreans have always hated one another. An old Japanese diplomat told me one day, with lucid cynicism, "They hate us because of history. We hate them because they are here."

Brutal, but true enough. That explains why Korean Japanese, vulnerable as they are, tend to keep to themselves.

On the large map pinned on the wall of Dr. Yamamoto's dispensary, the history, the hate, the isolation, materialize into thick clusters of red stickers glued right next to one another all along the river, on the edge of what, not so long ago, used to be fields.

Yamamoto is an old-style doctor, making ten, sometimes twenty, house calls a day, over and above his clinic consultations. In his early fifties, tall and thin, slightly stooped in his immaculate white uniform, he carries a heavy legacy. His father was a doctor too. He operated in the city working-class district. Those were the days when Kyoto was home to a flourishing silk-weaving cottage industry. Thousands of labourers toiled twelve hours a day in the deafening clatter of weaving machines. The working conditions were hard, the pay lean, and social services non-existent.

Yamamoto's father cared for the souls as much as for the bodies. He would even pull out his violin and play some Brahms for his patients when they were beyond the help of medicine.

But Yamamoto's grandfather, Senji, is the one whose legacy is the heaviest. He was one of the great humanitarian minds at the turn of the last century, and to this day, when people meet Dr. Yamamoto, they see him first as Senji's grandson, before they see him as their local doctor.

Senji Yamamoto (the grandfather) was trained as a biologist. He went into politics in order to improve the living conditions of the working classes. He was one of the original advocates of woman suffrage and birth control, and one of the most violent opponents to the Peace Preservation Law that, in 1925, established a de facto police regime in Japan. Assassinated by an extreme right-wing activist, he endures as a hero of the people and of democracy in the collective memory of the Japanese.

On occasion, Dr. Yamamoto has been told, as he assists a patient on his deathbed, "I am happy to be holding the hand of Great Senji's grandson as I leave this world!"

In such conditions, it would be unthinkable not to pursue the family tradition and devote one's life to the forgotten of society.

Nowadays, the forgotten are those who fall through the social security net – however efficient it may be. This is the case, for instance, for the three-hundred-odd residents of Zerobanchi, whom we are about to visit that morning.

First, we must walk through lower town, from beginning to end. In a vacant lot, surrounded with barbed wire, a large poster announces the construction of a luxurious hotel complex. The lot is invaded by nettles, the poster has been battered by the typhoons that blow every year in this area. We are contemplating a miserable fragment of the great collective dream of the 1980s. Those were the days of the economic bubble. Every Japanese thought that everything was possible, everybody was going to become rich, every single town was going to grow.

In order to prepare for this imminent prosperity, several blocks were levelled in lower town, the few hundred families who had been living there were summarily told to go be poor elsewhere, and most of them moved south of the river, where land is less expensive.

Then the bubble burst, the project died on paper, the evicted remained exiled in their "elsewhere," and the cleared lot remained empty, like an open wound in the urban landscape. Down here, on the electric poles, the greasy smiles are those of left-wing politicians.

We have reached our destination, in the area where the Koreans live.

It is the Japanese equivalent of Latin American *favellas*, European *bidonvilles*, North American *shantytowns*. The poverty that reigns here is more akin to a Third World country in South Asia than in the second-largest industrial power on the planet. This small enclave was created by three-hundred-odd Korean families, left behind after the Second World War. They settled here, on the riverbank – at the time, this was way beyond the edge of town – because they were unwanted anywhere else.

The municipality refused steadfastly to recognize their existence, to give a name to their streets and numbers to their homes. Eventually, the area was dubbed Zerobanchi, which means "the address number zero." The city that does not exist.

And, since Japanese administration is nothing if not methodical, this is the actual name printed on official maps of the city!

For a long time, the Koreans lived there in poverty, but also in relative peace, very officially ignored by the outside world. However, the city of Kyoto expanded, and new working-class neighbourhoods have been built all the way to the river. Well, almost. Between the last brand-new little houses and the river lies Zerobanchi, a squalid horror that blocks further urban development, and the municipality can no longer pretend that "the city that does not exist" indeed does not exist.

As a result, administrative hassles have been multiplying in the last few years. So have accidental fires. There are almost only old people left in Zerobanchi, and part of their social-security cheque has to be spent every month for protection against intrusions.

Dr. Yamamoto explains all this as we get closer to the forgotten quarter. Rejected and threatened by the outside world, the inhabitants have made their street into a kind of fortress that one does not enter without being invited. Even the good doctor and his guests have to wait for this invitation.

The two social workers who came with us scout ahead. A man and a woman, they always work as a team. They come here every morning and pay a visit to their flock. They know all the tragedies, large and small, hidden in this city of despair. They stop at each door to announce our arrival in a soft voice. If a single inhabitant objects to our visit, we will not be allowed in the nameless street.

At the head of the path, we wait in silence for the signal to enter the Korean slum.

Around us, the atmosphere is no longer the same: no more traffic, no vegetation, no human beings anywhere. The last houses of the city are resolutely turning their back on us. It is only nine o'clock in the morning, yet the heat is intense. That sun is not the sun of summer, holidays, beaches, and ice-cream cones. It is the white, blinding, crushing light of death. And the cicadas' buzzing, deafening, overwhelming, portends the sublime indifference of nature to the tragedies that unfold on this earth. One cannot remain an outside observer down here. The death that is hovering here is our own, is my own.

Dr. Yamamoto's tall silhouette is waiting, still, on the trail of despair. Finally, our two "sherpas" signal that the path is clear and, silently, we enter the cursed town. Town is a big word. One single street, a narrow dike rather, high above two streams. On our left, a steep escarpment and the river down below. On our right, a small moat at the bottom of an equally steep slope, a kind of putrid gully, which collects indiscriminately all the waste waters from this improvised village.

The narrow path on the ridge, that is the street. These two almost-vertical escarpments on either side, that is the town. The residents erected very high stilts, recovered steel sheets, plywood, windows, and old planks from some construction site, and somehow managed to build on the precipice two facing rows of houses, all snuggled against one another.

The city has provided them with electrical power and running water for two years. Gas is out of the question. As for sewers and garbage collection, all you need to do is look under the houses and between the stilts to understand how the problem has been handled.

On the spot where a house recently burned down, the municipal authorities have posted a stern warning: it is forbidden to build, expand, renovate, support, reinforce, clean up, or improve, under threat of punishments as terrifying as they are vague.

The authorities' attitude towards these permanent squatters is quintessentially Japanese. On the one hand, there are ruthless, rigid, inhumane, cold-hearted, inflexible regulations. Simultaneously, there are a series of pragmatic, compassionate measures coming from the very same authorities, to answer concrete human problems, the left hand pretending to ignore what the right hand is doing.

For instance, the Koreans are denied a street address, yet they receive their social-security cheques every month. They are not entitled to any social service, yet there is a phone in the street for emergencies. Their language is not recognized, yet the instructions are written in Korean. They have no civil rights, but an apartment building has recently been built just for them, not far from here, right at the end of the dike.

The older generation refuses to move there. They are wary of anything that comes from the Japanese authorities. For them a gift coming from officialdom cannot be other than a poisoned gift. Also, they have been living here for fifty years now; they built their homes and created a veritable little community above their sewer.

The time and place of religious services and public meetings are announced on handmade posters. A few representatives are in charge of relations with the outside world – that is the mafia and the municipal authorities.

They grow garlic and cabbage on the slope to make their kimchee, whose pungent smell permeates the street at meal time.

It is indeed a little corner of rural Korea that has been recreated here.

Muto-san greets us like a prince in his steel sheet and cardboard hut. We remove our shoes at the door, Japanese-style, and we settle on the floor at a low table supporting a huge ashtray.

On our right, a rag hangs from the ceiling to separate the kitchen corner. On our left, the window opens on the stinking gully and the new Japanese housing development beyond. In the centre of this one-room home is a monstrous television set with a VCR, and one single videotape, which Muto-san is anxious to show us.

Three years ago, he became famous. A Korean television crew came and filmed a documentary on the forgotten souls of Zerobanchi. Muto-san told them his story, and he is still reeling from the adventure. For the first time in his adult life, someone was interested in him, was listening to him, was treating him like an equal. Someone from the outside, someone he didn't know, was addressing him, not to insult, not to bark an order, nor to threaten. The novelty of the experience was a revelation, almost like a second birth.

The videotape is the tangible proof. And it is probably not a mere coincidence that in this poor, bare room, it rests precisely in the place where, in most average homes, one might expect to see a statue of Buddha.

For many years, Muto-san suffered in silence. Now that his story has been legitimized by television, he relishes telling it, again and again.

As with many Koreans, he was brought to Japan by force at the beginning of the war to work in the coal mines in the north of Kyushu.

"We worked twelve hours a day in the mine. At night, they locked us up, so we couldn't escape. Those who escaped were beaten up, then killed in front of our eyes in the morning, to serve as an example."

His voice rises as he gets into his story. He is again living through those years of hell, with memories similar to those of Japan's prisoners of war, memories horrible enough to give you nightmares every night for the rest of your life.

His testimony, and the documentary on the appalling living conditions in the slum of Zerobanchi, stirred Korean public opinion. Official protests followed. As often happens, the pressure coming from outside finally brought the municipal authorities to deal with the problem.

That is how they decided to build three apartment blocks to house the slum residents. The first was recently finished. It stands three hundred yards away at the end of the walkway. However – is it really a surprise? – the prospect of moving into this concrete box was not unanimously welcome. The younger generation, those who were born here, did not have to be coaxed very hard. They have no memory of the war. For them, flushing toilets and city gas are worth more than a sense of history, and it is time to turn the page.

But their parents are much more reticent. An old couple explains, as they welcome us in their home like family: "When we came here, there was nothing, not even fields. We built everything. This is home." Almost urbane, they invite us to sit around the low table. She brings iced tea from the fridge. He is sitting cross-legged on the plywood floor, his back very straight, his white hair carefully brushed, as he explains in detail the troubles they have with the administration, the 20,000-yen protection money they have to budget every month and which disappears into some mysterious pocket, the night fires, and also the creaking pains that come with age, but "They can't look after us in the hospital because officially, we are homeless. Thank God, we have the good doctor . . ."

The good doctor nods with a sad smile.

They also win the occasional victory. Last year, they received the authorization from the city to name their street – nothing official, of course, but for their own internal use.

Very formally, they named it "Pine Trees Avenue." There are no pines trees anywhere to be seen, nothing has changed, official city maps still show a blank space where their improvised street lies. When people talk about them at the post office, at the fire station, or at the police headquarters, they still say, "the Zerobanchi people."

But simply, when the Koreans talk among themselves about their slum, they are now allowed to call it "Pine Trees Avenue."

They feel a bit less like zeros, and they are happy.

These two old people under their sheet-metal roof, managed, despite all odds, to create a kind of normality in their life, a sort of balance, and their slum has a serene atmosphere about it.

A dark cupboard gives their home an almost bourgeois atmosphere. Someone has glued on the walls pictures cut out of a magazine: pretty Korean girls in the national costume, a Korean temple, fields of flowers. Near the hole that would be a window, between two planks, red purslanes are blooming in a rusty can. Outside, under the stilts, a very small cabbage patch, as in the Korean countryside, with guaranteed natural fertilizer. They are indeed at home.

Therefore, why should they leave Pine Trees Avenue and lock themselves up in a concrete box?

The building is brand new, yet it feels abandoned. The surroundings are deserted. Not a stray cat, not a bicycle leaning against a wall, no garbage either. We are entering a mineral universe.

The elevator stops on the fourth floor.

Here again, the two social workers go ahead to clear the way, whisper into doors barely ajar that it's all right, it is not the mafia collecting, nor the police threatening, nor the city ejecting.

One of the door opens wide to let us in, and in an instant I understand the reservations of the people down below: one single room, Japanese-style, bare and oh so sad, with a bad tatami mat on the floor.

In the middle of the room, a futon that the resident is now folding hastily to make some space for us. One nail in the wall, one wire hanger on the nail, one tattered T-shirt on the hanger. In the alcove, one tap, only one, used both for washing and for tea.

No table. In lieu of dishes, one tin mug on the floor. And, half-crouching on the floor, stunned by the unexpected visitors, a tragic old man, looking like an abandoned child. Frail, skinny, and bald, almost naked in pyjamas too large for him, tied with a string, he will retain the same weary position during the length of our visit, neither quite sitting or kneeling, as if he were not certain whether he should stay or leave, not certain at all that he is still welcome in his own home and that these important people are not about to throw him out like a dog.

His large eyes, blued with age, express the naivety of a very young boy. He has been in Japan for more than sixty years, and he has not fully grasped what happened to his life.

He came here of his own will, at the end of the 1930s, because he heard that he would find work in Japan. Once hired, he was treated exactly like those of his countrymen who had been brought by force: he received no salary, he was locked up, watched by armed guards, beaten up, undernourished . . . and he is still waiting for the land of plenty he came to find.

For fifty years, he lived in one of the slums we have been visiting. Then, people from city hall came and told him that he would be happier here, and he followed orders.

To be sure, his life could be worse. The apartment is clean and new, he receives a social-security cheque every month, and the good doctor pays him the occasional visit.

If he is so skinny, it is because, when one is that old and living alone, it is too much of an effort to go out, take the elevator (a novel and alarming experience), walk along hostile streets all the way to the corner store, cook some rice . . .

Several times in the course of the conversation, he will repeat, "I am alone," as if it were a sufficient explanation to all the questions.

I lean out of the window and look at the sheet-metal roofs of the slum down below, crushed under the sun, huddled together. And I realize that I am already beginning to refer to it mentally as "the village," with a hint of nostalgia.

Sometimes, people from the village come and visit. They bring him some rice with kimchee to remind him of home. When nobody comes, he simply pours some warm water over green tea leaves that spend several days at the bottom of his tin mug.

Squatting in the middle of the room, an uncertain look in his eyes, he is slowly losing his mind from loneliness.

The two social workers talk to him, talk to me, talk to one another, fill the space with human noises to attempt to recreate a semblance of a universe.

I glance at the good doctor. His smile is sadder than ever, and I am sure that, at this very moment, he regrets never having learned to play the violin.

CHAPTER 14

The Last Aboriginals

In their Adidas and Benetton T-shirts, electronic watches on their wrists and rubber dinosaurs in their skateboarders' pockets, they look like any other kid in Japan – in fact, they look like any other kid in the world.

Yet the children from Nibutani are not Japanese, and they carry on their shoulders a burden far heavier than their age should warrant. They are the last of the Ainu, the native people from the north of Japan.

On that particular Saturday morning, they are attending their bi-monthly class to learn the language of their ancestors. It is an uphill battle, because no adult uses the language any more. The last Ainu-speaking grandmother died two years ago, and there is nobody left to sing lullabies and tell tales from yesteryear, tales from the creation of the Ainu world, before the arrival of the abhorrent Japanese, who turned them into foreigners on their own land.

Fortunately, there are anthropologists.

A young Japanese anthropologist has taken up the task of teaching Ainu children their forefathers' language and culture, which her own ancestors tried steadfastly to eradicate from the face of the earth during three generations.

Yuko Yoneta invited me to attend her Saturday-morning class. It is early spring, and she is going to take the children for a walk in the woods and teach them how to identify useful plants from the forest. There are about twenty boys and girls between seven and fifteen years old. They regularly attend these sessions to familiarize themselves with their own culture. "They come on their own," she assures me. "No one forces them."

However, the villagers from Nibutani are imbued with such a strong sense of mission – to resuscitate a dying tradition – that almost all their children show up dutifully at the small community centre, week after week.

A very muddy trail winds up to the forest. The north of Japan receives a lot of snow during the winter months and, in May, there are still heavy snowbanks on either side.

Yoneta digs at the snow with the tip of her shoe and uncovers a pale green shoot barely peeping out of the earth. She cries in wonder, and the children gather around her.

She enunciates the name of the plant in Japanese, then in Ainu, and proceeds to give a short botany lesson: "What is it useful for?" Is it for fever? Sore throat? For "women problems"? To heal open wounds? To eliminate poisons? The fears, ailments, anxieties of their ancestors come alive before the eyes of these children of the twenty-first century, as they tramp in the woods.

They pick up plants one by one while the teacher quizzes them: "Which part would you use? The root? The leaf? Would you boil it? Dry it? Roast it? Crush it in a puree? Is it something to chew? To drink? To spread on the skin?"

She also asks them trick questions: "What about this root? Can you identify it?"

"It is to cure bear wounds," suggests a fourteen-year-old boy, dreaming of adventure.

"Not so! It is what your mother makes soup with!" Yoneta corrects with a smile.

The girls are giggling. The boy, embarrassed to have been led into such domestic terrain, walks away and feigns a sudden interest in a frog hiding under a dead leaf.

The young anthropologist is always smiling, encouraging. She never pokes fun. She leads with extreme deftness this vulnerable mission in the woods. For, if at times the situation seems innocuous – a school outing, a whiff of freedom, boys and girls horsing around when the teacher is not watching – it is also a political statement, a quasi-religious affirmation of each moment. The children are intensely aware that they are taking a stand – an important one – simply by being there, in the woods with Yoneta.

The younger ones are the most earnest. Seven or eight years old, imbued with their roles as Keepers of the Tradition, they clench their fists gravely around some insignificant root that drips a bit on their Benetton parkas.

The girls sense a hint of mystery in these recipes with curing powers. They do not quite belong to the world of the gods, but they are a way to bring back to the village the spirit of these famous grandmothers they have heard so much about. Plus, it may even be useful! The girls play along.

The attitude of the older boys is complex and ambivalent. It is romantically appealing, for these young peasants living at the end of the world, to tie their identity to a long tradition, to anoint themselves as Knights-Errant, Avengers of the Ancestors . . .

Yet each time they repeat aloud the new words taught by the teacher, in the language of those ancestors, they cast sidelong glances to see if their friends are making fun of them.

On the way home, we walk past a very old thatched-roof house, where mysterious things are unfolding. We watch as three young men, their faces hard with defiance, foreheads wrapped in bandanas like warriors off to a mission, ceremoniously set alight a bundle of sticks and grass and begin raucous, vaguely threatening, incantations, as a thin spiral of blue smoke rises towards the sky.

With a deliberate and slow gesture of welcome – yet with no hint of a smile – they invite me to enter the hut, black with smoke, where a patriarch with long grey hair prepares to celebrate an obscure cult around a stone fireplace. I am welcomed in the circle, I am allowed to film, I am forbidden to film, I am thrown out with as little explanation on the way out as on the way in. With my seven minutes on tape, I am floating in the seventh heaven of amateur ethnologists, dreaming already of making the cover of *National Geographic*.

Later, I will learn that this is the headquarters of the militant faction, the hard core of the Ainu Liberation Movement, those who are not willing to make the slightest concession to the Japanese and all they represent.

For the village children, though, what does it all mean? Yoneta is well aware that they are confused. How could they not be?

There are only twenty-four thousand Ainu left on the planet. Most of them are scattered in tiny fishing villages, spread out along the coasts of the northern island of Hokkaido, isolated from one another, trying their best to forget their origins and integrate into Japanese society.

The small community of Nibutani is the exception. Here, the Ainu are in the highest concentration anywhere (four out of five inhabitants), and they are determined to preserve their culture and keep their traditions alive, if only out of respect for their ancestors' spirits.

When he turned sixty-eight, Shigeru Kayano became the first and only Ainu ever to sit in the Japanese parliament. His life has been one long struggle for his people to have their identity recognized.

In his inaugural speech in the Diet, he spoke a few paragraphs in his ancestors' language, just for the pleasure of watching his Japanese colleagues wriggle with embarrassment on their benches. Two years later, he was still enjoying these little pleasures: "Every time they hear me speak with my accent, every time they bump into me in an elevator or in a corridor and see my hairy face, they are reminded of the Ainu issue," he says with a good-natured laugh.

The fact is that Japanese parliamentarians have spent numerous years avoiding very deliberately the "Ainu issue," because it represents a major thorn in their side.

Yet, they don't hate the Ainu as they hate the Koreans living in Japan. They don't despise them as they despise the Burakumins, the cast of untouchables that officially does not exist any more but is still kept carefully at bay. They are not wary of the Ainu as they are wary of all those immigrants (mostly from Southeast Asia) who come to Japan to do menial work.

But, more than any of these "alien" groups, the Ainu represent a threat to Japanese society. By their very existence, they challenge the theory that the Japanese are a unique race, rooted in their archipelago since the origin of time. This theory remains close to the heart of the Japanese to this day, despite all evidence to the contrary. Of course, they know that they share a common ancestry with the Koreans and the Chinese. They have heard of ethnographic research that established their blood links with South Pacific Polynesians. Naturally, they are aware of the troubling similarities between the Japanese and the Hungarian languages, and of the central European eastward displacement theories.

They also know that, to boast aloud about being a race-based state, in the twenty-first century, is simply not "politically correct," as their American friends never fail to remind them crassly.

No matter. The theory of the unique race lulled them in childhood, it comforts them when they feel unloved and misunderstood, it justifies them occasionally, and allows them to feel at home with their kin wherever they happen to be in the archipelago.

How should they be denied all that, just because of a few Ainu who demand the recognition of their status as native people? Such was the (unspoken) position of Japanese parliamentarians until Shigeru Kayano was elected.

When the feisty old militant, with his bushy eyebrows and his uncouth manners, arrived in Nagatacho (the part of Tokyo where the parliamentary buildings are located), things began to change. Not that Kayano is a particularly effective politician. "My main role is to be visible," he acknowledges readily. But his very presence has been a catalyst, and circumstances were propitious.

The previous year (1993) had been designated as "The Year of Aboriginals" by the United Nations, and, that summer, anthropologists from all over the world descended on the small village of Nibutani.

By coincidence, the Socialists had just come to power, for the first time in Japanese history.

In brief, six months after Kayano's arrival in the Diet, a commission of inquiry was created; a year later, Japan ratified the United Nations Charter on Human Rights (three decades after other industrialized countries). Within barely three years, in early May 1997, the Japanese government recognized the Ainu as a distinct society. It was the first time in its history that Japan acknowledged the existence of an ethnic minority in the country.

It was Kayano's crowning moment.

I met him for the first time at a very urbane reception in the capital city, where he looked and behaved like a bear in a zoo. Today, in his kitchen on the edge of the great woods of Biratori, his dignified demeanour is that of a prince, and he is anxious to welcome me into his kingdom.

His mark is everywhere in Nibutani. There are no less than two museums in this village of barely five hundred inhabitants: the municipal museum, brand new, built with government grants obtained by Kayano, where artifacts are exhibited to show what daily Ainu life was like not so long ago; and Kayano's own museum, where he exhibits his collection of artifacts from native people of the Pacific Rim. The family traits are unmistakable.

In the clearing next to his home, he rebuilt two traditional houses, as well as a rice granary, in order to show the children how their grandparents lived. Over the square stone hearth in the centre, a kettle of hot water boils for tea; all around, blankets hang on a wire to dry; at the door, a woman weaves bark bags as she greets visitors.

A few steps away is the small community centre, where villagers gather for traditional dance practices before seasonal festivals, for weaving classes on weekday afternoons, for political meetings to protest the latest aggravation from the Japanese administration, and for language classes for children every second Saturday.

Kayano's home completes the circle in the clearing. From his kitchen window, he observes his small universe with obvious contentment.

But his life was not always that peaceful.

He remembers the day – he was still a young boy – when his own father was taken away by two constables and thrown into jail like a thief, because he had caught a salmon. "Only one! And it was not even for himself, but for a poor widow who had nothing to feed her children!"

His own mother had passed away, so he was raised by his grandmother. She spoke only Ainu, and her mouth was decorated all around with traditional tattoos – a daily reminder that the spoken word is sacred.

When she died, Shigeru Kayano, in full adolescent rebellion, ruthlessly cut all his ties with the Ainu culture. He left the village and tried to forget his language and traditions, to become a good Japanese.

For seven years, he lived in shame about his roots and felt alone in the world.

However, thanks to the anthropologists (them again!), he found the light on his road to Damascus. As he was watching them foraging in his grandmother's kitchen drawers, marvelling over the utensils they were discovering, labelling, cataloguing, and taking abundant notes, he started to realize that his culture was not a source of embarrassment but a source of pride.

The day he discovered the existence of an unfinished collection of tales and legends, he finally launched into what was to become a lifelong adventure. If an old lady from his people had spent twenty years (from 1927 to 1947) putting on paper these stories from the past, if an illustrious Japanese linguist had devoted the last years of his life to the translation of the first eighteen volumes, if after the linguist died his heirs had applied themselves to find someone to finish the task, if a major Tokyo publishing house had already published nine of the volumes, certainly the whole enterprise was worthy of Kayano's interest.

As he reacquainted himself with the language of his childhood and rediscovered with adult ears the stories his grandmother had told him when he was little, he began to measure the extent of the loss, and, slowly, a deep anger rose in his heart, a holy anger that would sustain him for the rest of his life.

The first Japanese pioneers arrived in Hokkaido around 1868, and began to exploit its immense forests and started commercial fisheries. In order to protect their concessions, they passed a law forbidding anyone to cut trees and catch salmon in the rivers. This was a twin catastrophe for the Ainu, the ultimate forest people, whose main god is the spirit of the bear, and for whom the word "salmon" translates as "primary food."

It was nothing less than a form of genocide.

They were cornered into planting rice, because it was the only way to receive plots of land from the governor of the province. But the Ainu are hunters and fishermen, not farmers. And rice is not part of their traditional diet. Furthermore, the Japanese were taking away not only their land but their men.

Kayano recounts, as if it happened yesterday, the outrage they were still recalling with anger when he was a child: how, one fine day, the Japanese had come to the village and taken away his grandfather, who was only twelve at the time, together with all the able-bodied males, to work in the fisheries cooperative.

"It was an invasion, pure and simple!" he fumes.

What happened to the Ainu after that sounds dreadfully similar to what happened to colonized people elsewhere in the world: they became destitute; they lost all sense of belonging; they found solace in alcohol and government subsidies. During almost a century (until 1997), their status was defined by a law (adopted in 1899) whose very title says it all: the Hokkaido Former Natives Protection Law.

"We are not former natives! We are natives, period!" growls Kayano. "And we don't want to be protected, we want to be recognized!

"The Japanese consider us as an extinct people. In schoolbooks they mention us in the past tense. Go visit the Sapporo museum! [In the provincial capital.] All the explanations relating to the Ainu are written in the past tense. As if we were already dead!"

The fact is that they were very close to dead.

It is only the frenzy with which ethnologists and anthropologists were gathering last-minute evidence of their existence before it was too late that shook the Ainu out of their torpor and gave them back a taste for life and a taste for a fight.

Today, they are finally rid of the abhorred law that kept them in an infantile dependency, they are recognized as a people – yet, their relations with the Japanese authorities remain profoundly ambiguous. On the one hand, the government has been raining subsidies on them over the last few years. Tokyo created a fund to help the Ainu reestablish their way of life. It finances language and history classes, a research centre on Ainu culture at the University of Hokkaido, exchange trips with other native peoples, the participation of Ainu representatives in international conferences, visits by academics from all over the world, and the publication of a new dictionary.

Also, it helps the Ainu purchase land and build houses. It offers interest-free loans to farmers, study grants for young people . . .

"It is bad-conscience money," village people mutter.

Still, it is always good to take.

Simultaneously, the same central government deliberately provokes the people of Biratori. The authorities built a dam right across the valley, a dam nobody wanted. Its justification had disappeared (an industrial park project that had long been abandoned), it threatens the ecology of the forest upstream, and, to add insult to injury, it flooded one of the Ainu's most sacred sites.

"They had not used that site for years and years!" argue the public servants from Hokkaido development office.

"This is where we celebrate our funeral rites," retorts Kayano, who is suing the government.

Such are the tribulations of a people in the process of resurrecting themselves. The Ainu are rediscovering rites they had almost abandoned. Men are once again hunting deer the way their ancestors did, without weapons, by circling the animal until it backs into a river or off the top of a cliff. Women are learning again the art of weaving a kind of hemp taken from tree bark. Everybody takes part in traditional dances that often evoke the bear (king of animals) and various birds from the forest. And children learn a few words of their language, every second Saturday, thanks to Yuko Yoneta.

However, one wonders where the revival of traditions end and a living museum begins. If they chase deer, it is no longer to put food on the table, but for the pleasure of the hunt. The main outlets for the women's woven crafts are ethnology museums.

And no one nurses any illusions: Ainu children will never use their ancestors' language to communicate. "Still, it teaches them where they come from and who they are. It gives them a pride that we adults never knew," comments Kayano thoughtfully.

He put Nibutani on the map. Anthropologists and aboriginal representatives come there from all over. Their words of encouragement, scribbled right on the pine walls of the community centre, confirm to Yuko Yoneta's students that they are not alone in the world.

From Tibet, Indonesia, Thailand, Lapland, and the Canadian North, from Egypt, and France, and Russia, they all left their scholarly graffiti on the wall.

"Northern gods inspire and prolong the great Ainu people," wrote somebody from the University of Paris.

"The voice of Ainu is the voice of humanity," declares an Indonesian.

"Keep up the fight!" encourages an Egyptian academic.

A French visitor quotes a Chinese proverb: *Perseverance is advantageous.*

Language class is over for the day. The girls are lingering around the old upright piano, playing "Chopsticks" with two fingers. One of them plants herself in front of me, looks at me straight in the eye, and, after a moment of intense concentration, declares carefully, "Hello-how-are-you."

As for the boys, they are already long gone. The minute class was over, they bolted out all at once. Baseball caps pushed low over their eyes, they hopped on their red bicycles and pedalled away like the wind in the countryside.

CHAPTER 15

Angry Old Lady

Once upon a time, in Tokyo, there was a very old lady who spent her days watching parliamentary debates on her television screen, looking stern, pen in hand. She would take copious notes, then, the way schoolteachers did in the old days, she would send a "report card" to those parliamentarians who rated an A.

On pink paper.

And the happy few would openly cry with emotion as they read the laudatory comments inscribed in that unusual report card.

At the age of ninety-nine, Shidzue Kato, a long-retired parliamentarian, was still enjoying an unquestionable influence in the Japanese political landscape. I had had a first inkling of her unusual authority on the occasion of the launch of the New Frontier Party, in December 1994.

The event had received a lot of attention from the public and the media, for it was the first time in thirty-seven years that a new political party was attempting to compete with the venerable Liberal Democratic Party.

For many observers, it signalled the opening of a new era in Japanese politics: a genuine opposition party in the Diet, authentic debates, new blood, fresh oxygen, and hopefully a new breed of politicians.

How does one go about launching a new party? It was a totally unprecedented event. For months, organizers had been studying how political conventions are organized in other countries (meaning in the United States) to make sure they would do the right thing (in the right form).

What they had retained was just that: the right form, American-style. There was fanfare, banners, balloons, lighting effects, and, for the grand finale, the strange and magic spectacle of a giant blue veil floating down from the ceiling over the awestruck audience, while an invisible orchestra, without obvious justification, broke out into Beethoven's Ninth.

It was a memorable day. Yet, there was hardly a mention of the party platform, no input from the members, no election of the executive, no hint of substance. It was simply a big social event, one to remember, carefully scripted to project the image of a new political party tuned to the future, and whose members are young, modern, and dynamic. The stars of the new party had all paraded onstage, sporting their freshly crafted new images like suits straight out of the tailor's, hoping to erase, in the audience's memory, the fact that they were recycled from the bosom of the crusty old Liberal Democratic Party, where they had learned all they knew about politics.

It was at the end of this long parade, good-humoured and cynical all at once, that Shidzue Kato's fragile, aristocratic figure had appeared on stage, sitting very straight in her wheelchair. A respectful silence had fallen over the room, while microphones were lowered to the old lady's height.

With royal demeanour, she took a few seconds to survey the audience from behind her giant blue-tinted glasses, very deliberately, openly enjoying the power she still exerted. Then, in a deep and powerful voice that was surprising coming from such a frail body, she started to speak.

She congratulated the three former prime ministers, who were sitting in the front row alongside the founder of the new party, Ichiro Ozawa, for the courage they had shown in leaving the familiar ranks of their former political party, and their audacity in trying to change the status quo.

She had a few personal words for each one of them, in the same affectionate tone used by grandmothers: "I still remember, it was not so long ago, he was only that high . . . !"

Except it soon became clear that this particular grandmother was anything but sentimental. As she remembered anecdotes and moments from their respective careers, the faces of these political veterans, projected on a giant screen at the back of the stage, reflected, in quick succession, pride, embarrassment, and confusion, for the old lady was indeed relating and revealing all their past pranks.

Soon, she was addressing them directly from the height of her wheelchair, the way an elementary-school teacher addresses a group of promising but unruly pupils. And she had these four men, three of whom had occupied the position of prime minister of Japan, all of whom were in their sixties and had success written all over their faces, blushing, lowering their heads, squirming on their chairs, and laughing too loud trying not to show their embarrassment.

The whole assembly was relishing the spectacle of these four heavyweights of national politics reduced to the rank of bumbling schoolboys.

What was the power of this diminutive matriarch?

In this country caught in a confusion of ill-digested political ideologies, Shidzue Kato was an icon.

The vicissitudes of her personal life reflect the chaos of a whole generation: she endorsed just about all the ideologies across the board before concluding that ideologies were not her forte; she was elected as a member of a political party, yet ended up sitting as an independent; she fought all her life for women's rights, yet never associated with any of the feminist movements of the century; she displayed a boundless admiration for America and all it represents, yet had definite reservations towards Americans.

The only thing that never changed was the vigour with which she always demanded the right to say what was on her mind.

She had already gone down in history in her lifetime. She had become one of those very few characters in which the Japanese truly recognize themselves and of whom they can be proud, without reticence or mental reservation.

The story of her life sounds like a great adventure novel. Shidzue was born with a silver spoon in her mouth, to one of Tokyo's oldest aristocratic families. She enjoyed a privileged, if traditional, childhood, and was married off to a rich baron at age seventeen.

This baron husband was a free thinker, most interested in current Western thoughts on social reforms, a rather novel idea enhanced by a whiff of exoticism.

Two babies later, he decided that he didn't want a traditional Japanese wife as a spouse, but one of those "new women," as they were called then in America. So, he ordered Shidzue off to New York to learn how to become a "new woman," while he travelled the world and the children were left in the care of their grandparents.

Overnight, the very young baroness found herself alone in a big city where she knew not a soul, living in a small furnished apartment, learning with docility how to type and take dictation in order to become independent and please her husband, which is the first and foremost duty of any good Japanese wife.

During this first stay in New York, she met birth-control pioneer Margaret Sanger. She decided to endorse her cause and went back to Japan to preach the gospel of family planning.

This was in the 1920s, a population explosion was threatening economic growth in Japan, and, at first, Shidzue's efforts to open birth-control clinics in deprived neighbourhoods fell right into line with government policy.

But times soon changed. The military were asserting their power, the army needed soldiers to expand the empire, and, progressively, Shidzue's project became suspect. Soon, any attempt to reduce the size of Japanese families was perceived as genocide, pure and simple, fomented by foreign powers with the deliberate purpose of stopping the expansion of the Empire of the Rising Sun.

At about the same time, the baron husband changed ideological tack, concluded that the future of Japan resided in its traditional values, chided Shidzue for not behaving according to her station, abandoned his "new woman," and set off for Manchuria and the construction of the colonial empire.

Disowned by her family, left alone to raise her children, and constantly under the watch of the "thought police" because of her socialist affinities, that is how young Shidzue lived through the dark 1930s. As happened in so many Japanese homes, she saw one of her sons die of tuberculosis and the other go off to war. She spent some time in jail in 1937, together with 472 other people suspected of communist sympathies.

During those troubled years, she remained in contact with her American friends, wrote two autobiographies that were very well received in the United States, and married one of her socialist companions, Kanju Kato.

All of this provided solid credentials for her with the American authorities. As a result, when the war ended, she was quite naturally invited to work alongside the occupation forces to establish a democratic regime in the country.

Suddenly, Shidzue had wind in her sails. She was the first woman to run in the 1945 elections (it was the first time women were allowed to run), and one of the first women to sit in the Diet.

Since her husband had been elected too, they were also the first couple sitting together on the benches.

With this series of firsts, Shidzue Kato was becoming a star. The following two years marked a period of intense and heady activity, with public opinion solidly behind her.

The immediate postwar years were extraordinarily memorable for the Japanese. Those who lived through these two critical years still remember them as a page of history marked simultaneously by a sense of cataclysmic collapse and by an ethereal feeling of boundless renewal.

On the one hand, it felt like the apocalypse. The country was in ruins, people went hungry, every family had dead to mourn. Demobilized soldiers in tattered uniforms were begging on the sidewalks, while foreign military were parading in the streets.

Furthermore, the Japanese had experienced the ultimate trauma on the fateful day when they heard Emperor Hirohito announce the surrender of Japan on the radio. To make matters worse, a few days later, Hirohito paid a visit to the head of the Allied Forces, General MacArthur, and a photograph of the encounter was published. It was the first time the Japanese saw their Emperor. Never before in history had anyone been allowed to cast their eyes on the descendant of the Sun. On that historic day when, for the first time, they were allowed to take a look at this man many still viewed as a god, they saw an unattractive, frail-looking little man, bundled up in a black European outfit, vaguely ridiculous, in painful contrast to General MacArthur's imposing figure, all white uniform and military decorations.

There could be no mistake. This Emperor, whose existence had justified all the sacrifices, consoled them for all the pains, soothed all their anxieties during the long war years, this Emperor did not cut it. Short and homely, he simply did not measure up next to the American.

This image of the historical encounter took on symbolic dimensions and shaped the perception the Japanese had of themselves during the postwar years. For now, it pushed them a little deeper still into despair.

God was indeed dead.

But paradoxically, with the totality of destruction all around, came an exhilarating sense that they had a clean slate before them. Suddenly, for the first time, the future looked limitless. Everything had to be rebuilt, everything had to be reinvented. It was a unique opportunity to create a model country, an ideal society that would integrate the best of Japanese traditions and of American democracy.

In trains and buses, in the street, strangers would talk to one another: "Democracy . . . democracy . . . we hear the word everywhere, what is the democracy they keep talking about on the radio?"

A kind of euphoria floated above the misery.

All of this, thanks to the Americans. They were counting on them, they needed them to help Japan with its transition to a new future.

Shidzue Kato represented this transition. She was the Americans' friend, she spoke their language, and, like them, she dared say aloud what was on her mind. Yet she retained her ladylike manners, her traditional behaviour, the way taught since childhood to stand very straight, to bow very low, to keep a serene face and an even voice, to keep pains and worries to oneself. The Japanese recognized themselves in her, they admired her courage and audacity, they were reassured by her aristocratic manners. Everything was going her way, and the birth of a little girl in March 1945 added to the sense of a new beginning – in her life as in her country.

For three years, Shidzue Kato was in the centre of all the debates and of all the causes, starting with constitutional reform. The very fact that she sat as a member of the prestigious Committee on Constitutional Reform attracted a lot of attention. Furthermore, when she, a woman, dared speak in public before the said committee, she was front-page news. When, to top it all off, she demonstrated undeniable qualities as an orator, a definite taste for controversy, structured thought processes, and furthermore, presented a concrete program (the abolition of the civil code), she quite simply became a star.

Yet the debate was far from simple: Japanese lawmakers were facing the challenge of writing a new constitution modelled on the American version, while preserving their customs and traditions.

What were those "customs"? There lay the big question. For men, it was a non-issue: the whole Japanese ethical system was founded on the power of the paterfamilias, and that power should be the one thing to be preserved from the old regime. For women, on the other hand, it was a once-in-a-lifetime opportunity to get rid of a feudal regime that did not recognize their legal existence. The controversy was one of the hottest of the postwar years.

The new constitution, which proclaimed that all are equal before the law, was adopted in November 1946. For a while, Japanese women faced the absurd prospect of being equal to their husbands according to the constitution, while remaining totally dependant according to the civil code. Indeed, they had to wait more than a year (to January 1948) for the revised civil code that finally recognized them as persons before the law.

During that year, Shidzue Kato and women's groups struggled furiously to prevent equal rights from being swept under the rug. She could not hope to be heard in the Diet: her elected colleagues did not see any urgency in the matter, their officials played deaf, and opportunities to speak were few and far between.

She could have turned to her American friends, who had no qualms about dictating to the Japanese when they felt like it. But occupation forces knew enough to stay away from the sensitive issue of women's emancipation in a society as fundamentally patriarchal as Japan.

With no place to turn, Kato discovered the power of the media. She published articles and editorials in newspapers and hosted a weekly radio show for women. She would invite ministers to her show and confront them on the air, since she could not do it in the Diet. She eventually succeeded in shifting public opinion.

It was no easy victory, and the whole episode left her with a deep bitterness towards public servants, which would stay with her for the rest of her life. In the meantime, though, her name, her voice, and her face had become familiar to the Japanese.

She had another battle to fight: birth control. Even though she had been active in this area for so many years, her final victory sounded strangely like a defeat. Yet, in the beginning, things went very well. She had no difficulty convincing her colleagues that something had to be done to keep the population pressure in check. The country was devastated by war, everything had to be rebuilt, yet all organized efforts would be condemned to failure because of the demographic explosion.

Women's anguish over the daily challenge of finding something to feed their families gave rise to an active abortion black market, involving medical doctors and even veterinarians. The numbers of children abandoned at birth and of infanticides were multiplying. That particular year, there were three times as many as in 1940, when the war was raging.

Circumstances seemed ideal for Shidzue Kato to push the bill she had been dreaming about for so long, and which would set in place a birth-control program throughout the country.

Yet, she failed miserably.

In Japan, the issue of birth control and abortion never carried the same ethical and religious dimensions as it did in Western countries. Traditionally, the Japanese used abortion to limit the size of their families. The practice had been officially abolished at the time of the Meiji revolution in 1868; yet, it was the one lawmakers turned to, very naturally, in 1948, when they had to find an urgent solution to the imminent peril of a population explosion.

However, to launch a family-planning campaign, to open preventive clinics in rural areas, to educate men as well as women on how to avoid another child – in other words, to talk about "those things" – was beyond them. It was women's stuff. Therefore, they granted the ladies the right to abort, whereupon, figuring they had dealt with the problem, they firmly and deliberately proceeded to forget the whole issue.

For Shidzue Kato, abortion was a necessary but regrettable shortcut, a primitive solution that would have to do for the time being, and she was very disappointed.

At first, she hoped that this was only a beginning and that she would soon get the green light to deal with prevention and put in place the project she had been pushing for so long: a national birth-control program.

Fifty years later, that project remained a dream. Until the turn of the twenty-first century, Japanese women had no access to the Pill, and had no recourse other than condoms and abortion in order to avoid pregnancy – the way their great-grandmothers had.

From that fateful day in July 1948, when Japanese parliamentarians legalized abortion, Shidzue Kato's political career started to decline. She would keep a keen interest in population issues for the rest of her life, she would create the Family Planning Federation in 1954, would get the distribution of condoms legalized in 1955, would attend international conventions, publish, and be heard, but from then on she was going against the flow of Japanese political life.

She was also going against the flow of her American friends. As most Japanese liberals, she had invested immense hopes in the Americans after the war: they were going to teach the Japanese the fundamentals of great liberties; guarantee education for all; spell out their duties and responsibilities to politicians; remind public servants that they were at the service of elected representatives and not the reverse; in short, put in place the first Asian democratic model.

In actual fact, the honeymoon lasted less than two years.

As early as 1947, Americans started worrying about the influence of the left on unions. From 1948 on, they were haunted with the fear of communism in Asia. When the Korean War started in June 1950, they lost whatever interest they still had for establishing democratic values in Japan. They had put in place the framework and institutions, and figured that the Japanese would manage by themselves from then on.

Japanese liberals felt they had been coldly abandoned in mid-flight. They had wished for an Allied victory during the war; they welcomed them as liberators after the war; they had placed all their hopes in them; they felt betrayed.

"They let us go too soon," they were still wailing half a century later. "We were not yet able to fly by ourselves. Institutions were too recent, new ideas had not yet made their way. New habits had not yet taken root. Worse, we hadn't had time to get rid of the old guard. They took back the reins of power as soon as the Americans were gone, and things went back to the way they were before."

The blow was particularly hard for Shidzue Kato. She felt her dearest friends were turning their backs on her. Yet she remained attracted by the democratic and liberal ideal they represented, and she went on looking for new beacons.

Paradoxically, this radical activist-socialist, married to a left-wing militant, turned to the Moral Rearmament movement that was blossoming in the United States at that time to give a new direction to her life. Her political career became increasingly erratic. She found herself progressively marginalized within her own party. Her affinity with the Socialists had been circumstantial, her political activism before, during, and after the war was always dictated by pragmatic rather than ideological considerations. In the Manichean universe of the Cold War, there was no room for Shidzue Kato.

She spent the balance of her parliamentary career – more than a quarter-century – without much political influence. Still, she kept busy; she wrote, she gave lectures, she was heard. People liked her. Whatever the cause she was endorsing at any given time, be it environmental protection, the Pill, or cruelty to animals, this angry old lady always spoke with refreshing sincerity.

People wanted to hear her, if only to remind themselves that that is the way all politicians should talk. They envied her freedom; she was no longer a member of any political group, she did not owe anything to anybody, she could afford to speak her mind.

People also admired her ruthlessness when she was vilifying bureaucrats:

"These rotten and irresponsible bureaucrats interfere with the progress of new policies," she fulminated at the time of the abortion law. "In a democracy, bureaucrats are not the ones to decide on fundamental government policies."

Fifty years later, her feelings had not changed:

"Bureaucrats from the Finance Department are the ones who actually run this country, rather than the elected representatives. Our politicians are weak. We don't have any great statesmen. Political parties are corrupt. The Japanese feel they can't trust anybody."

Such was her opening diatribe the day I went to pay a visit to Shidzue Kato.

She presented a surprising picture: almost a hundred years old, regal in her impeccable blue suit with white lace trimmings, sitting upright in the centre of her sofa, very straight, as if to compensate for the extreme frailty of her body.

"I can no longer trust my legs to carry me, but don't worry, I can still trust my brain!" she explained in lieu of welcome.

Immediately after the obligatory cup of green tea, she began to speak, and I felt that her cool anger was what kept her alive.

"The problem is that politicians are intimidated by bureaucrats. Especially by the Ministry of Finance bureaucrats, because they are all graduates from the Tokyo University."

One needs to be familiar with this strict hierarchy: a graduate from a provincial university will always bow lower than a graduate from Tokyo University, whatever their relative positions in life. In general, senior officials went to Todai (that's the familiar name for Tokyo University), while politicians tend to come with lesser academic credentials. On that basis alone, most of them would never even think of contradicting a bureaucrat. All the more that these same bureaucrats are the ones who grant or do not grant credits and regional subsidies. Their support is invaluable when it comes the time to be re-elected!

Such is the symbiotic relationship that Shidzue Kato spent her life denouncing. The country needed its politicians to be strong, yet they could not assert themselves because of the undue influence of the public service. The vicious circle had to be broken. Politicians had to be taught how to fight for their ideas and dare defend them in public.

That is why she came up with the idea of sending a congratulatory note, in writing, each time one of them demonstrated his independence in a speech to the Diet.

"Why the pink paper?"

"You know, I was an elected member. I know what it is like. You receive boxes full of mail every day. It is impossible to read them all. But Diet members recognize mine. When they gave a good speech, the following day they wait anxiously for the mail, hoping for the pink envelope; if they find it, they call me to thank me; some of them cry with emotion . . ."

That is how, in her hundredth year, Shidzue Kato was still fighting, from her wheelchair, the battle she could never win from her bench in the Diet.

CHAPTER 16

New Politicians, Same Old Ruts

I was privileged to witness the early days of a new politician's career – privileged because new politicians are a rare breed in Japan.

At that time – in the mid-1990s – sclerosis of the political process was almost a required topic in all conversations. The Liberal Democratic Party (LDP) had been in power, almost uninterrupted, for thirty-five years, and had been governing as a one-party regime. A handful of self-proclaimed "Young Turks" had recently split from the old party in order to create a new political movement: modern, energetic, and focused on the future.

However, the electorate was not fooled. These "Young Turks" were as old as the LDP "old guard"; they had shared the same benches for years, belonged to the same factions, mingled in the same corruption. By seceding from the old party, they were simply hoping to grab the reins of power without waiting for their turn.

Two parties from the centre-right, peopled with the same stock, two Socialist parties at odds with one another, one marginal Communist party, such were the unappetizing choices offered to the Japanese every time they were called to the voting booth.

Akiko Yamanaka had the archetypical profile of the new generation so sorely needed by the Japanese political system. She was teaching sociology in university, had recently returned from a sabbatical at Harvard, and was full of ideas on internationalization, dialogue between cultures, and modernization in her home province of Hokkaido.

Our first meeting, at a very social cocktail party, was an exercise in naivety – my own shortsighted naivety – when, after chatting for a few minutes, I exclaimed enthusiastically, "Did you ever consider a career in politics?" And her highly polished feigned naivety, suggesting that the thought had never, could never, cross her mind: "Me? In politics? What a preposterous idea! What would my husband think? And my children? Who would be looking after them?" The whole thing delivered in a high-pitched voice, with her hand over her mouth to hide that typical childish smile Japanese women commonly use to mask their true feelings.

Later, I would learn that Yamanaka was already campaigning, though unofficially. I should have guessed from her Harvard business card: "Here is my business card. So sorry, it is not up to date . . . just came back from Boston . . . you will understand . . . just off the plane . . . haven't had a chance to get organized yet . . ." She had been apologizing for three months, handing out with a flourish the out-of-date business card with the prestigious crest.

The children she kept referring to in every conversation were adult, and had long left home. As for the husband ("Who would cook him dinner if I went into politics?"), he was in fact her most ardent supporter. A well-established lawyer in Sapporo, he had been urging his wife to go into public life and had been preparing his own meals for years.

However, such is the recipe for success for a woman who wants to get elected: she must exhibit a constant concern about her family responsibilities, feign reluctance, present a caricature of femininity. With her convent-girl looks, powder-blue dress, well-ordered curls on her shoulders, high-pitched voice, Yamanaka had achieved a perfect mastery of the character, and I had fallen headfirst for her act.

After this basic decoding, we became best friends. Akiko had established solid foundations in her community, but she needed a riding. I remember spending a whole afternoon with her, going through the political chessboard in her region.

"Logically, I should run in the number-one district, because that's where I live. The problem is that the former governor of the province, an old-style Socialist, wants to run there too. My only chance would be for him to get caught in a corruption scandal . . . but if he runs, the LDP [conservative] will vote for him, as well as his Socialist friends, of course."

I am confused: how can the same man collect votes from his party and from his sworn enemies? With a scandal looming over him to boot? But there is more: he might push a woman as an LDP candidate. This is strange, for this LDP woman started her career as a Communist, then became a Socialist, and at the present time she is courting the New Frontier Party (centre-right).

"Liberals don't want to have anything to do with her" Akiko explains. "She sleeps with everyone," she adds charitably. "Also, they claim that you can't trust women, because they change party constantly. It makes things more difficult for me . . ."

To complete the picture, one should add that the old Socialist ex-governor has also approached her to run under the LDP colours, if ever the scandal explodes and bars him from running as a Socialist. I understand less and less. And we are dealing only with the number-one district!

"The number-two district is Sapporo-North. The present representative is an old-school LDP. Everybody says he will be beaten. I could try my luck there, but I would need the support of the party executive in Tokyo, and they are all misogynous dinosaurs.

"The number-three district is where my university is located. My president would support me. There, the ideal for me would be to run as a candidate for the New Frontier Party, which is by far the best-positioned in that sector. Except that they already have someone . . .

and of course, there is always the risk that the ex-governor [him again!] will decide to run there under the Socialist banner. If he does, he will win, no question."

Incredulous, I have been trying to follow this mind-boggling criss-crossing. And there is more.

"There is of course the number-four district. At the present time, it is represented by two old-timers, one Liberal and one Socialist, both totally incompetent. The seat is up for grabs. I have some support among the LDP. I have some with the New Frontier Party too, but in my region, in the north, people don't trust that party because it is new."

Then she adds thoughtfully, "There is also the new Sakigake Party, recently created by my good friend Hatoyama. I have a lot of respect for him. He has a modern approach to politics; we think alike. But there is no grassroots organization yet, no support group, not even an office. Everything has to be organized from scratch. I don't want to waste my time pasting up posters on walls and looking for chairs every time we want to organize a public meeting."

The political portrait of her hometown is now complete. The burgeoning politician sums things up: "In any case, I have the support of the Chamber of Commerce and of the Unions [Socialist and Communist]. I must get the women's vote. That's easy; the recipe is always the same: I will produce a radio series about environmental protection."

Suddenly, Akiko's tone changes. From strategic and calculating, she becomes plaintive: "My hair, for television? Up or down? And the dress? Men prefer dresses. It reassures them; it reminds them of their mothers. But women expect me to wear a suit, it looks more professional, like American women politicians they see on television." During the following weeks and months, Yamanaka will opt progressively for the compromise solution adopted by most Japanese women in public life: severe-looking suits (to please women), cut in pastel colours (to reassure men).

I have a question on the tip of my tongue: Nowhere in this panorama did she ever mention ideology, visions of society, programs, or at least political platform. My new friend envisages just as serenely the prospect of becoming a Socialist representative or of sitting at the opposite extreme with the LDP, whom she herself calls dinosaurs.

I dare ask: "Deep down, you don't seem to care much about any political party's credo?"

She laughs, slightly embarrassed. "You know, in Japan, these things don't matter too much. In any case, ordinary elected representatives have no power. The only thing that matters is to be elected . . . and even then, the only way you can have any influence is to be in the cabinet. I don't want to vegetate on the opposition benches for the rest of my career. The challenge is to bet on the party that has the best chance to win, get them to nominate you, and then be parachuted into a riding where I cannot lose."

She then adds with transparent cynicism, "If I am elected, they will have to give me a portfolio, because I am a woman, I have a Ph.D., and most of all, I know how to use the media."

Whew! The whole thing is delivered in an even voice, sweet and innocent like a little girl's.

In the end, events will unfold almost exactly the way Akiko had hoped. She will be parachuted softly into the political arena, and will not even have to campaign. Thanks to proportional representation that was inaugurated that year, she will find herself first on a list, with the blessing of the party leader. Victory guaranteed.

Hers is a strategic position: even though, in the end, the party she opted for is not the party in power, it has so many family links with the old Liberal Democrats that she can still hope to become a minister sooner or later.

Today is the big day!

The opening of the parliamentary session is a very formal affair, and widely covered by the media. From my living room, I follow the ceremony, broadcast live on television.

Without admitting it, I feel a twinge of concern for Akiko. I have followed her accession to active politics from the beginning, I have shared her hopes, doubts, and uncertainties. Now that she has reached her goal, I want to see her succeed. As I wait to see her step for the first time into the Japanese Diet, I wonder. How will this young provincial woman survive in this hard, cynical world, dominated by males the age of her father, a world where the only rules that count are the unwritten ones?

I shouldn't worry. Akiko is everywhere on the screen. For the occasion, she is wearing a new crisp white outfit that makes her stand out instantly in the ocean of dark suits. The most seasoned politicians would envy her sixth sense for television: wherever the cameras are pointing, the slim white silhouette is sure to be in the frame, together with more familiar figures. Here she is posing with her leader, paying her respects to the prime minister, smiling to a minister, smiling to everyone. Nobody knows who she is but not to worry, soon everybody will. She is talking, turning, moving around, and somehow she manages to remain in the eye of the camera, always. It is truly a high-flying performance.

Alone in front of my TV screen, I smile, reassured. Once more, I have fallen victim to Akiko's feigned vulnerability, as I have to that of so many other Japanese women. Their powerless, distraught look often masks an iron will, a totally focused concentration on their goal, and a formidable obsession with excellence. Unless something goes drastically wrong, Akiko should get, some day, the minister's portfolio she is coveting.

For now, Akiko is going to have to learn her new profession. To begin with, she must settle in the big city. The central administration has thought of everything for these newcomers, freshly elected, arriving from their remote regions the day after the general elections. No way they are going to let them scatter at random in the capital. A few steps away from the parliament building, there is a residence for parliamentarians, and Akiko has invited me to join her in her first visit to her new home: four high concrete buildings around an inner court-yard. At the door, a stern-looking guard, not in the least impressed by Madam the Representative from Sapporo.

"Identification papers!" he orders.

He walks to his office to consult his list and check that this little woman is indeed a legitimate parliamentarian, and comes back with a heavy bunch of keys, slightly more respectful, but no more friendly.

We take a small elevator with steel walls sprayed with rust-proof paint, and land on the fourth floor: long corridors, grey walls, anony-mous doors on either side, threadbare runners, bare bulbs on the ceiling. The similarity to a jail is overwhelming.

Apartments are assigned according to need and status: Akiko will live alone in Tokyo, therefore she is entitled to only the smaller model. And since she has no seniority and she sits in opposition, her only window opens on the courtyard, facing north.

She does not seem to mind. She is delighted with her new quar-ters. Thanks to some high-ranking support, she will convince the administration to put on a fresh coat of paint and, after filling in some more forms, she might even be allowed to change the rugs – at her own expense, and provided she picks a regulation colour.

She must show her ID every time she goes in and out of the build-ing. "It is for my own safety," she explains. But she has no illusions: parliamentarians are watched day and night. Akiko is entitled to a chauffeur, as are all her other colleagues. All she has to do is reserve several days ahead, indicate in writing where she intends to go, and whom she intends to meet and why. Madame Future Minister is held on a very short leash.

It is the same thing in the parliament buildings: in the under-ground corridors connecting the various wings, young uniformed guards, who manage to look both obsequious and arrogant at the same time, check the new member's identity at each corner, under the pretence of helping her find her way.

"Whose wife is this?" mutters an old member to a colleague, as he sees the skirt go by. Then, noting on the pink lapel the red pin that identifies Diet members, he corrects himself, "Ah? No, it is somebody," he grumbles aloud. And he gives Akiko a perfunctory wave of recognition before going on his way.

My friend remains impervious to these small indignities. She is radiant, she floats on a cloud, she won, she has entered the fortress, everything else is of no consequence.

A few days later, she calls me, brimming with indignation. Party caucuses are in the process of deciding on who will sit on which parliamentary committees, and they asked each member to list their preferences.

"Finance and International Trade," wrote Akiko on the form. "Education and Environment," corrected an imperious hand.

In everybody's mind, education and environment are the ghettos in which one keeps women parliamentarians to get rid of them. These two portfolios are considered "soft." It is all right to let the ladies make speeches about children and little birds, while the senior mandarins manage and decide. Akiko is furious. No way will she be pushed into the ladies' ghetto.

"The saddest part is that, in fact, these topics are very interesting. Education and environment, what could be more relevant? But first, I have to establish my credibility with the dinosaurs, and for this, I must make my mark in files with hard figures."

I note the frequency with which she is using the word "dinosaur." Finally, by some mysterious manoeuvre, she will get her way and sit on the Finance and Foreign Affairs committees.

"Well? How was the baptism of fire?"

I am impatient to hear Akiko's impressions after a few weeks of parliamentary life. We decided to meet in a fashionable French restaurant on Omotesando Avenue – which the Japanese like to call "Tokyo's Champs-Elysées." Akiko does not have much time for traditional Japanese restaurants, with their intimate atmosphere, their private little rooms, and the ability they have to make you feel as if you are their only honourable customers. That is not her cup of tea!

Freshly elected, her constant preoccupation is to be seen, to be known and recognized, to figure in all the right address books.

Here, the restaurant is wide open. One side faces the street, the other a delightful inside courtyard. We have been seated (at her request) right in the centre, and I would be very surprised if we did not bump into some acquaintance whom we will wave to, just a little too loudly, just a little too merrily; yet we are so charming, and pretty, and lively, we will be forgiven, people will smile at us, and everyone will remember Akiko and Akiko's name.

We order, and she giggles as she recounts her first few days.

"Did you know that on the benches of the Diet, members are seated according to seniority and birth date? The newcomers are right in front. Everybody is watching us, and we have no idea what is happening behind us. On the other hand, Yasuhiro Nakasone [who was prime minister for a long time and still orchestrates most major intrigues] is sitting way at the back on the upper benches. From up there, he can keep an eye on everybody, just like the Godfather."

New Diet members are entitled to information sessions to learn the ropes of their new profession. However, Akiko quickly realized that her instructors' priorities were elsewhere. "When might you have some time in your busy schedule to receive our visit?" an immensely respectful voice inquired on the phone.

It was just a few days before the first meeting of the Foreign Affairs committee, and the minister himself was to appear. Akiko saw this as a golden opportunity to establish her reputation as a solid, serious member. However, she needed to familiarize herself with the very precise rules that govern committee meetings: Which party speaks first? And who speaks first in each party? In what order? What are the time limits? As for questions, how must they be presented?

The wording of questions follows a precise protocol. One must be fluent in all the tongue-twisting techniques designed to avoid any loss of face for the minister. Akiko needed to learn these techniques as soon as possible in order to prepare herself for this first committee meeting. This information session was a crucial part of her basic training as a new parliamentarian.

"They walked into my office. There were two of them. Very polite. They greeted me, I invited them to take a seat, and I settled in my chair with a notebook and pen in hand, ready to take notes like a good pupil. They were watching me, without saying anything. After a short while, the silence became embarrassing and the older of the two said, 'Well?' as if he was expecting me to say something. I didn't understand.

"'Well? What are your questions?'

"'I have everything to learn. The procedure, and of course I presume you may want to brief me on the files we will deal with tomorrow. I'm listening.'

"He made a gesture as if to brush all this aside with the back of his hand. 'Which questions do you intend to ask the minister?'

"That's when I realized that the so-called information session was not designed for my own education. On the contrary. My instructors had only one preoccupation: to find out where I came from, what was on my mind, what were my hang-ups, if any, so they could write down the minister's answers ahead of time. Pen in hand, looking worried, they had come to *negotiate* my questions!"

I interrupt Akiko to inquire: "Did you submit the questions you intended to ask the minister?"

"Absolutely not! I did not enter politics to play those sorts of games! If I have something to ask the minister, I will do so directly. No way I will let some public servant orchestrate everything ahead of time! That's not democracy!"

In principle, public servants have no partisan affiliation; however, the same party has been in power for so long that no one is surprised to see them work openly with their political masters.

Akiko is totally shocked – or pretends to be shocked. As a good politician, she knows she cannot go wrong badmouthing public servants. The theme is universally popular, and, whatever her audience, she knows she will get cheered.

As for the unfortunate public servants, they probably regret the good old days when Diet members themselves came and asked, "Which questions should I ask the minister tomorrow?" Public servants would draw up both questions (for the members) and answers (for the minister) and life was a lot easier for everybody.

Akiko is not unhappy with her performance. Her questions established that she is bright and well informed; plus, she did not embarrass the minister. Quite the opposite, he enjoyed this refreshing exchange with the spirited newcomer.

She is satisfied: her colleagues were justly impressed, and the minister will remember her. This is paramount because in this coalition government the balance of power may change overnight; in a few months she might very well find herself in the same group as the minister, and then who knows?

I realize that, once more, I have been taken in by the smooth mask of her face, her playful laugh, and her childlike voice. Since the appetizers, I have been listening to the adventures of her first few days, and I thought I was hearing the adventures of the young recruit going from discovery to discovery. How wrong I was!

Akiko wants to become minister, her eyes are constantly focused on that objective. On the eminently unstable terrain of Japanese party politics, she moves with great caution. One must watch not only the parties and coalitions, but also the factions within the great parties, which get into merciless power struggles. Every day, the media are abuzz with rumours about coalitions, defections, new alliances, new groups and subgroups . . . At any time, a small shift of one of these tectonic plates can propel her towards the heights of power or bury her forever in irrelevance and oblivion. That is why Akiko calculates, weighs, and measures everything she says, everything she does. Her survival depends on it.

Yet, in the process, she has already given up on the dream that pushed her to enter politics in the first place: the dream to change the system from the inside.

CHAPTER 17

Three Rebels

"**B**unch of losers! Poor fuckers! Did you get a good look at your-selves and your miserable little lives?" In the smoke-filled bar, the drunken obscenities explode above the quiet drone of a Friday night.

"Brown-nosers at best! That's what you are. You call that living?"

The beer-drinkers raise their heads, surprised by this sudden fury, and vaguely embarrassed, because they are the ones being shouted at.

"When is the last time you had a good fuck? I am asking you? I bet you can't even keep it up! Miserable losers!" All this because one of the regulars, a young worker with solid shoulders and a friendly smile, gallantly offered to help Michiko into her seat.

"Do you really think I can't sit by myself?" The vulgar voice goes on. "You want to protect me? You are trying to be chivalrous? I don't need chivalrous! Fuck chivalrous! I don't need a Prince Charming. I need a lover! A real one! With a stiff one! Not a loser like you!"

The torrent of insults and obscenities keeps on. Everyone else in the small bar is deadly silent. The drinkers are not sure whether to be insulted by or sympathetic to this violent outburst. All eyes are turned towards Michiko, and yet they all desperately wish to be elsewhere, not to see this, not to hear this.

Michiko is having a fine time.

She loves to be the centre of attention. Most of all, she loves to emasculate men; these sane, healthy, well-meaning men, full of good intentions, always ready to help her, protect her, poor little thing . . .

Michiko is quadriplegic, though she has minimal use of her hands and toes. From her wheelchair, she noisily demands the right to live a normal life, including the right to have one drink too many on a Friday night in the local bar, the right to pick up men, even the right to regret her nights. She has been ranting and cursing for twenty years to obtain that right.

When you are deprived of the use of your arms and legs, are not even capable of holding your head straight, when you speak in grunts, using only a few muscles around the mouth, you keep quiet. You remain in an institution, where an attentive staff washes you, dresses you, feeds you; you spend your days moving along the corridors in a wheelchair or watching television, and on Sunday, with luck, your parents come to visit.

Or else, like Michiko, you find yourself a friend with feet, convince her to give you a leg up in the middle of the night; using your two hands, you somehow manage to turn triumphantly the main door handle, you run away in the dark, you go live your life and open a centre for the liberation of the handicapped.

In the early days, everybody thought Michiko was crazy. When she went to city hall in her wheelchair to request a subsidized apartment, or to the ministry's office for her pension cheque, she was ignored; she was kept waiting for hours in the hallway in the hope that she would get tired and go away.

"Now when I visit public servants, they are very polite and offer me tea. They are all afraid that I might talk about them in my books."

Before she reached that stage, Michiko had to fight long and hard. First, she demanded the right to live in her own place. Not with her parents. At home.

"How will you do the cooking, the housework . . . ?"

"With my toes."

"What about the rest? To get washed, to get dressed?"

"I have a handicapped pension. Instead of giving it to the institution, give me the cheque and send me a home-helper for those things I really cannot manage by myself."

Michiko was confronted with the paternalism of authorities and their lack of initiative. "There are some things I cannot do, but there are also many things I am *capable* of doing, and no one has the right to prevent me from doing them."

That was the hardest, but she proved she was right. She lived alone. She got married; she had a son. "When he was a baby, I changed the diapers with my toes."

She is divorced. She has custody of her child, attends the PTA meetings, and does all she can to bring an appearance of normality to her life. "The most important thing one can do in life is to provide children with a good education."

Her goal is to prove to other handicapped people that they, too, can contribute to society. The foundation she created helps them settle in their own homes and find a realistic level of autonomy. Three vans offer a pickup service, and there is a call centre for emergencies. Volunteers lend their arms and hands to the whole enterprise, but all decisions are taken in committee by people in wheelchairs.

"We don't get a penny from the authorities," boasts Michiko. "All the money comes from fundraising and from my books."

She gives lectures to explain to handicapped people what they are entitled to, how to look for an apartment, how to apply for financial assistance.

And also how to find a lover. "He must be rich, not a penny-pincher. The kind of guy who tells you, 'Let's go, I'm taking you to the movies.'" She treats me to a foxy wink as she enumerates those criteria.

To wink is a major undertaking for a quadriplegic. The nape of her neck is propped on a white lace-covered headrest. Her neck does not support her head, which rolls on the side; when she speaks, she looks at you sideways, and all her facial muscles contract from the effort required – all this just to make a conversation, to chat, plus to make a small wink from time to time when she is talking dirty.

And yet, she is talkative! She has a sense of humour, she makes jokes – dirty, salacious, definitely incorrect – the kind of jokes that would discourage anyone from ever thinking "Poor little thing!"

She published a book on how to pick up men from a wheelchair; another whose title translates roughly as: *Breakfast in bed in a wheelchair, or how to make love when you are handicapped.*

With her tough language, boldness, and truculence, she has become something of a national celebrity.

"When I got married, I gave endless interviews. They all wanted to ask me the same questions, they wanted me to keep a diary. When my son was born, the house became a regular movie studio."

For a long time, the authorities gave her what she wanted, just to get rid of her. Now they are listening. Social workers come and ask her advice on how to prepare the handicapped to integrate into society.

"Government services are beginning to realize that locking them up in institutions is very expensive. It is much more economical to let them live independently, with the occasional assistance of home-helpers."

What she demanded for so long is now becoming a model for society. This is how Michiko Osanai, who, at the age of twenty, was trying to figure out ways to commit suicide, realized the impossible – getting the Japanese administration to change its ways.

He is an exhausted man. He climbs the mountain trail heavily, dragging his tall tired frame, head deep in his shoulders. With each step, he pulls his boots from the mud, moving slowly, in a daze. He is immensely sleepy. His whole body wants to sleep.

"There! A black woodpecker!"

His voice, sharp as a slash – though whispered – instantly freezes the small group of hikers who have been climbing a few steps ahead of him on the trail. With deliberate, slow moves, we all adjust our binoculars and scrutinize the undergrowth through the budding foliage. The privilege of spotting that bird on the verge of extinction will not be granted to all, as it stands twenty feet away, motionless, flat against the trunk, its colour the same as the bark's.

Those of us who missed it feel sheepish. How could this unusual guide, who is dragging behind the group, who looks so bored, who moves reluctantly, gazing at the tip of his shoes, and who, to make matters worse, wears thick glasses, how could this man spot the rare bird?

We will live through more humbling scenes during our climb: a bamboo shoot barely sprouting out and entirely covered with snow; a beetle larva, sleeping under layers of dead leaves. It seems as if no living thing can escape the sharp eye of our guide.

On this mountain in the north of Japan, Fubomichi Kudo acts like a landowner. This forest of tall white beech trees is his empire. He has covered its trails so many times that he knows every bush and, it seems, every wild goat.

Kudo was trained as a biologist. Circumstances turned him into a formidable militant. Thanks to his efforts, this beech forest, which was destined for the woodsman's axe, is now a United Nations World Heritage site. That achievement was the end result of ten years of epic battles with the Japanese administration.

All day, as we ascend Mount Shirakami, we hear about the beeches' longevity (three hundred years), the songbirds, flycatchers, and cuckoos that fly from South Asia in the spring, the thrushes and buntings that fly from the north in the fall, the macaques who live above the tree line, the two thousand insect species . . . "An ecosystem five times richer than that of European beech forests!" Kudo claims triumphantly. It is also a paradise for naturalists.

At the end of the day, the naturalist makes way for the militant. After soaking leisurely in the hot sulphuric waters of a natural spring and drinking a few cups of hot sake, Kudo embarks on his war stories.

"In 1982, I started getting panicked letters from farmers who live at the foot of these mountains. The local authorities had just decided to build a forest road. The inhabitants were worried about landslides, floods, and, most of all, irreparable damage to the ecology of their beloved mountain. Eventually, I took a trip up north to see for myself. I was stunned by the immensity of the forest. It was like a cathedral! Adult beeches one hundred feet high, an undergrowth the likes of which have become a rarity in the world; no survey had ever been done of its flora and fauna. What was standing before me was one of the last natural forests not only in Japan but in the world. It was the equivalent of making a major archaeological discovery."

Sprawled out on the tatami floor in the small restaurant in this isolated fishermen's village, the low table littered with leftovers of sushi, Kudo is looking more exhausted than ever as he recalls the many vicissitudes of what became his life crusade.

"I started giving lectures and organizing symposiums in the country. I created a fund for the protection of the Shirakami virgin forest. I presented a report to the government to stop the forest road. I was fighting on all fronts simultaneously: with the Agriculture Ministry, the Environment Agency, and the two prefectures covering the Shirakami mountains.

"I was alone. That was before the Rio summit, and environment was still a relatively novel concept in Japan. Finally, to get rid of me more than out of conviction, the Agriculture Ministry committed to protect forty thousand acres of forest from the axe. But I knew that in their mind, it was only a temporary measure until after the local elections. As proof, the construction of the forest road was going ahead."

As I listen, I am reminded of other encounters in other villages on the Japan Sea, where inhabitants are still paying today the price of the massive deforestation that took place right after the war, when Japan was still a very poor country: tons of mud coming down from

bare mountains with the slightest rainfall, rice fields threatened by
flooding, a fishing industry endangered by pollution. Such was the
fate facing Shirakami farmers and fishermen.

"What a battle! The prime minister had no interest whatsoever
in forestry protection. Even at the Environment Agency, I made
enemies. One of my few allies ended up in the hospital with a nervous
breakdown, another one came close to resigning more than once, out
of sheer frustration . . ."

Then came what Kudo calls "the Toronto miracle."

Canada was hosting the Group of Seven Economic Summit that
year (1988). For the first time, environment figured on the agenda in
a substantial way and the concept of sustainable development was
about to receive the formal support of participating governments.
There was one exception, however: Japan, which had made no reference to environmental issues in its preparatory documents. According
to Kudo, the Japanese delegation only realized their isolation once
they reached Toronto, and did not want to look as if they were
lagging behind other countries.

"Overnight, Prime Minister Takeshita made a complete about-
turn. To hear his speech in Toronto, it sounded as though he had
always been a champion of environmental protection. I couldn't
believe my ears!" recalls Kudo.

Less than a year later, the tall beeches of Shirakami acquired the
status of protected forest.

Others might have celebrated their victory and gone back to
teaching. But Kudo knew better. From his years of fighting the
authorities, he had developed a bottomless distrust for the Japanese
administration.

"As long as we don't have an international body to protect the
forest, Shirakami will not be safe," he explains darkly. "You can't trust
the Japanese authorities."

The following year, he started hassling the government to desig-
nate Shirakami as a World Heritage Site candidate. Three years later,
after more epic cliff-hangers, his dream became reality.

I watch with new respect this heavy-set, hard-headed man who took on, all by himself and for so long, an adversary thought to be invincible.

He lost his house in the melée, as well as his private life. And, for added irony, he is now concluding casually that, deep down, he does not even like beech trees that much!

He is no longer sprawled on the tatami, but seated very straight, his legs crossed like a dishevelled Buddha, and stark sober.

"What I wanted to tell the world is that we are as responsible for our forests as we are responsible for our own lives. The Japanese think only of their well-being, yet we are all interdependent on this planet. The Japanese must understand that. They must learn to be concerned about others' well-being."

That is why he went on a crusade – and why he cannot stop. With his momentum, he has undertaken a new, gigantic project, so huge that even UNESCO was intimidated: camera and microphone in hand, he has decided to survey all the sites, in the whole world, which are important in human history, yet have been forgotten or ignored, and are threatened with disappearance. He counted 358 of them, on all five continents. He gave himself ten years to produce a twenty-minute documentary on each of them for the benefit of the United Nations. He has no organization behind him, little public financing (though he does have UNESCO's blessing). Kudo does not stop. Kudo cannot stop, for life is short and the world is vast. Exhausted, alone, and stubborn, he has taken it upon himself to save the memory for the whole planet.

"Welcome to the musical sands of Maki City."

On this bright Saturday afternoon, the banner in front of the community hall and the vans cruising the streets with their loudspeakers are inviting the good people of Maki to come and play in a sandbox.

On the border between the town and the rice fields, the one-room community hall has been turned into an exhibition gallery, where you can learn everything you ever wanted to know about sand, and a lot more.

There is indeed a sandbox in the centre of the room for children to play in. All around, microscopes set on low tables allow visitors to examine at leisure sand samples collected from beaches of the world. Serious-looking students, polite, soft-spoken, and deliberate, offer detailed explanations on the geology, the physics, the chemistry of sands from various parts of the planet. This is a thorough exhibit, designed to demonstrate that Maki city beaches are blessed with the best sand in the world. So fine, so white, so pure, in fact, that, when you press on it, ever so lightly, it gives out a high-pitched sound, like some primitive Noh flute.

"Just imagine yourself walking barefoot on the beach, the sun setting on the horizon, your footsteps making soft, forlorn music in the sand at dusk over the Sea of Japan?"

I find it difficult indeed to imagine anything more romantic.

"You wouldn't want to sacrifice such a God-given marvel of purity for the sake of some nuclear-power plant, would you?"

That is what it is all about. The inhabitants of this quiet small town are fighting to stop the construction of a nuclear-power plant on their shores. And they are about to enter history, for they decided to organize a referendum, the first ever in the country.

Twenty-five years earlier, the North-East Electric Power Company identified a favourable site for a nuclear-power plant here. It was a narrow strip of land along the seashore, useless and unused, separated from the town by a high ridge, with a solid rock base, far from seismic faults and earthquake risks. It was the perfect spot. At the time, Maki was an isolated rural community, its farmers and fishermen had been compensated, and their retirement years looked after. However, the land-assembly process dragged on and, in the meantime, the population of Maki changed. City people working in nearby Niigata started moving in to raise their families in a rural setting. From a sleepy rural community, Maki turned into a quietly prosperous residential suburb with a country feeling. The new residents, vocal and articulate, were not going to take the nuclear-power project lying down.

It is often said that Japanese people are not keenly interested in politics, and suffer as inevitable the decisions from the central agencies. However, the day when a pro-power-plant mayor was elected, almost by accident (the anti-plant vote had been split between two candidates), the inhabitants of Maki city developed a sudden burning interest in public affairs.

Within a few weeks, they introduced and adopted amendments to municipal regulations, to allow for referenda. Within a year, they got rid of the mayor. They then organized a referendum to decide on whether they wanted a nuclear plant in their backyard.

The news had spread like brush fire in the country. Could it be true? Was it actually possible to use this thing with a foreign-sounding name, "referendum"? Was it actually possible to stand against a central government decision, rather than grumble and keep one's head down?

The citizens from Maki city had launched into the unknown, and the adventure was opening new, unforeseen prospects from one end of the archipelago to the other.

As for regional power companies, they were also watching events as they unfolded in Maki – with undisguised concern. There is practically no natural source of energy on the Japanese territory. No oil, little coal, and all the rivers have already been dammed. Nuclear power provides one-third of all the energy needs of the country, and that proportion is sure to increase with time.

Very simply, the people from Maki city were threatening the whole national energy policy. Which explains why, in the week preceding the referendum, a continuous flow of engineers, fresh from a crash course in public relations, started streaming from the minuscule train station. Their mission was to speak to the population, organize information sessions in public schools, answer questions, explain and reassure.

The people of Maki attend all public meetings, those with the engineers and those with the environmentalists. They listen, ask questions, and go home. They carry no pins, plant no signs on their lawns, stick no posters in their windows; it is impossible to know which way public opinion is going.

"The Japanese are always worried about what the neighbours might think," explains lawyer Tamiyo Takashima. "They campaign actively, but they don't want their name to be known, or used."

Takashima and his wife are the ones who came up with the idea of a referendum to decide on the town's future. In their bungalow, crammed full of books, the couple are waiting for the big day with the serenity of two Zen monks.

"For us, it is not the result that matters. It may be that, despite this whole campaign, the power-plant project will go ahead anyway. But at least it will be because people have decided on it, not because some agents from Tokyo tampered with local politics."

Takashima concludes: "My purpose is to teach the Japanese that it is in their power to decide their own fate."

In the rice fields surrounding the town, "protest trees" have sprouted in the last few weeks: these tall masts are held with thin ropes, on which families tie bright-coloured handkerchiefs, one for each one of their children. These makeshift sails are now flapping in the wind by the hundreds. Even before referendum day, Takashima has already won one battle: the battle against fatalism and electors' apathy.

Certainly the most astonishing aspect of this pre-referendum campaign that is fascinating the country is that the referendum has no legal standing. None whatsoever. Whatever the outcome, the power company could legally go ahead, ignore the referendum, and build the power plant as if nothing happened.

So why is everyone campaigning so hard?

"Because we are in Japan," explain Takashima and his wife.

"Because we are in Japan," add the journalists who have been following the story.

"Because we are in Japan," says Isao Nakamura, project direct for the North-East Electric Power Company. "Our lawyers may remind us every day that the referendum has no legal value. But they are talking like foreigners. In fact, we must respect the popular consensus. If in the end the plant is built, we will ourselves become citizens of Maki city: myself, the engineers, other employees, and our families. We will be part of this community. It would be unthinkable to go ahead without our neighbours' support!"

On August 4, 1996, the citizens of Maki city held the first referendum in the history of Japan and rejected the nuclear-power plant. The power company kept its word and suspended the project until further notice.

In the weeks that followed, other small towns held their own referenda; since then, they have become the weapon of choice to fight against large public works planned by the central agencies. They usually deal with very local issues and, as happened in Maki, they tend to oppose long-term global interests and short-sighted local interests. However, in the debates preceding these village referenda, the sense of duty to country is not totally absent. The ensuing reflection, too, has an influence, and everybody is getting a hands-on education on citizens' responsibility and the democratic process.

The Japanese are known for the low regard in which they hold political life, and too often they do not bother to vote in general elections. However, the emergence of local referenda is providing them with a fresh opportunity to get interested in public life.

More than fifty years after the democratic process was instituted in their country, the Japanese are just beginning to realize how it can actually change their lives.

CHAPTER 18

Geishas

Their universe is a secret one, closed, hierarchical, full of codes, passwords, and ciphers for insiders only. "The world of flowers and willows" evokes simultaneously the convent, the house of ill repute, and secret societies. The curiosity it arouses can only compare with its legendary mystery, and it would be a mistake to assume that this curiosity is felt by Westerners alone. The Japanese, too, know very little about their national icons.

Geishas belong to show business; their makeup and costume stem from Kabuki theatre, their music from Noh theatre. They are accomplished dancers and musicians. They are exquisite hostesses, mastering the art of banter and light conversation.

They are also ladies who work at night, are paid by the hour, and are expected to push drinks on customers. Prostitutes? Definitely not. Yet, there is undoubtedly sex in the air as soon as one talks about geishas.

In the transparent light of a sunny autumn morning, two young women are kneeling, naked under a thin cotton yukata, open palms resting on their laps, motionless, about to offer their bodies in one of the most praised rites of initiation in Japan.

Barely do they quiver when the mistress enters the room. They have already learned stillness. The owner of the place scrutinizes them, then addresses them in a voice both warm and imperious. She is in her fifties, handsome and earthy, dressed in black corduroy and a turtleneck, a woman with a mission.

With fast and precise moves, she spreads her material on the tatami floor, takes a block of vegetal wax in her hands, softens it with her body warmth, and applies the wax to the two impassive faces in long, heavy, insistent strokes.

"You must always begin with wax," she explains, "to make sure the makeup will hold for a whole evening. And you must wait until the wax has cooled before you go on to the next step."

The two young women wait.

Then comes the famous white paste, spread with a thick brush on the whole face, including the eyes, the mouth, the throat all the way to the breasts, and, most important, the nape of the neck, where she draws an elegant white curve in one single stroke.

"This is the most erotic part of the female body," the mistress comments. "This is where all body movements stem from, and a woman must be able to express all her feelings and emotions through her neck."

A fragile-looking girl, almost a child, enters the room. With an expert hand, she draws the eyes with a black brush on the white mask, traces a thin red line with a pencil from the inside corner of the eye, and steps back to see the result: the two faces are now identical.

The mouth is for the mistress. One doesn't take chances with such things.

"First-year *maikos* [apprentices] wear rouge in the centre of the lower lip only, to symbolize innocence. In the second year, they put rouge on the centre of the upper lip as well, to suggest a rosebud. Only when they graduate after three or four years and become *geikos* will they be allowed to put rouge on the whole mouth."

She explains in passing that one does not say *geisha* but *geiko* – at least, when one hails from Kyoto. Country bumpkins, on the other hand . . .

The time has come to adjust the wigs. There are at least forty of them, each in its own box, piled up in a corner. For geishas – sorry, for *geikos* – the wig covers the whole head. Apprentices, on the other hand, are entitled to only a half-wig, while, in the front, their own hair is brushed, back-combed, and sprayed heavily to finish the look.

There are many things under a kimono: first, a cotton tube (white for *geikos*, red for *maikos*) tied at the waist with a cord; on the shoulders, a brief shirt made of the same cotton, white or red, held by another cord. Another slip over the first, another shirt crossed in front, two more cords. Elasticized waists do not exist in the world of geishas.

Then, a long band of white cotton is wrapped several times around the torso, in order to erase breasts, waist, and hips, and construct the shape of a live rag doll.

This foundation is then covered with a short, ankle-length kimono, held with a small cord. And finally, the Object, the supreme object for which the tightly wrapped body is only a dummy: the glorious kimono, spread out on the floor like a silk puddle around the feet.

"Only silk will do," comments the mistress. "Silk reflects light, silk falls better, silk moves with the body. Remember that the lower part of the kimono must follow your moves when you walk, it should not open!"

The two young women, intimidated by their sudden magnificence, remain standing, arms slightly apart, while a first belt is tied to hold the kimono in place. Then, two pillows – real stuffed pillows – are tied around their waist. And at last, the pièce de resistance, the famous *obi*: five yards of stiff padded silk, wrapped several times around the waist, then knotted in a figure as complex as it is loaded with symbolic meaning.

Traditionally, tying the *obi* is man's work, but as there is no male around, the mistress and her assistant grab it with four hands, put a foot flat on the backs of the geisha apprentices, and pull together with all their might. Nothing dainty here!

From inside their straitjackets, the two young women radiate pure, unadulterated happiness. They do not recognize themselves in the full-length mirror. They are these splendid princesses in the mirror, haughty and hieratic – and again they are not. The reflection the mirror sends them is the picture of Japan eternal, the incarnation of centuries of history and tradition, the confirmation that they belong to something deeper and more meaningful than the dullness of their daily life.

For they are not *geishas*. Nor *geikos*. Nor *maikos*. These two young *office-ladies* in a large Tokyo corporation took two days off to visit Kyoto, the old capital, cradle of Japanese culture, and paid a lot of money (U.S.$300) to be "*maikos* for a day" in this "transformation room."

The initiated will recognize them in a flash: they have none of the professionals' fluidity, their necks do not lean at the regulation angle, and their gait, that of city girls used to running to catch the last subway, is ill adapted to the high wooden *getas* in which they are now climbing, before they go clattering on the paving stones.

It is part of the package: to strut in the streets of Gion, the pleasure quarter, to pose for pictures in front of one those ancient wooden houses miraculously preserved from American bombings during the war, to pose one more time in front of a weeping willow by the river, maybe turn the head of a foreign tourist, who knows, and, for a few moments, to dream of another life . . .

In the sunny upstairs room of Maison Hanafusa, the mistress has already undertaken the transformation of another customer – an eighty-year-old lady, wrinkled like an apple, who explains timidly that she wants to experience, once in her life "how it feels to be beautiful." Next comes a fifteen-year-old high-school girl, bright and lively. She is from a small mountain village in the northern part of the country. This foray into dreamland is a gift from her grandmother. The old farm woman, crouched in a corner, her face leathered by a lifetime in the rice fields, is attending, with an expression of sheer wonderment at her granddaughter's spectacular transformation.

"After I finish school," the girl informs us, "I will work in a factory. I would love to become a *maiko*, but my parents won't let me."

This unending fascination for geishas helps the owner of Maison Hanafusa pay her bills at the end of the month. Indeed, times have been hard lately. She supports two real geishas, who live under her roof and work in the evening in various *ochaya* (tea rooms) of the neighbourhood. Since the recession, she has been financially strapped. So, why not take advantage of the eternal attraction for this mysterious world and make some extra income during the day, while her two boarders, who work until the small hours of the morning, are still sleeping in the room next door?

The owner of Maison Hanafusa educates her customers as she transforms them for a day. As she applies the makeup, adjusts the wig, and ties the cords, she describes in detail the daily life in the narrow streets of Gion. She insists that *geikos* are genuine artists, just like in show business, that their professional life is demanding and austere, and that they are the ultimate guardians of an august tradition.

From the age of fifteen, *maikos* must attend a special school, where they will have dance classes every day as well as lessons in music, voice, and percussion; they will also learn flower arranging and tea ceremony. These disciplines all require great patience, infinite precision, a perfect mastery, and hours of practice. In the evening, *maikos* follow their "big sisters" on their rounds. The role of *maikos* is simple: they are expected only to be decorative and to bring to the table the freshness of extreme youth. In this world where everything is coded, the apprentices are the ones wearing the brightest colours (they alone are allowed to wear a red kimono) with long sleeves falling to knee level, giving aerial grace to their every move. They are not required to demonstrate any virtuosity yet, nor to entertain customers with their conversation. They are expected, however, to observe attentively how the adults do it, for it is the only

way to learn good manners as well as tricks of the trade. It is their
novitiate period.

The Hanafusa mistress is hoping that, by shedding some light on
the life of geishas, she is contributing to rehabilitating the image of a
world that, nowadays, is often perceived as old-fashioned and over-
rated. Her neighbours see her as a money-grabbing opportunist and
watch with open disapproval as Hanafusa clients parade awkwardly in
front of their door every morning.

The fact is that the transformation salons threaten the geishas'
image. On the eve of the new century, at least fifty salons had sprung
up in the streets of Kyoto within a short time. Most of them offer a
service far removed from the nostalgic authenticity of Maison
Hanafusa. Assembly-line work, long counters where a dozen customers are being made up all at the same time under neon lights, no
time for wax ("takes too long") and never mind the horror of wrin-
kles showing under the thick white paste; polyester kimonos, same
wig for everybody, same studio picture with the same cheap-looking
landscape painted on bad paper as a background . . .

People from the milieu are horrified. "We tried everything to
stop them," they complain, "but they are not doing anything illegal,
and we are powerless. The worst is that most tourists don't even see
the difference! The transformation girls wander in places highly privileged by history, places celebrated by generations of poets, places
highly charged with symbols from romantic literature, and they dare
have their picture taken as if they belonged to our world!"

Their only victory was a decree ordering all transformation girls
to be accompanied by a chaperone carrying a sign that says: "This is
not a real *maiko*." But nobody pays any attention. The sign is rarely
visible, and in any case, most foreigners cannot read Japanese.

As night falls, the milieu takes over and the lanes of Gion find again
their famed subdued sophistication. It is all in the atmosphere. From
the street, there is nothing to see. There are no windows in the old

wooden façades. Even doors are imagined rather than seen, at the far end of cobbled porches lit with invisible lanterns. At the entrance of each establishment, the names of the *geikos* who officiate inside are written in black letters on narrow wooden planks.

The evening schedule of a *geiko* is established by her *mama-san* of the *okiya* where she lives. The *mama-san* offers room and board, buys kimonos and accessories, pays for music and dance lessons. In exchange, she takes a percentage of the geisha's earnings, and organizes her appointments.

The first assignment of the evening is a flat rate, from six to nine o'clock. The geisha presents herself in the tea room that booked her. Despite the name, it is either a bar, where customers come for drinks, or a traditional restaurant, where everybody sits on the tatami floor around a low rectangular table.

Geishas take their place between the customers – they do not actually sit at the table, yet they are close enough to lean and fill the cups with sake. They keep conversation going to establish the right atmosphere, and inquire what might please the gentlemen. Maybe a dance or two? Some sentimental songs? Or would they rather sing themselves, as one of the girls plucks the strings of the *shamisen*?

The evening progresses according to these wishes, but the golden rule remains to keep the atmosphere convivial and the conversation flowing.

"The most important part of my work is neither dancing nor singing, but rather encouraging the honourable customers to talk among themselves," explains a young adult geisha. "Most of the time, they are businessmen entertaining clients; outside of the office, they don't know what to say. They taught us poems in school for that kind of situation, but frankly, I find it much more useful to read the baseball results in the paper before I leave for work."

Customers in the *ochaya* are the object of a constant watch, intense and unrelenting, both from the geishas around the table and from the owner of the establishment who runs the show like a regular conductor. Let one of these gentlemen look as if he might be getting bored, threaten to fall asleep, or simply abstain from the conversation for a few minutes, and immediately a silent choreography is set in motion. The geisha at his side fades away in a fluid move, barely visible, to be replaced by one of her colleagues, the way hockey players are replaced in mid-game.

It is a disconcerting experience for foreigners who are not familiar with those evenings. Imagine: you finally got used to this invading presence, too close, inserted between you and your neighbour, which makes all actual conversation impossible; you've finally adjusted to the uncomfortable proximity of this white mask with no expression, this unreal voice, high-pitched, artificial, unsufferably sweet, constantly inquiring about your well-being, without leaving you any respite; you are barely beginning to give up, give in, let go, and enjoy being treated like a spoiled baby – you sigh in comfort, you forget the wife and kids, you close your eyes to finally, fully enjoy the moment . . .

"How long have you been in Japan?" peeps a voice in your ear. "What is it like in America? My brother did an MBA in Michigan. Do you know Michigan?" A callow little girl with bad yellow teeth has been dispatched to the side of the foreigner-who-is-getting-bored to entertain him with her teenaged babble.

The mission of *maikos* is to be *kawai*: cute as rosebuds. And their conversation must be cute too. Therefore, MBAs in Michigan . . . from a distance the owner gives her a severe warning look, and the kid corrects herself immediately. "Do you like cherry blossoms?" she inquires cutely.

You will do with this what you want. You may get away with a banal comment on beauty, flowers, and cherry trees, or you may catch the overture and attempt some awkward play on words on the tired theme of blooming, flowering, and deflowering. In either case, everyone around the table will clap their hands and look positively enchanted.

Things won't go much further. Her mission (entertain the foreigner) accomplished, the young *maiko* will go back to the benches; a smooth and sophisticated *geiko* will take her place, while two ladies

who celebrated their seventy-fifth birthday a long time ago will start
a sad chant accompanying themselves on their *shamisens*.

   After nine o'clock, geishas are on overtime. In general, their first
assignment ends there. From then on, they run in shuffled steps from
bar to bar, spending an hour here, an hour there. Sometimes, the
owner of a bar calls them unexpectedly "to rekindle the atmosphere."
Other times, a regular customer demands the presence of a particular *geiko* for one hour, or two, or even more.

It is a small, popular neighbourhood restaurant. The husband is in
the kitchen, the wife behind the counter, the son makes deliveries on
his blue motorcycle. Neon lights, sumo match on television, plastic
flowers on the table, you can have noodle soup there, or hamburgers
– with chopsticks. Customers know one another, say hello to the
mama-san at the cash register, chat between tables, ask about children, comment about the weather. The house cat is moving from
table to table, The place is comfortable, warm, and familiar.

   Suddenly, the door flies open, a dream creature rushes in, collapses at the counter, orders "the usual," and fishes out her cellphone
from her *obi* to check for messages. She sucks her noodles noisily, the
way the Japanese do, leaves some coins on the counter, slips the cellphone back in place, and runs back into the night.

   Geishas never eat with customers. They will share a beer or a
sake, but never a meal. As a result, if they are having a long evening
and a little hunger, they grab a bite between two contracts in a familiar place where they can be sure no one will see them.

Where and how does the evening end for a geisha, a *geiko*, one of
these ladies who works at night, dances for men, sings for them,
makes them drink, and takes their money?

   How can we believe that, in the momentum, they will not end in
someone's bed, with money so easy to make!

   On that point, everyone in the milieu is definite: geishas would
be acting against their own interests if they slept with customers. In

a world where everybody knows everything, they would put an end to their careers, be denied access to the said clients, and would end up losing on both fronts.

On the other hand, it is perfectly acceptable to have a "patron." For a long time, it was the only way for a geisha to become independent and pay the huge debt accumulated towards her *okiya* during her apprenticeship.

A patron buys you an apartment, adds to your kimono collection, pays you an occasional visit, and showers you with little gifts. Everybody comes out ahead: the "patron" wins the exclusive favours of the lady, and also the prestige of having an artist for himself, just like the French bourgeois had their *danseuse*. The *mama-san* loses a boarder, but she benefits from a considerable sum of fresh cash. As for the geisha, she becomes a free agent, and it even gives added cachet to her presence in the town *ochayas* every night.

Such is the scenario all geishas dream of. Or rather, such was the dream scenario. Today, however, "patrons" are getting scarce. To keep a *geiko* is expensive, particularly since the recession. Hence a new phenomenon: the shared geisha. A few customers, determined to keep traditions alive, pool their resources to keep a geisha they way it should be done. They share the cost of the apartment, the formal kimonos, the small gifts . . .

"What about the visits?"

"Very simple. You take a calendar for the week. Mister X comes on Monday and Thursday, Mister Y on Tuesday and Friday, Mister Z on Wednesday and Saturday."

That makes for three happy patrons, a *geiko* no longer sure about her status, and a milieu that clams up in unison when anybody tries to broach the subject.

The phenomenon is embarrassing, but it remains marginal. Modern geisha hardly need a patron any more. The times are over when little girls were adopted or even bought by an *okiya*, and when the debt accumulated by the time they reached adulthood was such that they could never pay it back. The only way out of this form of slavery was the appearance of some miraculous "patron." Since 1945, child labour is forbidden by law, and school is compulsory until junior high. Therefore, a *maiko* is already fifteen or sixteen by the time she starts her apprenticeship. After three years of expensive music and dance classes, the young woman "turns her collar" (which means she becomes a full-fledged geisha). She can start paying back her debts and become financially independent within six years. No need for patrons!

No need either to suffer the oppressing atmosphere of this monastic milieu, jealous, secretive, run by embittered old women, unless she does it for the love of the art.

Such is the case of Ichisuzu-san.

As with all Gion establishments, Ochaya Nakagishi is barely noticeable from the street. Behind the narrow door, a long corridor leads to a small reception room; from there, another corridor takes you to a bar, small but opulent; a third goes on to a traditional sitting room, where Ichisuzu-san has agreed to see me.

This strange, lengthy layout dates from the days when property taxes were established according to the street frontage. To minimize the tax, people built houses barely wider than the door. Most houses in the old Kyoto are built that way. The locals call them their "eel's bed."

The young *geiko*, serene in a mauve day-kimono, welcomes me in her eel's bed. She is a privileged woman: in a milieu where obligations, debts, and duties play such an important role in defining relations between people, Ichisuzu-san does not owe anything to anybody. In her family, women are *geiko* from mother to daughter. This *ochaya* belongs to her grandmother. The small bar is run by her father. She grew up upstairs, with her parents. This is a small family business, and she is coddled like a rare, exotic plant. She is an accomplished dancer, she learned her manners from childhood, she represents the future and the survival not only of the profession but also of a tradition, a way of life, and a certain image that Japan has of itself.

She works every night ("I have only two Sundays off in a month"); she is very much in demand during the day as well, to mark the

opening of a convention, to promote the Chamber of Commerce or
the Tourism bureau. She accepts all requests, poses, smiles for the
cameras. She enjoys her work – but she will not spend her life doing
it. When she reaches thirty, she wants to get married and have children. "And I will certainly not marry a client," she laughs. "They are
all older than my father!"

"I am saving to do an M.B.A. in the United States," a *maiko* whispered in my ear one evening, when the *mama-san* was not watching.

And a provincial geisha explained to me that her dream was to
save enough money to buy a bus and drive tourists around. "I already
have the licence!" she exulted.

In Kyoto, as elsewhere, the new recruits, whether they call
themselves *geikos* or geishas, share the same prospect: work for a few
years in this brilliant, seductive profession, before going back to
private life.

Such is the world of geishas today: at one end, are young women in
their twenties who chose the profession deliberately, enjoy their work,
and manage their life like modern businesswomen. At the other
extreme, are women seventy years of age and more who were forced
into the "world of flowers and willows" from childhood, because their
parents were too poor to keep them at home; women who endured
the humiliation of *mizu-age* (ritual deflowering, offered to the highest
bidder), who spent their youth in slavery, who, as adults, became an
integral part of this secret society and its rites, and who, in the eve of
their life, elevate it into an apostolate.

"I belong to the Inoue tradition," the venerable Chikuyo-san
explains learnedly. This old lady with a stern yet serene face is
reputed to be one of the most accomplished dancers in Gion, and one
of the most severe Guardians of the Tradition.

Inoue is a dance style, particularly refined, developed in the
eighteenth century. All restraint and subtlety, its choreography is
akin to that of the Noh theatre. The dancer must avoid any expression on her face or in her eyes (that would be vulgar) and any sex

appeal (that would be coarse). One has to be a real expert to appreciate the subtleties of this abstract form of dancing. Gion people delight in this opacity.

"To dance in that style is to dance *ma-i*," I am told. "That where the word *maiko* comes from. A tradition dating from 1872 absolutely forbids teaching and dancing in *ma-i* style outside the Gion quarter."

The old lady adds sweetly: "Dance styles in other quarters are far more crude." It seems to matter little that, for the non-initiated, these dances all look alike.

For added emphasis, Chikuyo-san whispers condescendingly, "One could hardly expect the same degree of sophistication in Pontocho *ochiyas.*"

Pontocho is the area three hundred yards away, just on the other side of the river. Between Gion and Pontocho, there is a bridge, but it might as well be an abyss. *Geikos* hardly ever walk across that bridge, for there is nothing but contempt on each bank for the other.

There are five geisha quarters in the old capital. Five quarters, five schools, five traditions, five networks of *mama-san*, residences, bars, and regulars. To listen to insiders, you would think they are talking about five religions, five sects, five tribes, which coexist in icy tolerance.

These village wars seem futile when, in the same breath, the severe guardian of the tradition is deploring the fact that the world of geishas is threatened with extinction.

Such is the paradox: it is imperative that the "world of flowers and willows" remain subjugated to the rules and regulations of the milieu in order to keep its famed aura. Yet, the monastic rules from yesteryear scare away the young apprentices and dry up the new generation.

Between the two contradictory requirements, the sudden appearance of the grotesque transformation salons worries old-timers – but it also comforts them. If nothing else, the success of these salons proves that the Japanese are still proud of their geishas and what they represent.

As for the real geishas, beautiful and mysterious, they remain for the Japanese the icon, par excellence, of "their" Japan.

CHAPTER 19

Fireflies

A surprising invitation lands on my desk one fine June morning: we are invited to a firefly evening. Not only is it not a joke, but I am told it is a rare opportunity, a seasonal event that should not be missed. It is also one of these delicate situations in which declining the invitation would be acceptable by protocol rules, but would hurt our hosts deeply – which is unacceptable by protocol rules.

We meet them in one of the handsome reception rooms in the Four Seasons hotel. The style is Western-opulent, the sushi trays lavish, and we mellow into deep armchairs as the last rays of sunset linger in the tall trees down below. But there is anticipation in the air. For our hosts, this privileged moment is but a preamble. They can barely contain their impatience for what is to come.

Finally, the moon rises from behind the hill. It is the signal. We leave the table, slip on our shoes. "No high heels," I had been warned. "We are going in nature." We walk down a long corridor and emerge on a platform, where a small crowd is getting ready for the adventure.

A boardwalk slopes gently into the trees. On either side is a handrail, similar to those installed in high-mountain passes to assist climbers when the path is particularly challenging. We are now walking in the undergrowth, a babbling brook cascades deliciously through the ferns; suddenly, into a curve, our friends shout in unison, "Here! Right in front of us! Fireflies!" Hundreds, thousands, of fireflies, their greenish glow throbbing slowly in the coolness of the little grove.

On the boardwalk, the crowd has gone into a frenzy. They feign total surprise: "Look! Fireflies! Can you see them? There! There!" they all exclaim, pointing fingers in the night.

You can't miss them, they are everywhere around us. But still, visitors point at them, show them to one another, confirm loudly that indeed they are there. They marvel. Fathers crouch by their children, so their gazes are at the same height, to make sure the little ones don't miss anything and share their wonder. Young lovers, taking the most incalculable risks, lean over the handrail, catch a firefly despite the signs forbidding it, present it like a trophy to their sweet companions. With squeals of amazement, the young girls in galoshes and mini-skirts hold the insect ceremoniously in their joined hands the time of a picture, then raise their arms to the trees, to the sky, to the moon, and release them in the evening with the gestures of antique priestesses.

I glance at our hosts: they are in ecstasy.

This hardened businessman, whose conversations are all about turnover, export quotas, and productivity, this blue-rinsed woman whose life revolves around her bridge tournaments and her dwarf poodle . . . here they are, holding hands on the small bridge over the brook, melting with emotion before this idyllic scene.

And when a moonbeam glides along the branches and glitters on some water on a rock, a long sigh of happiness rises from the crowd. The instant is perfect.

Yet, it's all fake. The small grove and its undergrowth were created by a famous landscape architect. The water from the brook babbling through the ferns is recycled through a pump at the bottom of the hill. The hill itself was the result of a vast earth-moving project at the time the hotel was built. As for the fireflies, they are brought up every morning by the truckful, from distant Shikoku Island.

This remote province, forgotten by industrial development, is the last place where fireflies can still feel at home. For a few weeks every summer, they nurture an active cottage industry: locals go to catch fireflies on the riverbanks and sell them to these strange men in their big trucks who then drive all night to recreate a bit of the countryside in the big city.

The memory of lying in the grass by a small creek as a child, watching fireflies glow softly in the warm summer night, casts a strong picture in the mind of the Japanese. They are willing to pay good money for a firefly package at an international hotel in downtown Tokyo, in order to rediscover some of that lost happiness, to share it with their children and occasionally with visiting foreign friends.

Except that . . . our hosts that night were inveterate city dwellers, and there was nothing rural about their childhood memories. In the crowd around us, there was not anyone under the age of fifty for whom this bucolic spectacle could have possibly been a reminder of their childhood.

What people came looking for at the Four Seasons Hotel was not so much some personal nostalgia as the echo of bygone days, a time they never knew, but which survives as a background in their collective memory, and refuses to die away.

Some time later, I was attending a pleasant dinner party hosted by an American businessman long expatriated in Japan. Around the table were politicians, senior public servants, academics, all comfortable people, well established, with no serious worries in life. The conversation, flowing with ease among Japanese, English, and French, was a mirror of the group: serious and enlightened, but also light and entertaining. We had been talking about politics, Mount Fuji, holidays in Switzerland, Buddhism renewal, when somebody mentioned *konnyakus*.

Suddenly, the energy turned up several notches around the table. The Japanese launched into a passionate debate, at an accelerated pace, forgetting that, even for the most Japanophile of Westerners, their language remains an eternal challenge. Non-Japanese guests were getting lost, except for the word *konnyakus* that kept being repeated in this flow of words. Could it be a recently discovered African tribe? An avant-garde artist? A new sect, possibly?

Finally, taking advantage of the indulgence granted to newcomers, I dared to ask, timidly, "What is a *konnyaku*?"

New torrent of words. They were all talking at the same time. Each one wanted to be first to share with me the magic of *konnyakus*; the symbolism of *konnyakus*; what you can do with *konnyakus*; the origins of *konnyakus*; how to use *konnyakus*.

Yes, but . . .

"What is a *konnyaku*?"

It tastes very good, it has no taste, it is very pretty, it has no colour, it has no smell, and it has no taste, it's delicious, it's during the summer . . .

The parliamentarian to my left pulls out his four-colour pen to draw this colourless thing; the sociologist across the table undertakes to give me a delicious recipe for this tasteless thing. They are all brimming with enthusiasm. I am confused.

Little by little, some light is shed on *konnyakus*. A *konnyaku* is a vegetable. Or rather, it is a mountain plant whose tubers are crushed and pureed into a consistent gelatine (no colour, no smell, no taste), which is used to make fat noodles, which are eaten cold during the summer, and also a variety of sweets and desserts for children.

Konnyakus instantly trigger images of languid summers, cool country restaurants smelling of wood fire and fresh grass, and also those quiet summer days with Grandma as she pickled, sliced, crushed the precious bulbs for the pleasure of little children.

Here again, there is a gap. Except for very senior citizens, few Japanese can claim they went for *konnyakus* in the woods with their grandmother when they were little. These childhood memories are borrowed, drawn from a common core memory that allows them to claim legitimate ownership of experiences they never lived.

No matter. When they hear the word *konnyaku*, the Japanese melt with emotion for a certain image of what their childhood memories should be.

This immense nostalgia for a Japan that does not exist, that no longer exists, that may never have existed, has brought fame and fortune to author Koji Nakano.

Is he an old fool or a visionary? He refuses modern amenities, considers the consumer society as the source of all evils, and science as an evil Western import; he shakes his head in despair when he talks about today's youth, moans over the disappearance of traditional values and the good old days; he behaves like all curmudgeons have always done at all times in all latitudes.

Yet, his books sell like hot cakes. In particular, *The Philosophy of Noble Poverty*, published on the fiftieth anniversary of the end of the war, was an unprecedented commercial success.

What a strange book! Koji Nakano lectures, scolds, reprimands his contemporaries for selling their souls to the consumer society.

"Foreigners wonder whether the Japanese is nothing but an *homo faber*, who makes and sell things," he laments in his introduction. And he concludes his book with this warning: "We won't recover our pride by exporting more cars."

In the meantime, he is inviting his countrymen to make use of their ancestors' wisdom in order to solve modern problems such as pollution, as well as to find their identity. He calls to the rescue some of the most famous Japanese poets, artists, and authors from the tenth to the nineteenth century, and demonstrates that being detached from material possessions is the essence of the Japanese soul.

And he tells them stories – the kind of legends that everybody knows, which are woven into the culture of a people, which little children learn from their grandmothers and rediscover later in school.

Except that, in modern Japan, the school curriculum does not cover those stories, children don't read much, and grandmothers don't talk much either. Students in classic literature are the only ones still familiar with these stories, and that's exactly what worries old Nakano. That's why he undertakes to tell some edifying episodes from the lives of major poets and artists. The message is not only that money meant nothing then, but also that it was an obstacle to their creativity; that the refined elegance of their minimalist poems and their transparent brushstrokes mirrored an inner elegance, detached from material goods. That is what characterizes Japan, and that is what must be found again.

A number of these great names in the Japanese firmament lived as hermits. One of them (Kamo no Chomei) celebrated life in a nine-foot-square hut; another one (Ryokan) played on a stringless *koto* in order to better appreciate the sounds of the forest. A third one (Basho) wandered on northern roads, knapsack on his back, not a penny in his pocket. He celebrated the ecstasy of stretching one's legs in a straw hut and listening to the rain, the peace that comes from owning nothing but three spoonfuls of rice in the evening. This is a fry cry from the frenzied tourists pouring out of tour buses to clean out luxury boutiques in major capitals!

"Grotesque contradiction!" fulminates Nakano.

According to him, when they fell into the trappings of consumer society, the Japanese did a lot worse than just aping the Americans; they betrayed their ancestors, literally. They are in the process of forgetting where they come from and who they are.

Nakano joins the chorus in the anxious search for identity that has been tormenting the inhabitants of the archipelago since they decided to join the West in 1868.

His book is not easy. When he is not quoting some Zen poet from the thirteenth century, he quotes pell-mell Kant, Seneca, St. Francis of Assisi, Meister Eckhart, and Erich Fromm.

To top it all off, he tends to write in archaic Japanese.

The title, *The Philosophy of Noble Poverty*, borrowed from an eighteenth-century Zen poem, uses an ancient Chinese pictogram, "so archaic that word processors can't read it," his editor laments.

Despite all this, his book has been an unprecedented success. It was first published in Japan in September 1992 and remained on the best-seller list for nine months; sales were twenty times bigger than the publishers' most optimist forecast, and, three years later, the book was still doing a brisk business. Economic and financial papers recommended it to their readers. The Japanese edition of the very influential *Forbes* magazine reviewed it when it first came out. Several large corporations added it to the required reading for their new recruits.

Bookstore owners are unanimous in saying that, in general, women are the ones who read and who "make" best-sellers. In the case of *Noble Poverty*, men were the ones who made the book a success. And not just any men: executives in their forties and fifties, old enough to remember the days when there really was nothing to eat, but young enough to be the artisans of the Japanese miracle; men who gave themselves fully to their employer, who accepted all the sacrifices during close to thirty years, until Japan became the second world power; men who worked very hard, who accumulated savings, whose children studied in the better schools, but who, at the time when one starts taking stock of one's accomplishments, draw no satisfaction from their success. Something is missing from their lives. They don't recognize their country, nor their children. Worst of all, they don't recognize themselves.

Nakano's publisher, Masaki Kitamura, is one of these men. A youthful forty-five years old, he greets his guests in offices designed by an architect friend: a three-storey stone building in the heart of Shibuya's maze of chic little lanes. Elegant open spaces, deep leather seats, skylights and indoor trees, a young, serious, and efficient staff, a stable of successful authors on the shelves and ever-increasing sales figures, what more could a man want? Yet, when Kitamura stumbled upon some of Nakano's articles lamenting the loss of the Japanese spirit, he did a double take.

This old fool with his ancient Zen-monk stories, his ranting and raving against consumer society, was touching a sensitive chord, reviving a dull, ill-defined pain with no apparent cause that he had been keeping deep inside. It was not so much a pain as an unease –

and Nakano was talking about it, giving it a name and a shape, and, better still, he was suggesting a remedy.

"I phoned him immediately to ask him to write a book about it," Kitamura explains, "and he accepted right away. For me, in the beginning, this project was nothing but a small, personal luxury," he adds. "One of these projects you launch not to make money but only for sheer pleasure."

When *The Philosophy of Noble Poverty* made a killing in Tokyo bookstores, he was the first to be surprised. Then, he realized that he had unearthed a societal phenomenon.

"Nakano appeared just in time to call to mind the unease of men in my generation. His appeal is that the remedies he is suggesting draw from Japan's deepest roots."

On the surface, there is nothing terribly novel in Nakano's message. The notion that economic growth is not an end in itself, that it may trigger a degradation of the environment and a worsening of the quality of life, has been the object of many economic treatises and political programs in all industrialized countries during the second half of the twentieth century.

From E. F. Schumacher's *Small Is Beautiful* to Alan Durning's *How Much Is Enough?*, from the Canadian Greenpeace organization to the Green parties of Europe, people everywhere are rediscovering this wisdom that money does not buy happiness.

But there ends the parallel between Nakano and Western thinkers.

In the West, the problem is approached as a simple issue of good husbandry: we must limit our consumption so that there will be enough resources for everybody, because the degradation of the environment is costly, because the ecological balance is threatened when a species disappears, because we must think of the welfare of future generations. Whether consciously or unconsciously, we are obeying the ancient command from Genesis: "Replenish the earth, and subdue it." In other words, Westerners start from the principle that they have a planet to manage.

Nakano's approach is diametrically opposed. He starts from the human being: we must consume less because stuffing one's face is not Zen. To consume is unethical, to consume lessens man, diminishes his spiritual dimension.

When he offers as models some of the starving artists and homeless hermits scattered through Japan's cultural heritage, his purpose is to demonstrate that the most admirable works of art, the most venerated texts, stem from an intense spiritual search.

Nakano practises what he preaches. In his bungalow, set in a forgettable Yokohama suburb, the telephone is his only concession to modern life: "to talk to my publishers," he explains slightly apologetic. No car, no television set; to enter his house is to enter a silent and focused world, a world deliberately slowed.

Koji Nakano did not play hard-to-get. In fact, he is openly delighted that a foreigner is interested in his work; he will jump at every opportunity to let the rest of the world know that the Japanese are not all monsters of consumerism.

At first sight, his small house looks like any other; yet, it is built the old-fashioned way, with a post-and-beam frame made of the same rare cypress wood as the Ise Shrine, using the same techniques as did his carpenter father.

Given the price of specialized labour, this house cost him a fortune. Obviously, the main room has a tatami floor. Predictably, each cup in the kitchen has been created individually by a potter friend. The luxury is in the details. The pleasure is in the deliberate slowness.

Nakano measures the passage of seasons with the changing hues of plants in his garden. He writes his books entirely by hand, with a brush, in calligraphy. It leaves no room for correction, but, on the other hand, it leaves ample time to think ahead!

How does he explain his book's unprecedented success?

The question is banal, yet its effect is surprising: suddenly the poised, modest sage gives way to the prophet: the war was actually lost when the Japanese adopted the American way of life; the fact that his book sells is a good thing; it means that the Japanese, having caught up with the West, are looking for something more substantial to give value to their lives. His book is a success because it offers the Japanese a fresh and worthy reason to be proud of their heritage. Indeed, it may be their turn to offer the rest of the planet solutions to modern problems.

These solutions are to be found in their ancestors' view of the world, in which man and nature are part and parcel of the same universal harmony. Western thinkers, philosophers, and scientists are slowly discovering the power of that vision. As for the Japanese, all they have to do is to rediscover it, to smooth over the fault, and reconnect with their own roots.

And so be it, if getting back to this symbiotic relationship, this universal harmony, implies, as a first step, delivering truckloads of fireflies to the big city during the summer.

CHAPTER 20

Fashion, Post–Miyake

"Issey Miyake? I saw some of his creations in a gallery, and I finally understood why he became so famous in his day. But now, his stuff is rather passé, don't you think?"

The young man who casually just relegated to a museum the couturier who was called "the greatest creator of our time" sports a leather vest over a red jogging suit, bright yellow nail polish, and an angelic smile. Around the table, his colleagues nod gravely in assent.

We are in Ventan, the most trendy school of fashion and design among the younger generation. It is also the most expensive, yet there are twenty-five-hundred full-time students, and a long waiting list. Such is Ventan's reputation that 70 per cent of its graduates have already found a job six months before the end of their studies. Situated in the heart of bustling Shibuya, this school claims to be training the Rei Kawakubo, the Yohji Yamamoto, and the Issey Miyake of tomorrow. Around the table are some of its more promising students, and here they are, devouring these ancestors!

A boy with a shaved head and rings in all visible orifices announces shyly that he purchased his blue-and-red-striped blazer in a vintage second-hand store especially for my visit; a nineteen-year-old girl brags about her jean jacket with fringes and checkered pants ("From the seventies! Authentic! I found it in my mother's closet!"); another student simply wore her T-shirt inside out for the day. She is confused about her gaping lack of creativity, and apologized profusely as she came in: "I had an assignment to finish for this morning, I didn't have time to do any better..." in other words, no time to invent from scratch a brand-new arrangement of old pieces to honour my visit.

This seems to be their constant preoccupation. Ventan students spend their day being on the lookout, ears pricked up, smelling, feeling, sensing what is in the air, arranging, rearranging elements of costume, sketching, drawing, searching for the look that will best express the atmosphere at a given time.

The young creators find it immensely difficult to find a style and make their mark, while outside, right under the windows, street fashion, in perpetual motion, is reinvented every morning and suffers no labelling.

Patiently, the future couturiers explain the nature of the challenge:

"'It' is as elusive as water. What young people feel like wearing is constantly changing – almost from one day to the next. The stream is so fast, we almost don't have time to see 'it' flow by. Each one of us is looking for what he thinks is best; we don't even have time to imitate, 'it' goes so fast!"

"It" is the unbelievable, mind-boggling, staggering, breathtaking energy that emanates from Tokyo lanes. Between Shibuya and Harajuku in particular, the audacity, boldness, humour, imagination, dishevelled creativity hit you at every corner, on the sidewalks, in cafés and boutiques. What emanates from it all is the sense of a continuous turnover, a permanent re-creation, a never-ending quest. For apprentice designers, the challenge is somehow to harness that energy, and it demands their constant, undivided attention.

International fashion writers face a similar challenge. At collections time, they all descend on Tokyo to attend the fashion shows of established designers; they write their pieces, send them to their newspapers; then, having done their required homework, they form a beeline to Harajuku to find out what is really happening in the streets of the immense metropolis.

International publicists have long recognized that energy. For instance, Shibuya girls were the object of a Benetton campaign, their miniskirts found their way to the catwalk of the Chanel spring collection in 2000, and Max Factor created a line of makeup to imitate the style that was all the rage that year and that gave them their name: the "black-faced girls." Deeply tanned face, chalk-white eye-shadow, such were the famous *Ganguro girls*, whose look became famous all over the world for one season.

"To see the *Ganguro girls*, you must go to Shibuya 109," I was told. "That's where they all hang out." This department store sits on a sharp street corner in front of the Shibuya station; it is the high temple of the "black-faced" teenagers. Behind each counter, through six storeys, *charisma* salesladies (that's what they are called) offer live demonstrations on how to become a perfect little rebel. One must look very tanned whatever the season ("Max Factor cosmetics are on the ground floor"), with very white makeup all around the eyes; the finishing touch is the hair: back-combed, blown-up, huge, it must be dyed lighter than the skin; the skirt is almost non-existent, and as for the boots ("on sale on the basement floor"), there is only one acceptable model: beige like the hair, with platform soles so thick the girls must watch every one of their steps.

It matters little, for the *Ganguro girls* don't walk much. These teenagers, who for a few months became role models for a whole generation, are perched like birds, two by two, on the nearby sidewalks. Motionless, they stand in front of the temple. They stand, defiance on their faces, and they wait. They may be waiting for some photographer boyfriend to show up with very professional and expensive-looking equipment and shoot a few pictures for some new magazine that may or may not be published; they may be waiting for passersby to stop and gawk at the scene; they wait for tourists to turn their head and surreptitiously shoot pictures of these *Ganguro girls* they have read about in their guidebooks; they wait for schoolgirls in their uniforms to stare at them with envy.

The "black-faced girls" have positioned themselves there to be looked at. Is it possible to talk to them, despite their sullen faces?

Surprise! Faces brighten up, they love being the centre of attention, being asked questions, particularly when one comes equipped with a camera, a microphone, all instruments that will allow them to leave a trace behind, prove their existence . . .

They are seventeen years old. They come from Saitama. It seems they all come from Saitama! In this drab suburb north of Tokyo, life is grey and so is the future. The "black-faced girls" live with their parents; several times a week, they come to the heart of the big city. On their way over, in the train, they spread out their makeup kits and apply foundation and white shadow with the utmost care; when, after an hour and a half, they disembark at Shibuya station, the transformation is complete. Their appearance is no longer that of suburban kids ready to die of boredom, but that of superb city slickers, of dangerous, mysterious man-eaters.

"They look as if there are walking the streets waiting for a client, but in fact they scare men," explains Mihoko Iida, a *Vogue* editor, who has been following the phenomenon. "To please? To attract? They don't give a damn. In truth, they are not interested in men. They will sleep with one occasionally, but in their mind, it is not prostitution, it is just another way of taking money from adults when all the parents' pocket money is gone. All they want is to escape their reality, pretend they are someone else for a little while, until the unavoidable moment when, at the age of twenty-two, they will have to reintegrate into society and live a normal adult life, as boring, tedious, mindless as their parents'."

The energy they invest in shocking the good citizens of Japan may be the energy of despair, but they certainly succeed in drawing attention. The whole world comes to Shibuya to stare at them.

Clop! Clop! Clop! Clop!

A surprising vision appears suddenly from a street corner. Four girls, all dressed in black, long ample skirts and leg-of-mutton sleeves, white-lace jabots and matching collars, pale faces and Goldilocks curls, minuscule doll hats perched on top of their heads, come marching elbow to elbow, occupying the whole sidewalk, vaguely threatening.

"Here come the *Gothics*!"

Surprised passersby turn their heads. Fashion editors pull out their notebooks – again. Nice girls-next-door who had finally convinced their mothers to buy them high beige boots in order to look *cool* stop dead in their tracks.

Ganguros are no more. Long live the *Gothics*!

Such is life in Tokyo streets, where the fundamental rule, the only one that counts, is "impermanence." A style falls out of style the second it is given a name. And when department stores hire *charisma* salesladies to teach customers how to master a given look, it is way past the time to move on! For *Gothics* too, life will be short. Each new trend reflects an atmosphere, and the atmosphere is in a constant state of flux.

"They are *zokus*, tribes," explains Emiko Oku. Twice a year, this independent fashion writer covers the new collections in Paris and Milan, London and New York for *Vogue-Japan* and other fashion magazines. She follows what happens on the sidewalks of Tokyo with the same exacting attention.

"Each tribe has its themes and models. The *Ganguro girls* were inspired by a young singer called Namie Amuro, whose tragic life struck popular imagination. She has the tanned look of Southerners, because she comes from Okinawa. She married a famous hip-hop dancer, whose traditional family rejected their union. Namie's mother, an Italian-American, was killed in violent circumstances, which contributed to the exoticism of her legend."

So much for the *Ganguro girls* tribe. The *Gothics*, also called *Lolitas*, are musicians' girlfriends. But not just any musicians! Visual musicians, who constitute their own tribe, not to be confused with the rock tribe, rap tribe, hip-hop tribe, Stanley Kubrick tribe, the digital-animation tribe, surfers tribe, and computer-nerds tribe, the vintage-clothes tribe, Hong-Kong-movies tribe, and . . . the hairdressers's tribe. Each tribe has its stars, its *charisma* leaders, idolized by other tribe members, invisible to outsiders; they are the trendsetters. These trends are constantly changing. One must always be on the lookout, know how to recognize the signs. Sometimes, it can be as minute as a small logo on a collar, a piece of ribbon that goes from the right to the left, a pin that disappears . . . but it is enough to allow tribe members to recognize one another in the crowd, to be reassured that they are still bona fide members, that they are not alone.

Yet, they dream of individualism: *"Liberate yourself from mental slavery,"* claims an embroidered logo on a baseball cap. *"You and you alone can free your mind."*

"We go in search of our dreams with warm and happy hearts," announces another teenager on his T-shirt.

Kazuko Koike, who teaches art history and fashion anthropology at Musashino Fine Arts University, has a keen interest in what she calls "these human beings who are not yet part of established society."

"Young people are afraid of what lies ahead," she says. "They don't trust the adult world around them. They find some solace in their tribes, but deep down, they feel alone in the world. The dishevelled energy in their clothes is an attempt at survival. They reflect the failures of our society: failure of the education system, which systematically kills all creativity; failure of our families, where everyone has given up speaking. And, please understand, I am not talking here about the traditional lack of communication between generations. I am talking about something much deeper, a grave source of worry. Young people aged eighteen to twenty-two do not speak. They don't speak to anyone. They are concentrated on themselves. Their ability to communicate compares with that of elementary-school children. All university teachers make the same observation."

Koike was curator to the Japanese pavilion at the seventh architecture Venice biennale during the summer of 2000. She entitled the

Japanese exhibition *City of Girls*. It showed photographs of street fashion in Tokyo, together with the creations of a Japanese designer.

"The word 'girls' is symbolic of the human being in the city. Why girls? Because they are the ones generating this amazing energy you see in the streets. Boys are weak, crushed from childhood by the fear of not being equal to the task. Girls don't face the same expectations. They don't feel pressured to succeed, they are not constrained, their creativity is not nipped in the bud. They and they alone still have the strength to rebel against the society that was built around them, yet not for them. They don't find themselves in it, it does not mean anything to them. Their revolt against the older generation is diffuse in its object, yet specific in its means. See the famous *Ganguro girls*: their super-tanned faces are in direct defiance of tradition, which expects proper young ladies to stay away from the sun to protect their pale complexions; their aggressively blonde hair is a way of thumbing their nose at school regulations, which forbid coloured hair; as for miniskirts, they are the supreme insolence: their mothers simply did not have ten inches of leg to show above the knee! The young generation are tall; to show long legs represents the cruellest of revenges against adults."

How did Koike dare juxtapose in the same exhibit the eminently superficial and fugitive art that is fashion with the major and permanent art that is architecture?

The answer comes along with a sad smile: "If you think about it, the ultimate protection of the body against the elements is provided by clothes, not by buildings. When you can't count on anybody or anything, when you are totally alone in the world, when everything collapses around you, clothes become a cocoon, shelter, the ultimate habitat."

Her words ring particularly true in this country where earthquakes are part of daily life. Hardly a week goes by without at least a slight rumbling, reminding every Japanese that their familiar environment may indeed collapse and disappear at any time. Every home has an emergency kit, protection helmets, and a neighbourhood map marking the location of shelters and meeting places, should a catastrophe hit. Everybody remembers the Kobe earthquake, when forty-five seconds turned the residents of this modern, prosperous city into so many homeless. When Tokyoites come across one of the homeless who live by the thousands in parks and subway stations, that's what comes to their mind: it may be my turn someday – maybe tomorrow, maybe sooner.

Meanwhile, the earthquake is used as metaphor for the dramatic collapse in the relations between young people and their parents' generation. Kosuke Tsumura, the designer whose work was exhibited at the Venice biennale, named his company Final Home. The ultimate shelter. He creates high-tech clothes, made of nylon with zips, which can be used as a big comfortable coat for day and turn into a sleeping bag for night. One of his coats in particular – ample, warm, and cozy, with a big wide hood to protect you from the world's aggressions – was called, tragically *"The Mother."*

"Youth must have passion and courage," Issey Miyake wrote in 1977. "Our thoughts must materialize into acts."

Miyake was working with Guy Laroche in Paris when the events of May 1968 exploded. Within a few weeks, in the whole world, from Paris to Tokyo and America, students were climbing barricades, calling for a revolution, and marked one of the major caesura of our time: before 1968 and after 1968. For Miyake, it was a catalyst. He had just found his vocation, and came home to Tokyo.

In the West, clothes borrow the body shape. All fashions are but variations on the same theme: re-creating that shape. In Japan, on the other hand, the kimono (a word that means simply: "thing to be worn") is nothing but a series of long rectangles sewn together, that only take their shape and function once they hang from the body.

Miyake renewed with this traditional Japanese concept: it is the body – and the body movement – that gives its shape to the clothes, and not the opposite. The textile object gets a name and an identity only when it comes into contact with the person. This way of placing the human being at the starting point of the process reflected precisely Westerners' aspirations after 1968, and that explained Miyake's spectacular success. He was revealing Westerners to themselves, and, wonder of wonders, he was doing so by digging into the traditional aesthetics of ancient Japan. For the Japanese, it was an illumination, a consecration, a new birth: finally Japan was being understood; Japan had something to contribute to the world. Japan was no longer alone. In this country where people feel so acutely the need to build bridges between East and West, Miyake had found a passageway.

Zen entered the vocabulary of Parisians and New Yorkers, the Japanese discovered that it was possible to wear a kimono one day and pleats the next, to be simultaneously Japanese and modern. There were finally able to offer the world an image of themselves that was both audacious and coherent. Miyake had given them back their identity.

With the twenty-first century, a new chain of stores appeared in the streets of Tokyo and other large Japanese cities. The Uniqlo concept has the Gap, Agnes B, Benetton, and others afraid; it is "a new approach to marketing," I was told, maybe even a revolution for consumer society. Curious, I paid a visit to the Uniqlo store in Harajuku. A dense crowd on all three floors, a long patient line waiting before the cashiers, salespeople hurrying to refill the shelves by the boxful with the ever-popular merchandise: polar fleeces! Hundred per cent polyester fleeces! Fleeces of all sorts. Large, shapeless, cozy, fluffy, comfortable . . . And the colours! Light and pastel, soft and sweet, colours for a cocoon, for a nest, for a cradle, colour of milk, colour from my grandmother's eiderdown, colour of my mother's breast. All of this for the price of an ice-cream cone! In the heart of hearts of counterculture! No wonder the big brands are worried! Is it the last in the line of these fugitive fashions that come and go? Is it an echo of Tsumura's *Final Home*? Is it the end of fashion, period?

Such is the challenge to the apprentice designers from Ventan school: contrary to the great masters from the previous generation, their contemporaries have no passion nor courage. Everything has been smoothed out for them, they have no material worries, they are provided for, they don't have anything tangible against which to rebel. Only this desperate, stubborn, absolute certainty: "We don't want to live like our parents did."

Despite their amazing energy, they present to the world the picture of a disoriented generation, with no aim, no model, no aspirations, and saddened from not having any – so sad, in fact, that they might well give up on fashion, wrap themselves in a cozy polar fleece as in a cocoon, pull the drapes, and blot out the world.

CHAPTER 21

To Talk Cherry Blossoms
with the Emperor

Tomorrow, I meet the Emperor!

The whole household is jittery, and the staff flutter about like butterflies under the pretence of preparing me properly for the event. In fact, they are nervous, like a producer on the evening of the premiere. Will I be up to it? Will I be able to play my part? I shouldn't embarrass them! They suddenly remember that the angles of my bows are approximate, that the polite formulas I have been practising studiously are not to the standards of the Imperial Family, and that all my skirts are black. One does not wear black in the Imperial Palace.

Torn between their deep respect for "Madame" and the fear of being shamed by my inadequate behaviour, they mill about, pretending to fluff up a pillow, replacing a flower, providing me with small pieces of advice as they go, in light touches, in passing, as if it just crossed their minds.

They should not worry: the Imperial Household took the matter in hand and the Great Chamberlain is expected this morning to brief us prior to the event.

He enters with two acolytes, their arms full of files and documents, gets through the inevitable courtesies as fast as his impeccable education allows, and, with a worried look on his face, gets right down to work. There is not a minute to waste when one is in charge of polishing up foreigners, at least just enough to render them presentable.

This is the second time the Great Chamberlain has come to our home for a full rehearsal. A few days before my husband presented his credentials, he had to be familiarized with the scenario. As for a military campaign, the Great Chamberlain had spread a map on the table to take him through the event, minute by minute.

"You enter from this corner, you make five steps to the cross that you see marked here; at that point, you stop and bow. For three seconds. You rise up again. Then you walk to this other red mark, following the dotted line you see here, and you stop and stand right there." Large circled red cross.

In great detail, he had covered every instant, every step, every word of the ceremony that would turn my husband into a full-fledged ambassador.

"At that point," the Great Chamberlain added with a worried tone in his voice, "the program calls for a four-minute free-wheeling conversation with the Emperor."

Already, the future ambassador was exulting silently: "A private free-wheeling conversation with the Emperor! What a treat!"

However, the Great Chamberlain was briefing again: "The Emperor will inquire about the health of your prime minister, you will assure him that it is excellent; in turn, you will transmit wishes of good health from your prime minister. Then, he will ask you whether you have had a chance yet to admire our cherry blossoms. You will answer that you have been blessed to arrive in Japan just in time for cherry-blossom season, and that you have been deeply moved by their beauty."

All of this would take three minutes. The program called for four. The Great Chamberlain had hesitated for a split second, he had gazed around him, taken a look outside, and plunged: "Then you might mention that you have the great privilege to have several cherry trees right here in your own garden. These are double-blossom cherry trees, the Emperor will answer that there are similar ones in the historical gardens surrounding the palace."

Satisfied, he had concluded: "That should take care of the free-wheeling conversational segment."

Such are the briefings one has to go through before meeting the Imperial Family. Everything must be meticulously scripted, nothing, absolutely nothing, can be left to chance. Therefore, today, I am not really surprised to see the Great Chamberlain spread out on the table several detailed plans, with diagrams, to explain the choreography and protocol of the coming event.

We won't be alone: four other freshly arrived ambassadors with their spouses have been invited as well to meet the Emperor, the Empress, and two of their children: the Imperial Prince, and the little Princess, who is only twenty-two years old.

The challenge is for each newcomer couple to meet individually with each one of the Imperial Family members.

"No politics, and nothing personal!" Such is the rule, And we are advised to talk about cherry blossoms, since the season is upon us.

The big day has arrived. Here we are, five diplomat couples, freshly arrived in Japan, led ceremoniously through this modern palace, along bright corridors that run around an inner pebbled courtyard. We are invited into a bare and empty sitting room. We are offered a cup of tea and a petit four. It is a trap: don't touch the petit four. One mouthful, one crumb, and it is disgrace for you and your country. I risk taking a sip of tea. The Great Chamberlain, his acolytes, and several ladies-in-waiting are moving from couple to couple with ease and grace for a bit of small talk, taking great care to look relaxed. I have the definite feeling that I am going through some final exam. Glances at gold watches are getting more frequent, and suddenly, bru-tally, the atmosphere changes: we are no longer honourable visitors, but unknown interlopers to be kept under tight watch.

They order us to stand in line according to seniority (that is, according to our arrival date in the country). They have no qualms about pushing at a shoulder, pulling an elbow, in order to keep the line straight. They call the roll ("Present!") to make one last check. One final time, they go through the unfolding of the upcoming manoeuvres: six minutes and a half with each member of the Imperial Family, in the order that has been repeated many times. And they reassure us: "Don't worry, you will get a signal when your time is up."

The doors open and a shudder goes through the group as the Imperial Family enters the room. With a lightness and grace that would make a campaigning politician green with envy, the Emperor, Empress, Imperial Prince and Princess review the intimidated line, scatter effortlessly to the four corners of the room with their assigned interlocutors, and engage in conversation in silken voices.

The Emperor listens with exquisite patience as we wax poetic about the sublime beauty of cherry blossoms. As soon as we are through, he cues us on world events and international politics. Yet we had been told again and again: "No politics!" We tread carefully. His comments are informed, his questions, precise, he is interested in everything. At six minutes and thirty seconds on the dot, he ends a sentence and someone takes us away by the elbow.

We are led to the Imperial Prince, who has been expecting us with some eagerness, because he read in his files that we share with him a love for mountain climbing: here is something to talk about, he will not have to suffer another cherry-blossom litany! We compare notes on our respective climbs in the world, and he suggests some of the best summits in Japan. The next day, he will send us a book on the Japanese Alps. "This is a loan," a handwritten note will specify. Old trick, to manufacture an opportunity to meet again without depending on the vagaries of protocol. For, as we will realize later, members of the Imperial Family must absolutely justify all their moves, their outings, their travels in Japan, as well as abroad. Their latitude is just about nil, as if they were prisoners in their own palace.

Here we are, in front of the little Princess – the valiant little Princess for whom this exercise must surely be the ultimate bore. It suddenly dawns on me why the invitation card mentioned: "If you have a daughter twenty-one or over, she is welcome to attend." The little Princess is looking for friends!

In order to spare her the inevitable cherry-blossom recitation, I tell her about my own daughter, who is the same age and is at the moment doing social work, deep in rural China. I am gratified with a torrent of questions, all intelligent, interested, relevant, tinged with envy, perhaps? Then, the severe-looking lady-in-waiting who has been following the conversation catches her eye and the good little Princess gets back to the straight and narrow path of ornithology, wild-duck nesting habits, her field of specialization, in which she has been granted free rein.

My topic of conversation with the Empress is easy: we talk about our daughters, like any two mothers would. Then I remember my manners and I exclaim on the beauty of cherry blossoms.

Oddly, she listens politely, but without taking her cue, just as the Emperor did. She goes on to talk about the silkworms she raises within the confines of the Imperial Palace. I learn with ill-contained excitement that this is the time of the year when, by watching them very closely, one can predict which ones will produce a pink-tinged thread, a greenish one, or a pure white one.

A lady-in-waiting waves at me every so discreetly, to remind me of the time. But the Empress is now going strong about poetry, and the book she and her husband published together when they were newlyweds.

From behind me, someone brushes my elbow.

The Empress is still talking, without realizing that my six minutes and a half have elapsed. I am now listening to her in anguish, taking good care not to add anything that might fuel further conversation.

Another pressure, on my back this time, stronger.

The Empress is describing the poetry competition that takes place in the palace every year on New Year's Day.

That's when a definitely unfriendly hand grabs my arm and pulls me back, while another time-guard pushes Mister Slovakia and his wife towards the Empress – or was it Mister and Madam Luxembourg?

The whole thing lasted a split second. Behind her smiling mask, the Empress, unaware of the mini-drama, hasn't stirred. Slovakia attempts an awkward curtsy and launches into a gauche celebration of cherry blossoms.

I come out of the event perplexed and intrigued by the contrast between the Imperial Family's ease and grace – all speak impeccable English or French, and show a serious interest in everything – and the nervous stiffness of their entourage, haughty, uncomfortable, perpetually nervous, awkward manipulators, bordering on rudeness.

Why do these people, who come from the best families in the country, who have received the best education in Japan and abroad, who have gone through the exacting training of the Foreign Affairs Ministry, why do they feel the need to protect the Imperial Family to such an extent that they won't let them talk about anything but birds, fish, silkworms, and literature – provided it is very ancient? And why this apparent fixation on cherry blossoms in the spring time?

It is often said that in Japan, you are only shown what people want you to see, and that what you see is never more than an elaborate stage show. Reality is behind it. To see it, you need the codes. To understand the codes, you need a key. If you need a key for the codes, you are not entitled to it. That's how non-Japanese are kept in a cocoon of illusions out of which they are never seriously encouraged to venture.

It will take me a year to understand what it was I was actually witnessing the day of that first visit to the Imperial Palace. One year until I realized that, on that particular day, I had caught a glimpse of nothing less than the century-old tension between the Emperor and the samurais.

And that cherry trees were the key to the code.

Japanese cherry trees are not the fruit trees we know in North America and Europe. Taller, they do not bear fruit, and their abundant blooms are pale pink rather than white. In the wild, they grow in forests, and the effect of whole mountainsides covered in pink foam in March is striking. Planted in the cities, along rivers and canals, they form thick tunnels that magically keep the rest of the world out of sight.

When, after five or six days, the trees start losing their petals, it is in a slow and hesitating fall, which inevitably brings to mind snow and death.

The symbolism of the cherry blossom is universally shared by the Japanese. The homeless and ministers, rich heiresses and bar owners, jet-setters and country bumpkins use the same terms with the same veneration: "miracle of nature," "ineffable beauty," "purity," "ephemeral," "tragic," and, of course, "human condition."

It is all there, the words have not changed since the eighth century. The cherry blossom was celebrated by poets, reproduced by painters, evoked in dances and ballads, as well as in the sad song, "Sakura," which all Japanese know by heart, which brings tears to the eyes of the most hardened souls, and which might be considered as Japan's unofficial national anthem.

Cherry blossoms decorate ancient lacquer combs used by court ladies, contemporary formal kimonos, exquisite transparent porcelains, as well as, in plastic version, used car lots. All tourist brochures confirm cheerfully that the Japanese love their cherry trees; they wait for the blooming season with excited anticipation, and one must have witnessed the frenzy that catches the whole archipelago in the spring to measure the amplitude of the phenomenon.

From the beginning of March, newspapers have been competing for the scoop: the first bloom in the southern prefecture of Nagasaki. It will make the front page, and it marks the beginning of the countdown: day by day, the whole nation follows the "cherry-blossom front" as it moves northward.

"They have reached Hiroshima." "They should arrive in Kyoto

within forty-eight hours," "if mild temperatures keep up, the first ones will be seen in Tokyo within three days." During a five-week period, it is not only accepted but required to open conversations with some comment on the progress of the blossoms, the way other people talk about the weather.

Every night on the evening news, the newscast ends with an overview of the cherry-blossom situation. As the time approaches, tension mounts in the streets of Tokyo. People hold their breath, projects are put on hold, no one wants to miss the instant when the *sakuras* are going to start blooming.

D-day. Cherry trees open all the television newscasts. Whatever else may be happening in the world, be it an international crisis or the latest political scandal, cherry trees come first, and give the green light for the Big Bacchanals.

At dawn the next morning, a curious scene takes place in most city parks: young men dressed in suits and ties arrive one by one, bundles under their arms; they spread large blue plastic sheets on the ground, secure them on all four corners with heavy stones, and sit cross-legged in the centre.

No, they are not in deep *zazen* meditation, they are simply keeping the spot. They will not move from their position until the end of the working day. Around five o'clock, they are joined by their colleagues, carrying picnic baskets, ghetto-blasters, and many cases of beer. Ceremoniously, they remove their shoes before stepping on the blue plastic; with applied precision, they roll their ties and stuff them in their pockets, drop their jackets, undo their belts, and start drinking.

And can they drink!

Since morning, the blue plastic sheets have multiplied under the cherry trees. There are now hundreds, thousands, of people swilling indifferently canned beer and sake straight from the bottle, bawling romantic songs into portable karaoke machines, trying a few dance steps between the leftovers of sushi, and sighing in rapture every time the breeze blows a flight of pink petals over the carousing crowd, sprawled in drunken ecstasy.

Whole families walk about in the thick smell of fried foods. Children with Mickey Mouse ears hang on to their ice-cream cones. Grandmothers spy with expert eyes the best angle for a picture of their grandchildren in front of a cherry tree.

Foreign tourists, too, are meandering in the park, taking pictures of Japanese taking pictures, Japanese getting drunk, Japanese howling obscene songs, Japanese laughing, Japanese slapping their stomachs, in short Japanese being "so un-Japanese!" That will create a fascinating contrast with the stiff kimono-clad young girls and indistinct Buddhas in their souvenir album.

For Westerners, it is immensely tempting to laugh at the sight of these millions of people coming all at once to commune with nature and meditate before the snow-like purity of the tall trees in bloom, among piles of litter and greasy wrapping papers. And yet, it is indeed a communion of a kind.

For a few hours, they all come to celebrate together something that unites all the Japanese: a profound veneration, quasi-religious and universal, for their cherry blossoms.

Universal? A member of the Imperial Family gave me a hint otherwise, much later.

"You know, originally, it was the plum-tree blossom that symbolized purity in Japan." Originally, that is, in the sixth century, a long, long time before the Shogun military regime.

"The plum tree is the first one to bloom, in mid-February. It signals the arrival of spring, the renewal of life, the regeneration of nature. Its blooms are virginal white, much purer than the pinky-white of cherry blossoms. In ancient China, the plum blossom was the one favoured by artists because of the perfect simplicity of its outline. It is the one found on the crests of the oldest families, on tenth-century court coats, as well as on the most formal clothes of today's Imperial Family."

The whole thing was suggested more than spelled out by a prince who, discreetly, is trying to hand me the keys.

"But . . . what about the cherry tree, then?

"The cherry blossom is the symbol of the samurais. It is the image of their life: pure, beautiful, and ephemeral."

Samurais are those warriors who devoted their life to their lord and for whom death was a hundred times preferable to dishonour. The symbolism attached to the cherry tree is that of the samurai spirit: petals as white as their honour, with lines as red as their blood; a blossom as gloriously beautiful as their life, which, like their life, can fly away with the slightest breeze; most of all, a blossom that doesn't resist death, that would rather disappear in full beauty than remain attached to life and rot on its feet, as the vulgar rose does!

The samurai code of ethics – simple, strong, and romantic – was that of a small élite class of warriors. Yet it was endorsed as a protective mantel by the whole population at the time of the Meiji revolution in the middle of the nineteenth century. The country had just decided to gamble on westernization, its executives, engineers, educators, senior public servants were dispatched as explorers to study British, French, German, American institutions, and were given carte blanche upon their return to reconstitute those Western models. That's how Japan equipped itself with German-style secondary schools, a French-style civil code, a British railway network . . .

This revolution may have been a necessary step to becoming a modern country, yet it was also threatening Japanese culture: was it necessary to adopt Westerners' values together with their institutions? Did this new step imply abandoning "Japanicity"? In either case, what was it that was specifically Japanese? Whatever it was, would it be an obstacle to modernization? Who would evaluate the consequences and how?

Time was running out to embark in such a fundamental debate. Faced with the wave of new ideas, practices, and technologies they both welcomed and feared, the Japanese hung on to the samurai ethics as to a lifesaver.

And a whole population of merchants, farmers, and fishermen found itself endorsing awkwardly what had been for centuries the rarefied code of a haughty class of feudal warriors. The Japanese common people were more Rabelaisian than Zen, but no matter: honour, death, blood, the ephemeral, was all transferred higgledy-piggledy into their cultural baggage. And with it, too, was the symbolism of the cherry blossom.

Samurais have long disappeared, but their descendants are still actively present in Japanese society. As did their ancestors, they still behave in a quasi-proprietorial way vis-à-vis the Emperor and the Imperial Household, and they still propagate the notion that the cherry blossom is Japan, Japan is the cherry blossom.

Only erudite historians and princes still care to remember that the plum-tree blossom was forgotten in that great saga.

CHAPTER 22

A Country with No Heroes

Samurai dramas represent a very specific genre in Japanese television.

Drawn from historical events, largely romanticized, they present demanding, imperious feudal lords, servile and calculating vassals, fearless, chivalrous heroes, beautiful, merciless ladies, pure heroines with a tragic fate. The recipe is universal.

Over the years, the genre became rigid, to the extent that, today, they have become but a caricature of their former selves: feudal lords are more cruel than ever, loyal samurais even more fanatical, heroines even more tearful, and dialogues are reduced to sobs and guttural barks. The formula has become old-fashioned and outdated, and only grandmothers and idle retirees are still watching these shows, broadcast in the afternoon while children are in school and no one else is sitting in front of the screen.

Yet, in 1996, Japanese public television launched into the unknown and produced an expensive new historical drama. It even gambled on broadcasting it during the very sought-after Sunday-night window.

It was a resounding success. *Hideyoshi* drew more than 30 per cent of the ratings from the beginning, and kept close to one-third of the Sunday-night audience during all forty-nine episodes.

At first sight, it was the same old tired formula: good guys and bad guys, pure heros and traitors, agonizing conflicts, love and death, fire and tears, and gorgeous costumes. Except that . . . the hero was ugly.

Ugly, vulgar, and ridiculous to boot. He would win battles, but he often lost them too; he occasionally sank into despair; he cried; he goofed up; he humiliated himself abjectly before his master.

To top it all off, he would lie and cheat, steal, conspire, betray . . . What kind of a hero was this?

Yet, week after week, in Japanese homes, sarcastic teenagers and blasé fathers were joining the grandmother in front of the family TV set to watch the next episode of *Hideyoshi* on Sunday night at eight o'clock.

What was this enigma?

Commonly called "the Founder of Modern Japan" and "Japan's architect," Hideyoshi Toyotomi united the country and made it what it is today. He was born towards the end of a long period of instability (from 1536 to 1598), which the Japanese refer to "the time of the long wars": fifty years of ferocious struggles between small feudal lords, with assorted alliances, marriages, dark plots, treasons, and fratricidal struggles for power.

He came from a peasant family with no name or fortune. Turbulent and unruly, young Tokichiro was kicked out of all the schools he attended and would retain his rough peasant manners all his life. However, he was blessed with a bright mind, a gift for war, and a sense of the psychology of the great and powerful. He was a near contemporary of Machiavelli and, even though he most certainly did not read his works, he just as certainly would have been his best student.

He took advantage of quarrels between feudal lords to unite them under one single authority – his own – established his power over the whole territory, and ended up as shogun, all-powerful dictator of the whole archipelago. His interests extended way beyond the military and political. He was a builder, an innovator curious about new technologies; his influence was felt in many fields, and he left an indelible mark on Japanese society.

The Japanese, intensely intrigued by the arrival of the first Western merchants, that's him; the ferocious persecution of the Christians, that's him too; so is the popularization of the tea ceremony, and also the passion for pottery and porcelain that the Japanese nurse to this day.

His character is so much larger than life, his adventures have been so thoroughly documented, spiced with so many legends, that his biography can be accommodated to fit just about any need, at any given time. For instance, in the nineteenth century, during the Meiji revolution, when the Japanese felt threatened by the import of Western thoughts and habits, Hideyoshi was presented as the guardian of eternal Japanese values.

In history books published during the military and imperialist regimes of the first half of the twentieth century, Hideyoshi was first and foremost an illustrious military leader, fighting for the unity of the country, the glory of the Emperor, and the hegemony of Japan in the world.

After the Second World War, a new identity had to be forged for Hideyoshi: builder of canals and other great public works, creator of official land surveys, genial administrator, implementer of modern technologies in agriculture and industry, such is the Hideyoshi of the "Japanese miracle" years.

He has been used as a mirror in every period in Japanese history, and the NHK televised series is no exception. The producer actually made it his point of honour.

Hoshiki Nishimura meets me in the main-entrance coffee shop of the massive national television building (NHK), one of the primary landmarks in Shibuya. A youthful forty-something, with long hair and a dangling cigarette à la French movies from the 1950s to assert his creative side, a buttoned-up two-piece suit for his executive side, he exudes the constant, quiet, contained impatience of the Japanese who have lived in America.

Without even consulting me, he orders three short espressos, two for him, one for me, lights a fresh cigarette, and launches into his story.

In lieu of preamble, he announces that he learned his trade in Hollywood, in the Twentieth Century Fox studios.

"What made the series a success," he explains, "is that I applied to the letter the lessons I learned in California. First thing: target the audience. My mission from senior management was to aim at young teenagers, boys and girls from the age of twelve. Well, one of the things I learned in Hollywood is that young people have a short attention span. If you don't want to lose them, you have to maintain a fast rhythm throughout. That rapid pace is almost more important than the story itself. Meanwhile, here in Tokyo, they are still showing a moon rise in real time!" He rolls his eyes in exasperation. "We had to kick out a lot of old practices."

Lesson number two: how to choose the main actor.

"In a dramatic series, the main actor should not be someone famous from the start," he recites studiously. "His notoriety must rise as the series moves along."

That is what happened to Naoto Takenaka. This young actor was a quasi-unknown, except as a comic, when Nishimura approached him. By accepting the main role in the series, he saw his career follow a path parallel to that of his character. Like Hideyoshi, he had a modest start, he established his respectability episode after episode, and reached the apogee of success at the same time, in forty-nine weeks.

"Now, Takenaka is as famous as Sean Connery," the producer declares proudly. He is all the more satisfied that he had to fight with NHK traditional managers to impose his candidate. Not only was the actor an unknown, but he was also far from seductive: short, with arched legs, a fat nose in a flat face, buffoon-like and grimacing, more at ease in vaudeville, he was a far cry from the traditional profile of a historical hero, destined to raise national pride among the young.

The fact that the real Hideyoshi was himself afflicted with a notoriously unfortunate physique (to the extent that he was nicknamed "The Monkey" by his contemporaries) did not carry enough weight to convince senior management. The producer had, once more, to brandish the Code of Success According to Hollywood: "The audience must identify with the hero. They must recognize their own story in his adventures, project on him their dreams, hopes, and frustrations."

Nishimura gambled and won. His hero is popular because of his imperfections. People admire his exploits all the more because they are aware of his foibles. They sympathize with him because his dilemmas have a familiar ring to them. His lightning career is the stuff *salarimen*'s dreams are made of. Yanked from their hometown, anonymous and vulnerable, bored senseless in some crowded office, modern *salarimen* visualize themselves climbing the ladder of their corporation, plotting like so many Machiavellis to beat the competition, reach the higher echelons, and end up as chief executive, feared and venerated by all.

That is how, during a whole season, the adventures of sixteenth-century Hideyoshi fed the dreams of millions of suburban samurais every Sunday night.

"Such is the recipe for success for a televised series," explains Nishimura very simply. "But the most important thing by far is to find a good scenario. I learned that, too, in Hollywood."

His starting point was a biography of Hideyoshi published during the "bubble years," in which our all-purpose hero was presented as a great entrepreneur. The author? Taichi Sakaiya, famous economist and prolific writer, who abandoned a successful senior public-servant career at MITI (the all-powerful Department of Industry and International Trade) to devote himself to the study of his country's history.

"According to Sakaiya, Hideyoshi was not a hero but a very ordinary man," explains the producer. "He was not a great soldier, nor even a great strategist. But he had the ability of surrounding himself with the talents he was lacking."

Then he adds, pensively, "Rather like Tanaka."

Tanaka: that is always a magic word in conversations. Tanaka was one of the most influential prime ministers of postwar Japan. He started from nothing, with no money, no contacts, and no education, and he reached power thanks to a very deliberate and sophisticated network of influences. Even after a very public scandal forced him to resign, he remained dear to the heart of the Japanese because of his humble origins.

Truly, the theme of the poor young man who reaches the heights of glory thanks to his tenacity and determination is an enduring theme! That is how the NHK producer became convinced that Hideyoshi's story, reinterpreted by a modern economist, presented all the necessary ingredients to become a commercial success.

Nishimura is still talking about future projects, ratings, budgets, market shares, but I am no longer listening; my ears have registered something that my brain has difficulty processing.

Something is not right. He did say "MITI?" He did say "high official"? Did I hear him say that Sakaiya *left* MITI?

It sounds impossible. MITI is one of the most prestigious departments in the Japanese administration. Peopled with the best graduates from the best universities, it makes the rest of the bureaucracy feel cowed, and politicians feel like bumbling college boys. A career at MITI is sheer power: power to influence elected officials, power to initiate major bills, power to design the main orientation of the whole country for years to come. One does not leave MITI. Except to go into politics, and even at that!

Therefore . . . Sakaiya . . . what motivated him, what unfathomable force pushed him to make this unprecedented move, to leave behind absolute power, and, very mundanely, start writing?

His office staff answers like a minister's: his time is scheduled to the minute, his program is established months ahead, and, yes, he will be willing to give me fifty minutes of his precious time in five weeks. Impressive, for someone who lives by the pen!

Five weeks later, then, I ring at his door, with a young political-science student in tow, who offered to act as interpreter. Sakaiya speaks perfect English but, as is often the case with politicians, he refuses to use it in public.

From his years in the higher spheres of power, he kept the quiet assurance of a prince. An elegant sixty-year-old, with silver hair, an impeccable grey suit, gold-rimmed glasses, Taichi Sakaiya welcomes me with exquisite efficiency.

I will not be given the luxury to ask questions. In fact, I will barely be allowed to talk at all. Sakaiya has a presentation to make, and fifty minutes to make it – the usual length of one of his speeches.

"Most of Japan's problems," he explains, "stem from the fact that the Japanese don't have enough heroes. As long as they don't have heroes they can identify with, they won't be able to pull it out."

This conviction was strong enough to motivate him to leave government, bury himself in history books, and go on a hunt for role models.

Hideyoshi Toyotomi and his multiple adventures provided him with all the necessary ingredients to construct a modern hero.

"His life marked a turning point in the history of Japan," he tells me. "When Hideyoshi was born, the system in place was crumbling. When he died, he left behind a new society, together with a blueprint that the Tokugawa dynasty would follow to the letter for the next two and a half centuries. What attracted my attention was a number of surprising parallels between the fifty years of Hideyoshi's career and the fifty-year span following the end of the Second World War."

Sakaiya rubs his hands in anticipation as he gets ready for his demonstration. To make sure that I follow him (for after all, I am not particularly well versed in the detailed history of sixteenth-century

Japan!), he hands me with authority a diagram, prepared especially for me, and which I am to follow throughout.

"In 1551, when young Tokichiro leaves his village looking for fame and fortune, his whole future is ahead of him, like Japan in 1946 at the time of the first general elections.

"In 1560, Tokichiro wins a first big strategic battle that changes the balance of power in the whole archipelago, as happened in Japan in 1955, when a new economic structure was put in place, marking the actual beginning of the postwar period.

"In 1570, our hero's boss, Nobunaga, marches into the old derelict capital of Kyoto and erects a new palace as a symbol of power and renewal. The Tokyo Olympics in 1964 had the exact same psychological effect on the Japanese.

"In 1582, when his leader dies, Hideyoshi [that's his new name] grabs the reins of power and gives himself the task of uniting Japan."

For my professor, this turning point can be compared to the 1979 oil shock, when Japan's economy started relying less on heavy industries and more on automotive and electronics.

"By 1590, the unity of Japan had been realized, thanks to land distribution. With this momentum, Hideyoshi invades Korea, in order to funnel the energy of his major feudal lords."

Sakaiya notes that this episode is strikingly similar to the period when the Japanese were buying anything and everything in the world, from the New York Rockefeller Centre to Hollywood movie studios, from Van Gogh's *Sunflowers* to various castles in Spain, in Scotland, and in France.

"He should have stopped right there," the historian comments. "He didn't. He was kicked out of Korea once; that didn't deter him, and he started planning a new Korean campaign, with the ultimate goal of conquering . . . China! No less! His diplomats were lying to him, drew him far too rosy a picture, exactly as bankers were lying to politicians in the 1980s to justify the untenable expansion of the bubble economy. In both cases, four centuries apart, the upcoming catastrophe was unavoidable."

Curled up on his chair, the young student who came with me has long given up on his interpreter's role. Looking frantic, he is avidly taking notes. No need to ask him what will be the topic of his next presentation!

The time seems opportune to risk a question: "Who are the Hideyoshis of today?"

"The generation of businessmen who cropped up after the war. Look at Toyoda, for instance: from a small spinning-mill, he and his successors built the Toyota empire known throughout the world! In barely fifty years! The same time it took Hideyoshi to transform Japan."

Sakaiya is having fun pushing the parallels further: "In one single generation, Hideyoshi transformed a whole warrior class [the small feudal nobility] into a class of businessmen preoccupied only with land production and management. Just like today's *salarimen!*"

The parallel still applies when it comes to women: "Look at Japanese males today! They work long hours, they look important, but in actual fact, their wives are the ones who make all major decisions and organize their life in all its details. Without them, they are lost. The women are the strong ones, in this country." Similarly, the correspondence of Hideyoshi confirmed that the shogun would not lift a finger without consulting first with his mother or his wife, and the historian made certain that this was adequately portrayed in the televised version of the biography.

At this precise moment, a gorgeous young woman with a delicious, smooth face pushes open the door respectfully and inquires with exquisite courtesy whether I would care for another cup of tea. In good Japanese, that means: "Get out!"

My fifty minutes have elapsed. However, the master is having a fine time and he invites me to stay a few minutes longer as he finishes his story.

"The Japanese desperately need role models. However, their heroes from the recent past are not politically correct in the eyes of the world. As for contemporary heroes, the Japanese are so jealous of one another that they destroy them as soon as they arise. Furthermore, only those with obvious shortcomings can qualify as potential heroes, because only then is it possible to sympathize with them."

Does this explain why Hideyoshi's appeal endures in the Japanese imagination?

"Indeed, this is part of the reason, but there is something else too."

The great Sakaiya leans forward, lowers his voice, and pronounces, in conspiratorial tones: "Hideyoshi passed through like lightning in Japan history. Nothing before him, nothing after him. He had no illustrious ascendency, we barely know his father's name. Once he reached the pinnacle of power, he dreamed of founding a dynasty. Yet, soon after his death, his only son, who had been groomed to succeed him, was killed in a great fire that levelled the family castle." As the result, the dynasty that would dominate Japan for two hundred and fifty years after him would be one other than his own. Such is the tragic destiny of the man who left such a major imprint in Japan's history.

"How romantic!" Sakaiya exclaims victoriously. "His passage was like that of the sun: brilliant and domineering during his life, yet leaving nothing behind him. That's the stuff popular heroes are made of!"

It is all there: the small peasant risen from the countryside, the great epics, love, tragedies, the founding of a country, supreme power, and to cap it all, the theme of the ephemeral, always present in Japanese literature.

With all these ingredients at his disposal, author Taichi Sakaiya was able to present his sad contemporaries with a historical figure to which to anchor their present, their past, and their national pride. That explains the immense success of his serialized biography on television.

Yet, what should we make of a people who have to go back in time all the way to the sixteenth century to find an acceptable hero?

And what should we make of a country that needs a senior official to manufacture heroes and reconstruct the past, tentatively, the way one reassembles a puzzle?

CHAPTER 23

Keredomo

Even the most casual visitor with no notion of the Japanese language cannot fail to notice this little word that pops up constantly in conversations. *Keredomo*: these four syllables are easy to identify for a Western ear. They are always clearly enunciated, well articulated, slightly isolated from the rest of the sentence. To make it easier yet, they are usually uttered on a rising pitch, as a question would be, even though there is really no question mark after *keredomo*. The voice remains suspended, as in a mute invitation, an opening, a glimpse over the immensity of the field of possibilities . . .

Keredomo means "however."

At least, that's what the dictionary says. But the way the Japanese use it, this little word carries much heavier responsibilities. At one level, it is a sort of polite formula for everyday talk, one of the many tools fashioned over the centuries to soften the harsh reality of life. *Keredomo* helps nuance the black and white, to soften the edges of the most benign assertions.

For instance: "I think it is going to rain this afternoon, *keredomo* . . ." However, it may well not rain, in which case please do not hold it against me.

"The weather report is forecasting rain for today. You might want to take your umbrella, *keredomo* . . ." However, I wouldn't want you to think that I might even consider telling you what to do.

The most telling illustration may well be this most mundane of daily situations: making a phone call. You dial the number, your correspondent picks up the phone, and you introduce yourself:

"Hello, this is Kenji Sato, *keredomo* . . ." I am telling you who I am, this is my name, but I am embarrassed to impose this assertion so crudely. I apologize for having to confront you with the reality of my name in such a brutal fashion. For, indeed, who is Kenji Sato? He introduces himself by enunciating the name his parents gave him at birth. Yet, he is *Kenji-san* to his father; his mother may still call him *Kenji-chan*, as she did when he was a baby; he is *Onisan* to his younger brother; classmates who have known him since kindergarten call him *Ken-kun*; to the teacher at the other end of the line he is "my student," "my employee" to his boss, and *Sato-san* to his colleagues.

Therefore, when he gives his name thoughtlessly by way of introduction, is he not imposing a given perspective on this Kenji Sato who is calling on the phone? Is he not guilty of an intolerable arrogance? *Keredomo*.

This little word is the exact opposite of the American phrase "in your face." It's a way of declaring to the world: "I am not imposing anything, not starting a debate, not opening a controversy, not creating a confrontation." Or should it be interpreted as: "I don't want a debate; I don't want a controversy; let's avoid a confrontation"?

Often, that's what is suggested by the slightly hesitant intonation, the exaggeratedly distinct enunciation, the four syllables, clearly separated from one another, isolated from the rest of the sentence, so that you can't miss them. You don't want any ambiguity when you are trying to tell the world you are not looking for a fight!

Of course, the Japanese do not think consciously about all these messages when, in their daily life, they add a *keredomo* (or a *kedo* for short) at the end of the most mundane statements. It is only a manner of speaking. It is part of everyday language.

Still, it does reflect a certain way of seeing the world: nothing is absolute; there is not one single way to interpret the world around us, not one single way to be in that world.

An eminent doctor in etymology came to my rescue and unveiled the root significance hidden in the Chinese pictogram of this innocent-looking word. *Keri* is a purely Japanese suffix, which means it dates from the beginning of time. It asserts that the matter at hand is over, finished, accomplished; it happened and there's no point going back over it. The affirmation is plain, blunt, and brutal. After which, one has a change of heart: "That is what I said" (*ie*), "however" (*domo*). Well, this *iedomo*, this way of soft-pedaling reality as it is, does not come from the Japanese, but from the Chinese. This purely Confucian concept is one of the most significant borrowings from Chinese civilization, and the fundamental principle of all intellectual proceedings, Chinese-style. According to this principle, there are four steps to developing an idea.

The first one consists of presenting the topic; it is then expanded upon and developed; for the third step, the tables are turned, the perspective is changed, the subject is observed under a new angle, a different viewpoint.

In conclusion, the whole thing is tied together with a pictogram that represents both a string and good luck.

The process strikes me as rather similar to the *thesis–antithesis–synthesis* we were taught in college. However, while it leads us Westerners to reach certainties, after having studied the question under all its angles, the same process leads the Japanese to the opposite conclusion: the biggest mistake would be to assert certainties, it is impossible to make definite statements on anything; all, absolutely all, is relative, it all depends on circumstances and your own standpoint.

That explains why the Japanese universe is never all black and white. Whether they deal with paintings or emotions, architecture or ethical norms, they see no discontinuity between the all white and the all black, but rather, a subtle gradation that leads progressively from one extreme to the other.

Good and evil, like the rest, are a matter of lighting, perspective, circumstances. In this world of chiaroscuro, our Western notions of good and evil sink like a stone in a lake.

Our favourite injunctions such as, "Let us be clear and concise," "Let us be brief," "Let us go straight to the point," are very simply incomprehensible to the Japanese, because they consider them to be non-operational.

Why should we be clear and concise when the real world around us is all blur and uncertain hues?

What would be the use of a scalpel in a fragrance garden?

The *keredomo* perspective may explain why the Japanese have such a difficult time dealing with their past, their present, and even their future.

It may also explain why they find it so difficult to define who they are.